HOLOCAUST LEARNING
AND MORALITY

Shay Efrat
Holocaust learning and morality

Publihsed by BooxAi
ISBN: 978-965-577-916-5

HOLOCAUST LEARNING AND MORALITY

SHAY EFRAT

preface by GIDEON GREIF
Edited by NAOMI GOLDSTEIN YALIN
Translated by NAOMI GOLDSTEIN YALIN

Dr. Shay Efrat

Holocaust learning and morality

Based on

DOCTORAL THESIS

Jewish Holocaust learning program as forming moral attitudes among Jewish-Israeli high school students

Scientific Supervisor: Prof. Univ. Dr. Adriana BABAN

BABEŞ-BOLYAI UNIVERSITY CLUJ-NAPOCA
ROMANIA

Faculty of Psychology and Educational Sciences

PhD School: Applied Cognitive Psychology

Cluj-Napoca

2017

CONTENTS

ACKNOWLEDGMENTS

First I would like to thank Professor Adriana Baban, my Scientific Coordinator, for her professional and wise guidance. In addition, I would like to thank Professor Sebastian Pintea and Professor Gideon Greif for their professional help and support.

I would like to express my gratitude to the internal committee members: Professor. univ. Dr. Adrian Opre, Lector. univ. Dr. Eva Kallay and Lector. univ. Dr. Robert Balazsi for the evaluation of my progress over the years.

Gratitude is also due to the staff of "AD Atid Lekidum" for their friendship and advice.

I would like to express my thanks, gratitude and appreciation to the research participants who provided the data for my study.

Last but by no means least, I am most grateful for the support of my beloved family throughout this journey, and especially to my wife Molly who joined me on this fascinating exploration.

PREFACE TO THE RESEARCH
CONDUCTED BY SHAY EFRAT

The following preface, written by Professor Gideon Greif, relates to the question whether it is morally permissible and worthwhile from an educational and pedagogical point of view to undertake research on the moral dilemmas faced by the Jews during the Holocaust.

"Dealing with the 'morality' of victims – all types of victims – is problematic by its very nature. It is more natural to talk about the "morality" of the criminals and murderers – the Nazi-Germans and their principal crime: the Holocaust that they inflicted on the Jewish people and other people from 1933 to 1945. If we do not remember this, we shall do a severe injustice to the victims, and this is something that cannot be permitted. The morality, or more accurately, the immorality of criminals is what should head the list of priorities in any discussion on morality and conscience.

The Holocaust placed the individual and the collective Jewish community in unprecedented extreme, extraordinary and exceptional human situations. Now, 70 years later it is perhaps possible to discuss these situations in order to consider how we should act in similar situations. Naturally, even this determination is very problematic, since no historical situation is exactly replicated. Circumstances, backgrounds and situations alter from moment to moment, and what happened yesterday will not occur today or tomorrow. It is in this spirit that we should see the research conducted by Shay Efrat. The consideration of moral questions and dilemmas discussed in the research does not in any way taint the Holocaust victims, the Jews. Furthermore, it does not lessen the enormity of the German crimes.

However, there is educational value in discussing questions of human behavioral practices in extreme situations, in order to examine ourselves, to think about these situations close-up, to try to reconstruct a particular historical reality and perhaps to come closer to the victims and to identify with them.

Thankfully, we do not need to cope with the issues that faced the Jews through the years of the Holocaust. They were forced to decide – sometimes within minutes – fateful matters, concerning their families and children, those most precious to them. In most cases they did not have essential information; they had no relevant empirical knowledge of any kind and no-one to consult. Each Jew had to make these fateful decisions, whatever they might be, by themselves; each individual and his conscience, each with his world of morals and values. We therefore relate to the research and the questions that it poses as a workshop on human behavioral sciences – and no more than that.

This is not a judgmental workshop, nor is anyone being put on trial. Anyone who has not faced similar situations should not be quick to judge others; nobody will authorize us to do so. The moral dilemmas that were raised in this research were drafted out of respect and admiration for the masses of Jews, who were humiliated, tortured and murdered cruelly and intentionally by the German Nazis and their collaborators".

Professor Gideon Greif, Givatayim, Israel, December, 2014

ABSTRACT

The research is an innovating attempt to examine Holocaust Learning Programs and their influence on the formation of moral attitudes among Jewish-Israeli high school students. It aspires to fill a gap in knowledge relating to two major questions: the first is what do Israeli high school students think about the way in which Jews coped with the moral dilemmas that they faced during and after the Holocaust? The second question is what effect present Holocaust learning programs in high school have on the formation of students' moral attitudes. Therefore the main aim of the research is to identify the level of agreement or disagreement with the different moral behaviors of Jews during and after the Holocaust among Israeli high school students who participated in a Holocaust Learning Program, and in addition to examine what moral lessons they may have gained from this learning.

Due to the fact that this research subject has not been investigated or clearly defined in previous research, an exploratory approach was chosen. The research is a longitudinal survey combining mixed methods. It was conducted in three high-schools in Israel and included 102 participants. It lasted from January 2015 until January 2016 over a period of two academic years, when the students were in the middle of Grade11 until they reached the middle of Grade 12.

Research procedure included attitudes' measurement at three points in time during this period: January 2015, September 2015 and January 2016. At these times participants filled in a "Moral Attitudes Questionnaire" relating to 14 moral dilemmas. Participants were asked to relate to each dilemma by choosing between two alternative solutions - solutions based on deontological morality in contrast to solutions based on survival morality. In January 2016, at the end of the research, participants answered one more questionnaire - the "Perceived Influences and Lessons Learned Questionnaire". In addition, thirteen of the questionnaire participants also participated in individual in-depth interviews. Main research results indicate that participants gradually increased their understanding towards the survival moral solutions that Jews had to take to stay alive during the Holocaust. They also gradually decreased their judgmental moral attitudes towards the "passive" resistance of the Jews to the Nazis. Following the presentation of the research results and conclusions, we propose a new model for Holocaust learning - the "Multidimensional Holocaust Learning Program".

Keywords: Holocaust Moral dilemmas, survival versus deontological moral solutions, Holocaust learning program, the journey to Holocaust memorial sites in Poland, Multidimensional Holocaust learning program.

INTRODUCTION

The Jewish Holocaust - the premeditated and systematic murder of more than six million Jews by the Nazis during World War II (1939-1945) is a very wide field of knowledge and research. It has been discussed, investigated, taught and learned from many perspectives and points of view over many years but there is still much more to learn regarding this terrible event (Browning, 2004; Farabstein, 2002; Goldhagen, 1998; Zimerman, 2013). One of the most interesting but less investigated aspects of the Holocaust is the moral perspective. From the Jewish point of view, morality is considered in relation to four main dimensions: the Nazis who exterminated the Jews, the governments and individuals who assisted the Nazis, the free world and especially the countries who fought against the Nazi Germany, who undertook or did not undertake actions to save the Jews and finally the Jews' own actions in order to cope with the Holocaust. This research discusses moral aspects of the behavior of Jews, who were forced to cope with dilemmas caused by the Holocaust. The high-school students who participated in the research were asked to express their moral attitudes not as a judgment on the moral decisions taken by Jews during and after the Holocaust but as if they themselves faced identical dilemmas. The rationale for consideration of both Holocaust era dilemmas (1939-1945) and Post-Holocaust era dilemmas (1945-2016) was that these are two parts of one story and we need to look at both parts in order to understand the entire story.

The research subject was chosen for two main reasons: the first is my personal interest in the Jewish Holocaust, as a Jew and a family relative of both Holocaust victims and survivors. This interest has emotional as well as intellectual aspects. It stems from a deep emotional-moral sense of personal obligation to do something about the Holocaust which was created in my childhood and more acutely in adolescence during many conversations with my grandfather about what happened, mainly to our family, in the Holocaust.

The second reason is that in recent years during my professional work as a teacher with adolescents and college students, I have found that the study and discussion of ethical, moral and value-related questions in class, became very interesting and meaningful when related to Holocaust moral dilemmas.

The importance of this research subject derives firstly from the influence of the Holocaust on Jews and Israelis over the last decades. Throughout this time it continues to influence and occupy the Jewish people and the State of Israel in various ways - education, social, culture, political, national etc. (Guterman, Yablonka, & Shalev, 2008; Weiss, 2013; Weitz, 1997). Second importance derives from the continuing attempts mainly by the Ministry of Education in Israel to find new ways to teach the Holocaust to the young generations and to preserve its memory (Ministry of Education, 2015a). The universal importance of this research subject stems from the fact that the Jewish Holocaust is one of the darkest and perhaps one of the most despicable and horrifying chapters of World War II (Barley, 2007; Greif, Weitz & Macman, 1983). It is important for humanity to teach and learn about the Jewish Holocaust as a part of the terrible historical phenomena of genocides (Oron, 2006).

Over the years, various aspects of the Holocaust have been studied in many ways and from many points of view (Machman, 1998). However, the ways in which the Jews coped with the moral dilemmas they had to face during the Holocaust is not one of them. Public and academic discourse in Israel including school Holocaust learning usually tends to ignore or underestimate moral issues and specifically the Jews' behavior in relation to moral dilemmas during and after the Holocaust (Aharonson, 1999; Weinrab, 1984).

Previous research studies on the Holocaust have not focused on the development of moral attitudes evolving through Holocaust learning and this subject has barely been explored (Mayseless & Solomon, 2005). The present research that investigates the consideration of moral dilemmas of the Holocaust as part of Holocaust learning and their effect on students' moral attitudes is therefore an innovative attempt to bridge this gap of knowledge. **Why did we choose to focus on the moral dilemmas?** The answer is that moral dilemmas enable us to touch upon the very core of the Holocaust – the human emotions, thoughts and reactions of its victims and survivors. Furthermore, a deep understanding of moral dilemmas and decisions will help us widen our knowledge on human behavior in genocide events.

The decision to investigate the moral attitudes of high school students was based on the consideration that most of these young students learn the subject of Holocaust in Grades 11 and 12. Although these students are the third and fourth generation after the Holocaust they will carry on its memory in the future. The Holocaust Learning Program of the Ministry of Education includes chapters dealing with the causes of the rise of the Nazis in Germany, Nazi ideology, the Jewish Holocaust and World War II. This formal education program focuses on regular academic studies based mostly on textbooks, and is taught in history lessons during school studies (Ministry of Education, 2015). In addition, students are strongly encouraged to participate voluntarily in the organized youth heritage expeditions (journeys) to Holocaust extermination and memorial sites including ghettoes, exter-mination camps, memorials, synagogues and additional sites in Poland. The goal of the journey is to foster the students' deep identification with the Holocaust and its victims (Lindenstrauss, 2012). The journey to Poland is the culmination of an educational and academic process, which lasts a full academic year and includes intensive preparation including academic studies, meetings with survivors/witnesses, visiting Holocaust museums and watching documentary and epic Holocaust films (Bitts, 2004; Bar Natan, 2004). Because all of the participants in this research took the Holocaust Learning Program and most of them (70%) also chose to participate in the journey to Poland the research investigated the outcomes of these two parallel axes of learning.

The main research question was how Israeli youth, who are members of the third and fourth generations after the Holocaust grasp the Holocaust from the Jewish moral perspective. Therefore, **the main aim** of this research is to explore the attitudes of Israeli youth towards the way Jews coped with the moral dilemmas of the Holocaust. The research participants were 102 Jewish-Israelis students aged 16-17 from three high-schools who volunteered to participate in the research. The study is a longitudinal survey investigating the participants' learning process over a chronologic period of one year, from January 2015 until January 2016 and over a learning period of two academic years, from the middle of Grade 11 until the middle of Grade 12. This is also an exploratory research since its deals with a new subject – the moral issues of the Holocaust, more specifically with the moral attitudes of the participants towards the Jews' ways of coping with Holocaust moral dilemmas.

A mixed methods research was conducted in order to collect a wide range of data. A questionnaire investigating the participants' moral attitudes towards Jewish moral dilemmas during and after the Holocaust was given to the participants at three points in time – January 2015 at the beginning of Holocaust learning, September 2015 in the middle of learning and January 2016 at the end of learning. The questionnaire related to 14 different Jewish moral dilemmas - seven from the Holocaust era (1939-1945) and seven from the post-Holocaust era (1945-2015). In addition, at the third point in time (January 2016) the participants filled out another questionnaire regarding perceived social and educational factors influencing their moral attitudes and perceived moral lessons they learned in their Holocaust studies. At this point 13 students also participated in an individual in-depth interview in order to deepen the researcher's understanding of their thoughts and feelings following their learning.

CHAPTER 1- LITERATURE REVIEW

1.1 The Holocaust as a critical historical event

1.1.1 The main events of the Jewish Holocaust

"In the Holocaust, worlds collapsed, the world of the individual, family and the community, and all the conventional rules were broken: the rules for daily living and society, rules of morality and thought" *(Faberstein, 2002, p. 133).*

The Second World War (1939-1945) is considered as one of the beigest, important and influential historical events for humanity in the twentieth century. Possibly it is also the most terrible of all. During the war and especially between 1941-1945 another terrible despicable event occurred - the Holocaust suffered by the Jews and other people in Europe; the premeditated and systematic murder of more than six million Jews and other people from other races and nations by the Nazis under the leadership and vision of their leader, the Fuhrer, Adolph Hitler (Greif, Weitz & Macman, 1983). Hitler first outlined this vision in general lines in his infamous book, "Mein Kampf" ("My struggle" in German), first published in 1925 (Gunnar, 2000). The book was written when he was imprisoned for leading an attempted military coup to overthrow the German regime in November, 1923. From that point on, he tried to fulfill this vision using the power of the German nation. The Second World War gave him the opportunity and was the key to fulfill this ideological ambition (Heilbrunner & Zimerman, 1995).

Nazi Germany initiated the war in order to fulfill its vision of world domination. Above all, the Nazi regime sought to conquer territories in Eastern Europe and the Soviet Union to provide the German people with a "living space", but in fact, Nazis armed forces invaded many countries all over Europe and North Africa. Their plans involved political, economic and military considerations. The primary goal was to establish a New "Third Reich" – a German empire that was to rule Europe and, if possible, the entire world. As the "dominant world empire" Nazis consider themselves as entitled to overtake territories and economic resources by force. The new world order that would be created through war would consequently include the racial subordination of "inferior" races, especially the Slavs - the people living in Eastern Europe - to serve the "superior race", the German people. A no less important goal was to ensure the victory of the "superior German Aryan race" in the "war of the races", achieving world domination and exterminating "injurious" and "inferior" races. These races were primarily the Jews and secondly, the Romani people, both of whom were victims of Nazi ideology and were slated to be exterminated. Although the Nazis' actions took the lives of many people from many nations, Jews were considered the main threat and were, therefore, the main target (Machman, 1998).

During the years 1941-1945, approximately 6,000,000 Jews and 300,000 Romani people were murdered by the Nazis solely for ideological reasons (Barley, 2007). Nazi plans for extermination were also aimed towards specific groups of German citizens – those people, who were found to be physically or mentally disabled according to medical standards. They were murdered in a special secret government operation, termed "Euthanasia" or under the code name "T-4", which took place in 1939-1941. Approximately 100,000 Germans including children were executed, using toxin shots (Snyder, 2012). These actions provide an accurate reflection of the Nazi regime's implementation of their ideas in practice that were performed thoroughly, faithfully, and sometimes even happily by ordinary Germans (Goldhagen, 1998). In order to gain some understanding about how such monstrous actions could have happened, we should look at the main concepts of this ideology:

- The superiority of the state over its citizens so that the individual is obliged to relinquish his own welfare and wishes (which are considered secondary to those of the state) for the benefit of the state, which he has a duty to serve with no questions even at the cost of his life.

- Complete and unquestionable obedience to authority and especially the supreme authority of the "Fuhrer" Adolf Hitler whose orders are stronger than any written law. From this perspective, the state and the "Fuehrer" are one and the same and any resistance or harm to the state and its laws, as embodied in the Fuehrer's wishes and orders, is considered to be treason against the homeland.

- There is always a "struggle for survival" between races, however only the strong are worthy of living and the weak should die. The "Aryan" race – the German race - is the superior race on earth and consequently should dominate all other races and use the "inferior" races (mostly the Slaves) for its benefit, regardless of the welfare or wishes of those races. The "injurious" races – the Jews and the Romani peoples should be exterminated because they interrupt world order and balance. In order to maintain its superiority, the Aryan race should be sustained as a "pure" race without any unhealthy people, for example, physical handicaps and mental illness and disabled populations should also be exterminated.

- With regard to the Jews they are considered to be the most "injurious" race and the most terrible enemies of the "Aryan" race. They should therefore be completely

obliterated, both physically and culturally from the face of
the earth (Browning, 1992).

The murderers' hostility towards the Jews which was such an important part of Nazi ideology derives from a combination of ancient murderous Christian anti-Semitism with racist concepts that developed during the 19th century in Germany. The Nazi innovation was that they enacted the realization of this combined ideology by attempting to exterminate the Jews during the Holocaust. In fact, this created a reversal of the moral dictate, "Thou shalt not kill" became "Thou shalt kill" and the shedding of Jewish blood became permissible by anyone in any place during that time in occupied Europe. The anti-Semitism that existed among the nations that Nazi Germany conquered served as a "gift" for the Nazis because they could easily enlist collaborators among the conquered populations to help them to murder the Jews – they permitted others to kill Jews and not be punished and even receive rewards for this. There were many people in the occupied countries that supported the Nazis' policy towards the Jews whether by independent killing of Jews or by handing them over to the Nazis or by enlisting to units that acted under the Nazis to murder Jews. Nevertheless, it is important to note that although this help was important, it was not essential for the Nazis to fulfill their plans to eliminate the Jews. For the Nazi military personnel and police, the murder of Jews was an order that they had to perform whether or not they supported it. However, the fact is that the large majority of these people fulfilled the order without question and usually tried to excel in murdering Jews including women, children and babies. This happened despite the fact that those who wished to be relieved of the duty of participation in the murder of Jews could have done so and would not have been punished for this (Browning, 1992, 2004).

The racial war waged by Nazi Germany against the Jews lasted from January 1933, when the Nazis took power in Germany until the end of World War II in May 1945. The first to suffer were the Jewish citizens of Germany. On April 1st, 1933, only a few months after the Nazis took power, a boycott was declared on Jewish stores. This was followed by the legislation of the "Race Laws" and the denial of Jews' civil rights in 1935 and with brutal attacks including the destruction of Jews' property, killings. Then, in November 1938, during and after the "Kristallnacht" ("Crystal night") events, the Nazis conducted mass arrests of Jews, who were sent to "concentration camps".

At the outbreak of World War II, on September 1st, 1939, the Nazis expanded their war against the Jews outside German territories, at first mostly in Poland. Until 1941, the Nazi regime encouraged the emigration of Jews out of Germany, but following the German invasion of the USSR on June 22, 1941, the policy turned towards mass murder of the Jews (Zimerman, 2013). This policy developed gradually during the war until it became an immense extermination operation that spread through the many countries occupied by Nazi Germany. The program to exterminate all the Jews is usually referred to as "The Final Solution". This program took the lives of approximately 6,000,000 Jews from all over Nazi occupied countries, including USSR, Poland, Romania, Hungary, Bulgaria, Yugoslavia, Czechoslovakia, Italy, Greece, Norway, The Netherlands, Belgium, France and North Africa. The actual murder took place in the main in occupied USSR and Poland. It is important to indicate that the German Nazis did not only murder the Jews; in the process that preceded the actual murder, they tortured them, starved them and humiliated them in many most evil and distorted ways (Goldhagen, 1998).

The Jews were murdered using various methods: at first from 1939 – 1941, mostly in Poland, Jews were confined in parts of towns known as "ghettos", where they were subjected to intentional starvation and negation of minimal living conditions that caused mass mortality. At this time many Jews were also imprisoned and enslaved in "concentration" and "work" camps where they were forced to perform hard labor and were starved to death. From 1941 Jews were massacred systematically in mass shootings by special S.S "death squads" called "Einsatzgruppen" together with Nazi police units and locally recruited units from occupied territories mostly Ukrainians and Latvians. All these groups were aided by the Nazi army – the "Wehrmacht". These shooting massacres took place in the USSR, eastern Poland, Latvia,

Lithuania, Estonia and northern Romania (Bukovina). From 1942 -1944 Jews were murdered with poisonous gas in special extermination camps which were located primarily in Poland. The most famous extermination camp is "Auschwitz - Birkenau" in west Poland. The Jews were sent to these death camps from all over occupied Europe. From the fall of 1944, as a result of the Soviet "red army" advance from the east into occupied Poland and other Eastern Europe countries, many more Jews died as the Nazis herded them in "death marches". The "death marches" were long and arduous forced marches, almost without nourishment, from the hard labor camps and extermination camps in Eastern Europe (mainly Poland) into Germany. At that time and until the end of the war on 8 May 1945, many Jews died of starvation, illness and executions in the concentration camps that were still operating in Germany until the last days of the war. To sum up, the main stages of the extermination program in occupied Europe were:

1. Identification, marking and registration of Jews and denial of their civil rights (1939-1940).
2. Expulsion of the Jews from their places of residence and enforced concentration in "ghettoes". This included the infliction of starvation and physical and mental exhaustion and anguish through enforced labor, abuse and humiliation (1940-1941).
3. Organized and systematic extermination by shooting in the villages or towns where Jews were concentrated performed by "death squads" (1941-1942).
4. Systematic extermination of the Jews with poisonous gas in special "death camps" which were located mostly in Poland (1942-1944).
5. Extermination during the "death marches" and in the "concentration camps" in Nazi Germany (1944-1945) (Barley, 2007).

A question often asked is: "how could it happen". To answer this question, we should first look at it from the Jewish perspective - the way, in which the Jews coped with the Holocaust. Indeed, in the first years of the war Jewish leaders unwillingly obeyed the Nazi regime hoping that this cooperation would improve Nazi consideration of the Jews. The main reasons for this approach (Gutman, 1990a; Machman, 1998) included:

- There had been a short lived German regime in Poland from 1917-1918 that had favored and been very positive for the Jews, and this fact together with the generally positive reputation of the Germans, led many Jews to believe that a new Nazi regime would also be positive despite the many worrying signs that had already appeared.
- The Jews had been accustomed to cooperate with gentile civilian governments for hundreds of years as the safest way to ensure their wellbeing and therefore they acted in the same way with the Nazis before they fully understood their true intentions.
- Even after the extermination began and the Jews understood the Nazis' intentions, there were many leaders who believed that by cooperating and working for the Nazis, Jews could gain time until the Allies would defeat the Nazis in the war and that they would be rescued.
- The Jews continually hoped until the last moment that cooperation would help them to be saved and assumed that aggression towards the Nazis would lead to the Nazis losing patience and immediately harming them.
- In most places, the Nazis cruelly tortured and terrorized the Jews in different ways through starvation, forced labor, executions, degradations and abuse even before they began their full extermination program. Thus they reduced the Jews' ability and desire to defend themselves when the mass exterminations began.
- The Nazis used many deceptive means and thus managed to deceive the Jews regarding their real intentions until the last

moment; while the Jews "wanted" to believe the fictitious promises they were given.

- The Jewish population was an unarmed civilian population, untrained in warfare and without any military leadership. It faced a huge army and an evil terror mechanism that imprisoned it in ghettoes and made it difficult for them to conduct any independent action.
- The Jews' adherence to their families meant that many of them who could escape or fight, chose to stay with their families until the bitter end.

Nevertheless, as Gutman (1990b) and Machman (1998) point out, it is very important to emphasize that many Jews did resist the Nazis in various ways, including armed rebellion. Approximately 250,000 Jews survived and were saved because they resisted and struggled to survive in any way they could, assisted by certain main factors:

- Jewish education promoted a tradition of cohesion, mutual assistance and guarantee in times of distress.
- Belief in the ability of the Jewish people to survive despite many enemies over the generations with the help of Almighty God.
- The common desire to resist the Nazis and to prevent or at least disrupt the realization of their plans to exterminate the people of Israel.
- The belief that the Allies would eventually win the war.
- A strong desire to survive in order to document and tell about what had happened.
- A strong desire to wreak vengeance against the Nazis.

Now let us examine the question: "how could it happen?" from the Nazi perspective. As noted, the motivation for the genocide of an entire people stemmed from Nazi ideology. The orders for the mass murder of the Jews, the Romani people and other victims of Nazi ideology came from the highest Nazi officials and these orders were perceived by the Germans as the implementation of the wishes and policy of the Nazi party and regime, led by the "Führer", Adolf Hitler. Nevertheless, these orders were carried out by the entire German Nazi chain of command and at its lower end, by simple S.S. soldiers, policemen and regular army soldiers all of them contributing to the fulfilment of this ideology and policy in practice. The question of how they were able to morally justify their acceptance of and participation in the mass murder has not been satisfactorily answered till today (Mazower, 2015).

After the end of the war, in 1945-1946, trials of Nazi war criminals were held in the city of Nuremberg in Germany by the victorious allies – the Soviet Union, the United States, Great Britain and France. The accused were senior members of the Nazi regime and military forces. Some of them were sentenced to death and some were imprisoned. Hitler himself and other senior members of Nazi regime committed suicide at the end of the war. Nevertheless, most Nazis associated with the terrible war crimes were never put on trial (Kochavi, 2006). Although Nazi Germany was the driving force and the main factor in causing the Holocaust, it did not bear sole responsibility. It was supported by the regimes of its allies that cooperated with Nazi Germany and helped by individuals in many places that supported and even participated in the implementation of its deadly racist ideology. Fortunately, the alliance that opposed Nazi Germany won the war and stopped this terrible outbreak of madness and evil. Nazi ideology and military practice did not only hurt the 'injurious' races". Millions of Russian prisoners died in POW (Prisoners of War) camps. Millions of POWs from other countries and ordinary civilians died while performing forced slave labor. Additional millions of civilians died in wild but systematic destruction of towns and other settlements all over Europe. So how could it happen?! 70 years after the end of the war and despite vast research, there is still no clear answer to this disturbing question, but we can indicate that dictatorship, terror, racism, lack of morality and the people's fear of standing up to resist these forces are essential components in creating this kind of universal tragedy (Mazower, 2015).

. . .

1.1.2 The historical-psychological context of the Holocaust for the Jewish people

Since the destruction of Jerusalem and the deportation of most of the Jewish people from ancient Israel by the Roman Empire in 73AD, there have been two more events that are seen by scholars as exceptional historical events in the history of the Jewish people. These events, or perhaps historical processes, are the Jewish Holocaust that occurred from 1939-1945 during the Second World War and the establishment of the State of Israel in 1948 (Gutman, 1983). The proximity of these two events is not random and there is a close affinity between them, although each holds a significant status of its own. From a chronological viewpoint, the establishment of the State of Israel occurred after the Holocaust and the Holocaust served as an important catalyst in the establishment of the new state. Therefore, it is not surprising that the Israeli Ministry of Education relates to this connection in its learning program and introduces the chapter on the establishment of the state immediately after the chapter on the Holocaust in its history textbooks (Guterman, 2008).

Although the Holocaust ended with the surrender of Nazi Germany on 9th May 1945, it continues to influence and occupy the Jewish people and the State of Israel in various educational, social, and cultural dimensions until today (Weitz, 1997). Thus too, the official establishment of the State of Israel on 14th May 1948, just three years after the end of the Holocaust, is a process that in a way has not ended until today. This is at least true in geo-political terms since the young state is under constant existential threat from some of its neighbor states (Klausner, 1975; Goren, 1997). This is exemplified by the fact that one day after the declaration of the establishment of the State of Israel on 15th May 1948, the armies of five Arab states, Egypt, Syria, Iraq, Jordan and Lebanon invaded the infant state and joined the Arab Palestinian "Liberation Forces" with the declared aim of wiping Israel off the face of the earth. Despite the changes which have occurred since then and the peace treaties that have been signed between Israel and two Arab states Egypt and Jordan, the Holocaust continues to serve as an inspiration for the evil designs of some states and organizations (Gelber, 2004). It is almost superfluous to note that until today there are some who still aspire to destroy the State of Israel and overtly declare this as their goal (Ben-Orveh, 1983; Lorach, 1976). In this context, it is also relevant to note that the Palestinian Arabs who lost their state in the War of Israeli Independence borrowed the concept "Holocaust" (in Arabic "Nakhba") to describe their own catastrophe. They define their fall in the Israeli War of Independence as a national Holocaust and note its anniversary as a special commemorative day, remembering their defeat and raising black flags as a sign of mourning (Gelber, 2004; Machman, 1996a; Oron, 2003).

In order to discuss the issues raised by the Holocaust in the context of the State of Israel, it is necessary to understand how this context is seen in Jewish and Israeli perceptions. In terms of the present study, it is also important to note the significant influence of Jewish and Israeli conceptions of the Holocaust on educational approaches to Holocaust studies in Israel. In a broad national-historical conceptualization, the predominant view of the Jewish people sees the Holocaust as an additional event along the sequence of continuous attempts by different empires, peoples and dictators to harm and destroy the Jewish people and now also the State of Israel. This orientation traces the persecution of the Jews from the times of the Assyrians and Babylonians, through the Persians and Greeks and the Romans, to the Spanish Inquisition, the "pogroms" that massacred Jews in Eastern Europe and of course, the Holocaust perpetrated by German Nazis and their collaborators among the European nations. The modern-day aspirations of some states and terror organizations to destroy the State of Israel are seen by most Jews and Israelis as simply a current stage in this continuous process (Machman, 1996b).

1.1.3 Survivors and Israeli society's dual trauma following the Holocaust

"A person who survived the Holocaust, believing that he had reached the very limit of suffering in the years of persecution and imprisonment in the hands of the Nazis, now becomes aware that suffering is infinite and that he is able to bear additional and even sharper suffering" (Frankl, 1981, p. 115).

This is how one Jewish survivor of the Auschwitz extermination camp, the psychiatrist Viktor Frankl described the emotional experience of a Holocaust survivor after his release. Many testimonies from the Holocaust testify that the victims in their last moments expressed one or both of the following requests: revenge against the Nazis and that the world would remember them and what happened to them (Frankl, 1981).

Those who did survive felt that they needed to fulfill these wishes of their dead relatives, but they also had a strong desire to rebuild their personal and family lives that had been destroyed. They felt the need to tell their personal, family and community story, but this was a secondary need at that time; first, they had to cope with the exhausting challenge of resuming their lives. Indeed, those who survived the Holocaust all went through terrible physical and mental suffering, in addition to their loss of most or even all of those who were dear to them. They survived, but the events that they had undergone left their mark on them and continued to influence them for their entire lifetimes. Despite the fact that the war ended in 1945, they had to continually cope with the memories and scars that they carried in their souls and bodies. Most of the survivors were very young, between the ages of 15-25, since older and younger Jews were the first to be murdered by the Nazis (Aharonson, 1992).

With the end of the war, survivors had to invest immense efforts to overcome the trauma they had experienced and most of them indeed succeeded. The majority of the survivors immigrated to Israel, established new families and became active and creative citizens who became engaged in social activity and achievements no less than the other residents of the state; however, others suffered from severe Post-Traumatic Syndrome and did not manage to overcome this malady. Even those who functioned well remained with mental scars that imposed subjective suffering for the rest of their lives and, of course, influenced their families and their close surroundings (Neuman, 2010).

Yet many of the survivors, like the public and medical institutions of Israel tended to ignore and even deny the influence of the Holocaust in a manner known in psychology as the initial and unhealthy response to loss. The young state established in 1948 was dominated by mixed feelings: on the one hand, a sense of guilt due to the lack of success in saving the Jews who had been massacred in Europe during the war, and on the other hand, prevalent opinions criticized the "surrender" of those Jews who "went like lambs to the slaughter" (Heskel, 2015). Later after the "Eichman trial" in 1961, a greater understanding developed towards the survivors. The "Eichman trial" was the court case against Adolf Eichman, the Nazi officer who was responsible for the logistics of the extermination of the Jews of Europe. He was caught in Argentina and brought to court in Israel. During the trial, the testimony provided by survivors was written up in full detail in the press and broadcast on the radio, so that Nazi crimes and the full extent of the horrors of the Holocaust became public knowledge (Machman, 1996b). Thus, for the first time the survivors' suffering was awarded a sort of legitimization and many of them began to speak about what they had endured during the war. This change in attitudes was a positive change from a clinical psychology aspect, helping survivors to cope with their loss. With the exposure of the survivors' experiences and stories, the dimensions of the mental anguish that they had undergone were revealed and clinical understanding of their state grew. These stages in the Israeli public's attitudes towards the Holocaust during and shortly after the Holocaust are noted by Machman (1996b) and Heskel (2015):

1. Disbelief in the reality of the Holocaust.
2. Guilt feelings about the insufficient aid provided to the Jews in Europe.
3. Irrational anger at Jews who it seemed did not sufficiently resist the Nazis.
4. Scorn for the survivors who were seen as weak and submissive in contrast to what were supposed to be the brave and militant "sabras" (native born Israelis).
5. Lack of desire to listen to the terrible things that had happened to the survivors.

These reactions were "assisted" by a lack of real information and research on the Holocaust and its effects and by the fact that survivors did not talk about what had happened, or only a very few told their stories. The main factors for the survivors' difficulty in talking about the Holocaust, especially before the "Eichman trial", included:

1. Guilt feelings due to the fact that they remained alive while their family perished.
2. The fear that no one would believe them and that they would be ridiculed.
3. Reactions of scorn, disbelief and derision by Israeli society.
4. Fear of being accused of different acts that they did or did not do during the Holocaust.
5. A sense that they needed to focus on the present and to leave the past behind as something less important.
6. Psychological defense mechanisms – repression, rejection, denial.
7. A sense of shame and guilt feelings regarding matters that they were forced to do during the Holocaust.
8. A desire to protect children and other family members from the horrors of the past.
9. Difficulty to turn the mental resources that they need in order to reconstruct their lives, to the telling of their stories about the Holocaust.
10. Difficulties involved in expressing themselves in writing and orally in Hebrew.

All these factors led to misunderstandings in Israel concerning the actual events and experiences of the Holocaust.

One of the most extreme mental phenomena suffered by the survivors became known as the "Concentration Camp Syndrome" (Neuman, 2010). Clinically, this syndrome resembles the main characteristics of chronic and prolonged Post-Traumatic Syndrome as noted in the DSM-5, classification of psychiatric diagnoses (American Psychiatric Association, 2015). Nevertheless, it should be seen as a phenomenon with its own particular characteristics. The most blatant symptoms include: fluctuating anxiety and depression, irritability and aggressiveness, apathy and indifference, concentration difficulties, nightmares and repetitive associations relating to traumatic events. Other prevalent phenomena are difficulties in interpersonal relationships, distrust and suspicion towards others, a sense of isolation and emptiness, difficult guilt feelings and shame, a tendency to distance themselves from society, inability to enjoy life and to enjoy a sense of real satisfaction (Neuman, 2010). In addition to these mental characteristics, physical symptoms are also exhibited, especially damage to the central nervous system and the hormonal system (Shasha, 2012). Guilt feelings are especially predominant among Holocaust survivors. These feelings are usually expressed overtly in a phenomenon known as "survivor's guilt". The survivors blame themselves for remaining alive due to actions that they had to do to survive but which were often amoral such as theft of food, escape while leaving family members behind, forced cooperation with the Nazis etc. (Neuman, 2010)

Studies relating to child survivors of the Holocaust, those who had not reached the age of 17 at the end of the war, show that as adults, they developed illnesses such as diabetes, heart disease, different types of cancer, dementia and depression. These diseases appeared among child survivors of the Holocaust at three times the rate that they appeared in the general population (Shasha, 2012). The mental state of child survivors has been called the "child-survivor complex". This definition refers to the fact that the child survivors of the Holocaust endure irreversible psychological and social damage throughout their lives. This is in addition to the educational and cultural deprivation that they suffered during the years of Nazi persecution. Prevalent psycho-pathological phenomena among the children are depression, grieving and anxiety. These children suffer from defective ability to realize their educational, social and professional potential (Solomon, 2012). It is noteworthy that most of the survivors, despite the fact that they suffered all these phenomena to some extent, have succeeded in coping with their difficulties and leading, at least ostensibly, a normal life, yet often accompanied by daily mental distress because of their experiences during the Holocaust. This is a splendid example of the ability of the human spirit to cope with suffering and to enlist resources and strengths.

The influences of the Holocaust are also visible among the second generation, children of Holocaust survivors. Since the survivors and their families constitute a large proportion of the population in Israel, this is very significant for Israeli society. The strong mental needs of parents who are Holocaust survivors have significantly influenced their children and created difficulties for the children such as anxieties, difficulty forming individuation and over-responsibility for their parents and others so that they become "parental children" (Neuman, 2010). In order to survive the Jews had to cope with the new twisted and incomprehensible reality of the Holocaust.

Drawing on the above literature review, we suggest that survivors underwent five main psychological reaction phases during the Holocaust. The time between phases could be seconds, minutes, days, weeks, months or years depending on the situation. Successful survival depended on moving forward from Phase 1 to Phase 5 and to make the right decision at the end. This involved decision-making and performance of the decisions in practice, together with consideration of moral dilemmas. The phases can be illustrated using the following table:

Table 1.1 – The different phases of reaction to Holocaust reality

Phase of reaction	Nature of the reaction
First reaction	Total shock when facing a terrible new reality
Second reaction	Understanding the new reality
Third reaction	Acceptance and adaptation to the new reality
Forth reaction	Decision making – what to do?
Fifth reaction	Actual Doing

The fifteen common factors that were found to influence an individual's ability to survive during the Holocaust were: age, physical strength, mental strength, personal skills, personal appearance, resourcefulness, repeated luck, the help of other people, the way of behavior, possession of assets and money, strong belief in personal survival, strong hope to survive, finding purpose for survival, strong survival instinct and survival morality. These components have been found to be common to almost all survivors and they can be found in almost any Holocaust survival story. The four main components among these are: resourcefulness, repeated luck, the help of other people and survival morality.

- **Resourcefulness** – is the ability to recover and overcome new everyday challenges.
- **Repeated Luck** – is being able to avoid many situations in which you could easily die.
- **Help of Other People** – is simply the fact that no one could have survived the Holocaust without getting some help from others.
- **Survival Morality** – relates to the actions that an individual must take in order to survive, even if they are contradicting his believes and values.

The following figure illustrates How to survive the Holocaust:

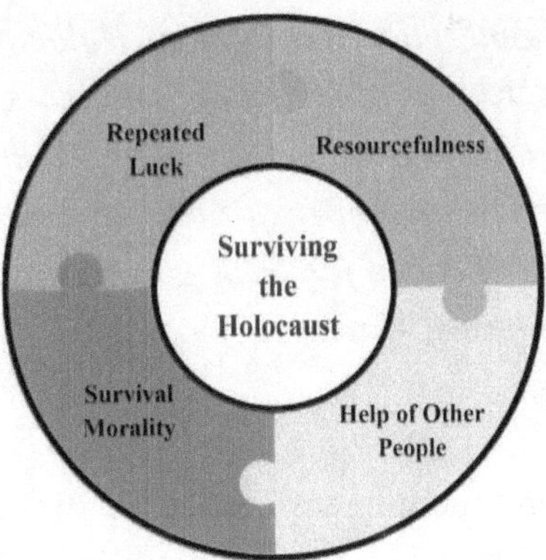

Figure 1.1 – Anchors for survival

· · ·

In order to recover from the trauma of the Holocaust and to build a
new life, the survivor had to cope with major mental and physical
injuries in addition to the loss of his family. Most of the survivors
needed to go through five phases of post-Holocaust reaction to achieve
successful recovery. Nevertheless, often the injuries were so severe that
they could not be never fully overcome. The following table describes
these five phases:

**Table 1.2 – The different phases of reaction to post-Holocaust
reality**

Phase of reaction	Nature of reaction
First reaction	Overcoming the confusing state of unexpected full freedom. A kind of shock
Second reaction	Overcoming the desire to die as a reaction to the loss of family
Third reaction	Repression of memories and feelings such as sorrow and shame
Forth reaction	Acceptance and adaptation
Fifth reaction	Catharsis using creative literary, oral or other means of expression

1.1.4 The inter-generational trauma of Holocaust

*"Among the generations of Holocaust survivors, the children of the
survivors, their grandchildren and great-grandchildren, there is an
inter-generational transmission of trauma and memory. This trauma
has most central significance for each generation and it influences a
variety of areas and levels"* (Fuchs, 2009, p. 12).

In order to understand the immense influence of the Jewish Holocaust
on the Jewish world and especially on the life experience of Israel to
which most of the survivors immigrated, it is important to understand
the influence of the Holocaust not only on the survivors but also on the
next generation. In April 1945, close to the end of the Second World
War, the Jewish population of Israel numbered 500,000 persons

(Hadawi, 1970). In the first years after the war, 150,000 Holocaust survivors arrived in the land of Israel and by the end of 1948, the year in which the state of Israel was established, the Jewish population had risen to 650.000. The increase in the number of Jews was a direct result of the immigration of Jewish Holocaust survivors from Europe (Orbach, 2010). Most of the residents of the Land of Israel before 1945 had arrived from Europe and they had relatives who had remained in Europe. After the establishment of the state in 1948, tens of thousands of Holocaust survivors immigrated to Israel, so that it becomes possible to understand that by the early 1950s, most of the Jews living in the State of Israel had relatives who had been murdered in the Holocaust or were themselves survivors (Steev, 2002). Second generation descendants of the survivors lived in and grew up in the new Israeli society that was being created. It was very different from the society in which their parents had lived in Europe before the Second World War. For them, the Holocaust was more a sort of myth than the continuous daily reality of the past and present endured by their parents - the generation of the survivors for whom the Holocaust never really ended. This family background shaped and continues to shape the children's perception of their reality. The difficult events of the Holocaust, which were experienced to a different extent and at different strengths through the medium of their parents, never disappeared and is continually influential till today (Bar-On, 1994). These influences were explained most succinctly by Gampel (2005):

"The Holocaust changed the meaning of our history, its effects are revealed in the long term, dispersed in space and time like 'radioactive fallout'; The parents who are Holocaust survivors, their children, grandchildren and grand-grandchildren cannot defend their children from their own anxieties" (p. 13).

An amazing example of the influence of the Holocaust on the second generation of survivors is given in "Warriors' discourse" – a discussion between Israel Defense Forces soldiers that participated in the Six Day War in 1967. Yariv ben Aharon, one of the soldiers, noted: *"it's true that people believed that there would be a massacre here if we do not succeed in the war ... the Holocaust granted or endowed us with this concept. This is a concrete concept for each person who grew up in Israel even if they themselves did not undergo the Holocaust. Genocide is a very real concept for us"*. Abba Kovner, who led this discussion - a Holocaust survivor and partisan who had fought the Nazis – responded: *"I can see that you (the fighters) unintentionally reveal here the existence of the Holocaust's effect on you. This should supposedly be strange but your reality leads you there"* (Yablonka, 2008, pp-33). Another interesting example is presented in the book by Kischke (2013), a second generation descendant of Holocaust survivors:

"At night I have nightmares. I dreamt that my father was lying dead between the train tracks and the chimney in Auschwitz" (the Auschwitz-Birkenau extermination camp was where million Jews were murdered). I woke crying. Father would come running to my bed and consoled me without asking any questions. And what could I have answered? He said: "it's not terrible, it's just a bad dream" (pp. 9-10).

The difference in the perceptions of the different generations of Holocaust survivors can be understood in psycho-social and historical terms: the first generation – the generation of the survivors had to struggle to be accepted and integrate into the harsh Israeli society that did not accept the survivors with much understanding. They had to participate in the construction and defense of the young state under attack by its Arab neighbors. This is the generation that lost its home, its land, its security and its old life. They arrived in Israel in order to find a sanctuary, home and healing. Members of the second generation were already "sabras" (the name given to those who are born in the Land of Israel). They felt the responsibility imposed upon them to continue the construction of Israel and its defense and to raise their own children in the land. They were also seriously influenced by the trauma of the Holocaust as embodied in the overt and covert messages that they received from their parents. This second generation reinforced the homeland and increased its security, but they still lived under the threat of the Holocaust. The third generation has stronger self-confidence and is, therefore, able and willing to ask itself questions that were seen as "taboo" by previous generations. This is also even truer with regard to the fourth generation. Members of the third and successive generations were born into a world that is relatively safer and more distant from the Holocaust and so they are influenced less by it. This weakening of the trauma passed on from generation to generation allows the opening of discussion on the Holocaust and goes deep into new territory in an atmosphere of existential security. From a psycho-social and historical aspect it is now more possible for the third and fourth generations to develop new perceptions of the Holocaust and new directions of thinking (Litvak-Hirsch & Brown, 2008).

The first generation was occupied with its pain, repression, revenge and maintaining its very survival against the influences of the trauma. In parallel, this generation also dealt with the commemoration of the memory of the Holocaust through the transmission of their testimonies and autobiographical novels. The second generation continued to deal with the memory of the Holocaust and its commemoration and developed research and national educational programs to study the Holocaust. This generation focused on the experience of the Holocaust as a national trauma revolving around the Nazi's attempt to exterminate the Jewish people. The third generation began to deal with questions of morality in relation to the Holocaust (Weiss, 2013). An example of this is described in the book "The banality of indifference":

"An essential condition for coping with evil of this sort (the Holocaust as genocide) is to be aware of the fact that evil intentions and the circumstances of its occurrence always exist. From a moral aspect it is impossible to sit by idly in the presence of the criminal acts of any genocide. Evil does not cease to be evil when it harms others" (Oron, 1995a, p. 11).

1.1.5 Summary of main events from 1933-2016

- *30th January 1933* – The Nazi Party becomes the governing party in Germany, Hitler is appointed Chancellor.
- *15th November 1935* – Enactment of the Race Laws against the Jews of Germany – "Nuremberg Laws".

- *9-10th November 1938* – "Kristallnacht" – a government organized pogrom against the Jews of Germany.
- *30th January 1939* – Hitler speaks against the Jews in a speech at the "Reichstag", threatening that they will "pay a price" if war breaks out "because of them". This is Hitler's clearest reference to the intention to harm the Jews. As far as we know, Hitler never gave a written order to exterminate the Jews. In fact, there was actually no need for this because Hitler's oral orders in Nazi Germany were stronger than any other written law or order.
- *1st September, 1939* – Germany invades Poland and the Second World War erupts. Jews are concentrated into and imprisoned in "ghettoes" and an un-declared policy of starvation, forced labor and mental and physical abuse is carried out against them.
- *22nd June 1941* – Nazi Germany attacks the Soviet Union. The S.S. butchers the Jews in the areas that the Nazi army occupies with extermination shooting units, employing local collaborators to assist them. This is the beginning of the planned mass murder. About 1.4 million Jews were murdered by the extermination shooting units.
- *20th January 1942* –The "Wannssee Conference": The Nazis plan the continuation and improvement of the organized annihilation of all the Jews of Europe using gas in special extermination camps. From 1942-1944 the new planned extermination program is carried out.
- *8th May 1945* – Nazi Germany surrenders to the Allies. The Second World War and the systematic extermination of the Jews end.
- *20th November 1945* – the opening of the "Nuremberg trials": the trial of the leaders of the Nazi regime, the S.S and the German army by the Allied Powers. The S.S was considered as a criminal organization in the trials which continued until 1949 (Gutman, 1990b; Kochavi, 2006; Levine, 2005; Friedland, 1997).

- ***14th May 1948*** - The Israeli War of Independence began.
- ***August 1950*** – The Law to exact Justice against Nazis and their Collaborators is enacted in Israel. Trials of Jews accused of collaborating with the Nazis begin in Israel.
- ***July 1951*** – Enactment of the first Holocaust Remembrance Day law in Israel: "Holocaust Day and the Ghetto Rebellion". In 1959 the law was renamed to become "The Memorial Day for the Holocaust and Heroism".
- ***August 1953*** – the "Memory of the Holocaust and Heroism – Yad Vashem Act" is enacted. The "Yad Vashem Institute", the authority for the commemoration of the Holocaust and Heroism is established as the main museum of the Holocaust on Mount Herzl, Jerusalem. It is declared to be an official Israeli state institution by a special law passed by the "Knesset" (Israeli Parliament).
- ***June, 1955*** –the first instance trial of Israel Kastner is completed. The judge Benjamin Halevi accuses Dr. Israel Kastner of having "sold his soul to the devil", in other words of having collaborated with the Nazis against the Jewish people. In March 1957 Kastner is murdered by Jews who sought vengeance against him. In January 1958, in a second instance trial Kastner is acquitted. In effect, this affair ended the era of trials against Jews for their acts during the Holocaust.
- ***January 1959*** – the "Holocaust and Heroism Memorial Day Act – State Memorial Day" is enactment. The date of the Memorial Day is determined as 27th Nissan according to the Hebrew calendar. This day is the sixth day after Passover during the days of the counting of the Omer which are days of bereavement for the Jewish people. The date is close to the date on which the Warsaw ghetto uprising began on 19th April 1943 and it takes place approximately a week before the Day of Remembrance for Soldiers Who Fell in Israel's Wars. The name of the new act was intended to combine the memorial for the extermination of the Jews

with the memory of their heroic stand against the Nazis in battle and in other forms of resistance.

- *July 1961* – the Eichman trial begins. Adolf Eichman, who was responsible for the administration of the extermination of European Jews was tried in Israel, found guilty and hung. For the first time - the testimonies of Holocaust survivors were heard in the court and shocked Israeli society. People began to understand the reality of the Holocaust and to alter what had previously been their alienating and disparaging consideration of Holocaust victims and survivors.

- *February, 1980* – the Knesset passes an amendment to the State Education Act, adding an additional goal to the goals for education in Israel as follows: education for "awareness of the Holocaust and Heroism". Since then the Holocaust has been taught officially as part of the Matriculation syllabus in history.

- *April 1983* – the Israeli youth journeys to Poland begins. As a result of political change in Poland Israelis were now authorized to visit Poland. One of the consequences of this was that it was possible to realize the aspiration to visit the Holocaust sites in Poland.

- *February 2014* - The Ministry of Education published a revised learning program on the subject of the Holocaust, known as "Memory for me". This is an organized set learning program from nursery to Grade 12 that came into operation from the school year 2014-2015 (Konforti, 2006; Shapira, 2009, Ministry of Education, General Manager's Directive, 2014).

1.2 The concept of morality

1.2.1 Morality - terms and definitions

Since the research described in this thesis relates to moral dilemmas during the Holocaust, certain fundamental concepts must be discussed in order to clarify the issue including the determination of exactly what is meant by the following terms: "morality", "ethics" "values", "universal morality", "moral dilemma", "deontological morality", "utilitarian morality" and "survival morality".

"Morality" relates to human behaviors that are considered to be "good", distinguishing them from behaviors that are considered to be "bad" or "immoral". This leads us to think about morality in terms of behaviors or judgments made in consideration of the principles or rules of appropriate conduct, and the distinction between right and wrong (Ring, 1999).

"Ethics", also known as moral philosophy, is a branch of philosophy that involves systematizing, defending and recommending concepts of right and wrong conduct. The term comes from the Greek word ethos which means "character". Ethics studies the moral behavior of humans and offers alternatives regarding how one should act (Kidder, 2003).

"Values" are actually the criteria (standards) that we choose to guide how we live, based on a worldview relating to questions of justice, morality and additional issues. Values determine what is and is not correct and appropriate for us in a particular society or organization. An example of a value might be "true friendship" or "human dignity". Values constitute the foundations on which society is constructed and these are considered fundamental values that dictate behavioral norms. This means that the value dictates what is and is not desirable in a particular society, or in other words, which behaviors are and are not accepted and desirable (Levine, 1979).

To summarize: The words "morality" and "ethics" are often used interchangeably; however, it is useful to make the following distinction:

- Morality is a collection of accepted rules of behavior in human society, in which one believes and which one normally obeys.
- Ethics is the philosophical study of morality which criticizes it and presents alternative moral behaviors. It is

also more related to professional concepts such as different codes.

- Values are the moral standards by which we want to live.

This study focuses on moral questions, issues and dilemmas and so the main concept discussed here will be morality. Is there a "universal morality"? Or are the criteria for morality completely dependent on the society, culture, location and time in which they are applied, so that they are context-related and vary according to time and space? We shall try to examine this question through a short historical review. Much of ancient moral philosophy, from the west to the east, was virtue-based. All societies valued benevolence and fairness, but they also emphasized group-level concerns about social order, authority, duty and loyalty to one's family or group (Larue, 1991; Schweder & Haidt, 1993).

When we think about universal moral behavior, we naturally and usually think of the Old Testament and the Ten Commandments. According to Weinfeld (2001), the Ten Commandments are actually moral commands that God delivered to the Jewish people to instruct them how to behave with one another and how to worship God. The commandments that establish social behavior are: Honor your father and mother, do not kill, do not commit adultery, do not steal, do not lie and do not covet (another man's property). These moral commands are considered universal moral commands, or guiding attitudes, or values both by Judaism and Christianity. The New Testament and Christianity, as one of the main monotheistic religions, adopted and developed this moral thinking (Leibovich & Lavie, 1997). The "Quran", the holy book of the third great monotheistic religion, Islam, which was influenced by both Judaism and Christianity, provides similar although not identical moral precepts for human behavior (Abrahamov, 2006).

Looking further, towards the Far East reveals that ancient eastern religions also relate in depth to issues of morality. For example, the Shinto religion in Japan sanctifies the value of life so greatly that even killing in order to survive (hunting, for example) should be conducted only according to a minimal essential extent. Killing for profit is considered a gross infringement, tainting the honor of the killer and the victim (Bowker, 2002).

Buddhism provides moral stipulations including: avoiding harming any living being; avoiding taking anything that is not yours, avoiding harmful use of sexuality, avoiding saying anything that is inappropriate or harmful, avoiding taking from those who are mentally challenged (Tal, 2006).

Hinduism with all its various sects emphasizes the multiplicity and variety of opinions, freedom of expression and toleration between different people (Greenspan, 2012). Hinduism also seriously opposes any expression of violence or aggression (Knott, 2008).

In modern times, civil law is the tool used by Western countries to consider moral issues, for example: The Eighth Amendment to the US Constitution (one of the first ten amendments to the Constitution known as the Bill of Rights) forbids the Federal Government from imposing "cruel and unusual punishment", in other words, it considers the extent of morality of punishment, especially with regard to capital punishment. The US Constitution has served and still serves as an example for other countries, especially throughout the Western world. But it should be noted that some of the amendments to the constitution were in turn inspired by the principles of the French revolution (1789) and by the earlier English Bill of Rights in 1689 (Bruns, 1986).

Israeli law relates to the issue of moral behavior of soldiers in the Israel Defense Forces. It stipulates explicitly that despite the accepted military rule that a soldier must obey orders and fulfill them in an optimal manner, and although this rule is essential to the proper functioning of the army, there is still an exception when an order is given to the soldier is obviously illegal. This exception was determined by Justice Benjamin Halevi in a verdict given at the trial of the Border Guard soldiers who massacred Arabs at Kfar Kassem after they had breached a curfew imposed on the village in 1957. This ruling was also applied in other trials (though rarely) during the following years, such as the trial of Ehud Yatom of the Intelligence Service, who killed Palestinian prisoners of war, captured after they had hijacked a bus. He had been obeying the orders of the head of the Intelligence Service, Avraham Shalom (Ilem, 1990).

German law, even during the Nazi regime, forbade certain actions such as murder. This was the reason that the comprehensive plan for mass murder of the disabled and mentally challenged populations, organized and performed by the Nazi state and known as the "Euthanasia" Program", was hidden from the German public (Barley, 2007).

In sum, it can be said that ethical codes universally guide moral behavior that sanctifies the value of life. This can be seen as a general historical, religious and cultural world perception. It, therefore, seems that it is possible and perhaps even necessary to use the term "universal morality".

The main focus of this research is on moral dilemmas. What are moral dilemmas? A dilemma is a situation in which an individual is faced by two or more alternatives and has to choose between them in order to decide how to act in a given situation or to respond to a question. The dilemma creates a state of deliberation as the individual examines their own considerations, and it may be very difficult and even sometimes impossible to resolve. In a moral dilemma, deliberation stems from the character of a person's conscience and their perception of what is the "correct" way to act. The dilemma is expressed by the fact that the individual finds it difficult to decide which alternative is the "moral" one (Weiner, 1995).

A moral dilemma is actually a moral conflict. It is a situation in which the individual is pulled in contrary directions by rival moral arguments which have different outcomes. We may experience moral conflicts of many different types, such as: moral conflicts between personal interests, moral values, different duties or moral principles. Typically, the scenario that we face in a moral dilemma is that there are important moral reasons to support both options (Sorensen, 1988). An example of moral dilemmas during the time of the Holocaust is portrayed in the book "Sophie's Choice" (Styron, 1979). The book describes a true story. A Jewish mother of two children was asked to make a fatal decision by a Nazi officer, which child would remain with her and survive at least in the meantime and which child would be taken away by the Nazis and killed. An example of the dilemmas that Holocaust survivors faced following the Holocaust-era is as follows: whether to overcome mental inhibitions and to tell the story of how they survived, despite their sense of shame due to the choice they were forced to make in difficult moral decisions during the Holocaust, or to avoid exposing their secrets (Kischke, 2013).

Moral dilemmas focus on the deliberation between a "deontological"- the "right moral" choice - and the "a-moral" or "utilitarian" choice (Christensen & Gomila 2012).

"Deontological morality" is a morality based on state and sometimes religious laws together with the values of the particular culture and society. It is accepted as normal in a specific society or societies and characterizes moral decisions in standard daily situations (Waller, 2005; Beauchamp, 1991; Kamm, 1996).

"Utilitarian morality" is a morality that grasps moral action as one that should maximize the benefit for the person who carries out a curtain action. As such, this kind of moral behavior could contradict deontological morality (Bredeson, 2011; Gay, 2002).

"Survival morality": In extreme moral situations facing the danger of death, a decision according to "utilitarian" morality can save a life (Koenigs et al., 2007). So we can say that "Survival morality" is actually a kind of utilitarian morality decision. Such a decision would completely contradict the substance of deontological morality. The main and perhaps the only goal of this morality is to preserve lives in the face of great danger. Survival morality is based on moral thinking that has an "instinctive" character and serves the basic human drive for survival. It is an expression of thinking that is often very hasty and sometimes instinctive as the individual tries to find ways to save his life. "Survival morality" is potentially relevant for all the Holocaust era dilemmas, because the solution to these dilemmas could lead to life or death. In these dilemmas, tension exists between solutions that are based on "deontological morality" versus solutions that are based on "survival morality". Survival morality very often characterized Jews' behavior during the Holocaust. Holocaust survivors would usually not have survived if they had acted otherwise (Greif, 1999; Wiesenthal, 2012).

1.2.2 The development of moral thinking

Since the research deals with adolescents aged 16-17 and the moral thinking of adolescents, this subject is now discussed in some depth.

Adolescence is a period that continues from age 12 until later teenage years and often even extends into the third decade of a young adult's life. This is a period of many changes and accelerated physical, mental, emotional, sexual and social development. Since adolescence spans almost a decade, it can be divided into the following stages: early adolescence, approximately 13-14 year olds, middle adolescence from 14-16 year olds, and later adolescence from approximately 16 to the beginning of the twenties (Sroufe, Cooper & DeHart, 1998). Most physical changes occur in the early stage of adolescence, especially for girls, and this period also involves changes in social relationships and relations with parents. During middle adolescence, the emphasis is on the growing development of the self and autonomy and the beginning of the search for the consolidation of identity and adopting adult functions. The period of later adolescence is one in which personal identity is formed in a clearer way, as are attitudes concerning a variety of domains and principles of social and political behavior (Elliott & Feldman, 1990).

Within these chronological boundaries of adolescence that relate to stages of general development, three main dimensions influence the development of moral thinking in adolescents at the later stage of development. These dimensions are (1) the consolidation of personal identity (2) social development and (3) development of thinking. According to Harter (1990), during late adolescence, the development of the self reaches a point that permits the creation of a consolidated personal identity. This identity includes moral values, adoption of principles of social behavior, attitudes concerning religion and nationality, together with political and gender identity.

The psychological theoretician, Eric Erikson (1968), dealt with this dimension of personal identity development, relating especially to psychosocial development. He was the first researcher to examine the formation processes for the development of the self and the formation of personal identity in a social context. The uniqueness of Erikson's theory was that he focused on the question of an individual's identity formation and through this explored the development of the personality. According to Erikson (1987), the formation of a sense of identity is a person's most important goal. If this goal is not attained, a situation of identity confusion evolves bringing difficulty and pain. In Erikson's opinion, the autonomous self is the basis for human behavior and one of the essential functions that construct it is the creation of a sense of identity and its maintenance. The sense of identity includes four components: uniqueness, identity completeness and synthesis, unity and continuity and social affiliation (Erikson 1987).

Identity includes a set of feelings that stem from and are maintained by the environment. If the environment encourages the development of identity and control, good and proper development will ensue, but if the environment impedes this development, confusion, impotency and deficient social assimilation will appear. Erikson saw society as a positive factor that could assist a person's development and functioning. Yet society may also have a negative influence if it teaches the individual negative values or values that contradict and confuse, making the formation of identity difficult or engendering the development of a negative identity.

Erikson described eight stages of human development in which identity is formed through a long series of reciprocal social relations. He described this development as "a life cycle" and believed that the personality develops over an entire lifetime, and at each stage, the "self" copes with a crisis that it must overcome in order to proceed to the next stage. The stage that interests us in this research is Stage 5 – identity versus role confusion. This stage of identity formation overlaps with the age of adolescence and according to Erikson relates to ages 12-18. The value noted at this stage, in terms of the formation of an independent identity, is "loyalty". At this stage, there is an acute crisis of identity for the adolescent that focuses on the question: "Who am I?" The goal at this stage is to consolidate identity or to consolidate different social identities such as sexual identity, social identity and later also political and moral identity (Erikson 1987).

The attainment of an independent identity means that the adolescent accumulates confidence to maintain internal unity and consistency that also correlates with the way they are seen by society. With the achievement of a sense of identity, the adolescent attains self-definition out of a sense of an integrated personality and affiliation to the social framework to which he belongs. This process has a decisive influence on the continuation of their lives. This is when the youth reaches a positive solution to the identity crisis; but when there is no such solution; development will be different (Erikson 1968). Negative childhood experiences or difficult and unsuitable environmental conditions may generate a state of confused identity and confused roles. This confusion is expressed in the adolescent's lack of success in choosing a self-definition out of the available options. This is liable to cause evasion of commitment and social affiliation, and hostile consideration towards the accepted social frameworks and people who belong to them. Another negative possibility is the choice of a negative identity. In this state, the adolescent who does not succeed in reaching a positive solution to confusion of roles and the identity crisis chooses as an alternative to identify with figures and attitudes considered negative and even forbidden in the society and family in which he lives. Adoption of this negative identity creates conflict between the adolescent and members of their families and social environment, such as teachers, classmates and family members. If a successful solution to the identity crisis in adolescence is attained, the adolescent can succeed in forming a clear positive identity and adopting the value of "loyalty". They will then be able to hold a consistent self-identity and sense of belonging to their family and society (Erikson, 1987). Erikson created important foundations for the understanding of psychosocial development, however, he did not relate to cognitive and moral aspects. Another most important researcher-Jan Piaget was the first to close a major part of this gap, the cognitive domain.

Piaget (1972) coined the term "formal operations" to describe a type or manner of thinking based on a system of principles of formal logic that lead to cognitive progress in adolescence. This "logic of arguments" acts by accumulating individual statements or arguments in order to reach a logical conclusion. Piaget & Inhelder (1973) claimed that formal operations assist the adolescent to practice thinking that is more abstract and systematic than in their past and to reach a level that enables them to make analogies and generalizations. It can be said that insofar as the level of thinking improves, the ability for more abstract and generalized thinking is enhanced. What then is the connection between such developed thinking and moral thinking? Piaget defined moral thinking as a process combining thinking and judgment that leads to the taking of action that is perceived as correct in a given situation. He believed that the development of moral thinking is a direct result of cognitive development and the broad social experiences that the child and adolescent experience.

According to Piaget (1972) model, moral thinking develops in stages, which are similar and, in fact, parallel to the stages of cognitive development. The first stage is the "moral absence" stage correlating with ages 5-7. At this stage, there is, in fact, no real moral thinking. The second stage, at approximately ages 7-12, is the stage of "moral realism". At this stage, the child sees behavior in a polarized way, as completely justified or completely unjustified. They think that if they act in an inappropriate manner, they will be punished by an external authority such as God or their parents or their teachers (Piaget, 1965) Children at this age base their moral attitudes on the implications of the action for them and not on the underlying intention of the act. The third stage begins in adolescence from approximately 12 years of age and is called "moral autonomy". At this stage, the young adolescent begins to see morality as something that is relative or connected to a particular situation so that it is seen as a changing reality. In moral judgments that the adolescent conducts at this stage, they take into account the intentions and not only the results of the action. They recognize the possibility of the existence of different attitudes concerning moral questions and no longer perceive moral rules as absolute, but rather as connected with social norms and values that can change. At this stage their moral thinking relates to morality as something founded on social consensus

(Piaget, 1965). Although Piaget was the first who outlined the most important theoretical model of moral development, it was really a pioneering work that needed more expansion and development, which was performed by Laurence Kohlberg.

Like Piaget, the theoretician and researcher Laurence Kohlberg (Kohlberg, 1969) developed a model to explain the development of moral thinking. Kohlberg did not see morality as a collection of behavioral criteria, but rather as different levels of understanding of justice. In contrast to Piaget he defined a model of moral development composed of three stages, each stage being divided into two and thus creating six sub-stages. This pioneering model was constructed through the presentation of moral dilemmas that were given to research participants at different ages. According to Kohlberg (1973) these stages are:

Stage 1: "Pre-conventional morality" - Early childhood'

At this stage, the child's judgment is not based on any conventions or social rules and he is unpredictable.

Sub-stage 1.1: "Obedience and punishment orientation". Good behavior is based on the child's desire to avoid punishment that could be imposed by an external authority (such as parents) if the behavior goes against the desire of that authority.

Sub-stage 1.2: "Hedonistic and instrumental orientation". Good behavior is anything that allows a material or other reward (emotional, social etc.) to be attained. The motivation for a moral decision is the aspiration for a reward for the behavior.

Stage 2: "Conventional morality" late childhood and beginning of adolescence.

At this age, moral judgment is based on impressions from the environment and from social experiences. The focus here is on the opinions of others and the official rules that other people have created.

Sub-stage 2.1: "The good child orientation". The goal is to gain approval of society due to moral decisions. The motivation for an action is the fear of social criticism.

Sub-stage 2.2: "Social conventions or law and order orientation". At this stage, moral decision is based on the young adolescent's concern to fulfill their duty as determined by the laws of society to their best understanding. The thinking is directed towards others, their welfare and respect.

Stage 3: "Post-conventional morality" (anchored in principles) – late adolescence and adulthood. At this stage, the adolescent passes the stage of conventional opinion and begins to focus on more abstract principles that determine what is good and what is bad.

Sub-stage 3.1: "The social declaration orientation". At this stage, the moral goal is to assist society and to run things smoothly. Thus, even if particular laws are seen as arbitrary, they are nevertheless also seen as being important since they allow people to live harmoniously and stably together. The motivation for a moral action is a person's desire to realize the respect that society, and especially their peer group, gives them, or in other words: social conformity.

Sub-stage 3.2: "Hierarchy of principles orientation". At this stage, the goal is to make the moral decision or to perform moral judgment according to the highest relevant moral principles. At this level of moral thinking and judgment, society's rules and laws are integrated with the dictates or instructions of the conscience to create a hierarchy of principles and moral judgment. The individual is motivated by the aspiration to comply with their principles, as they understand them, even if the society around them thinks or acts otherwise.

How did Kohlberg conduct his studies? Kohlberg (1969) gave his participants case descriptions containing moral dilemmas. The participants could choose to answer in one of two ways: "for" or "against", where each choice had an explanation, indicating why it should be chosen. Kohlberg sorted the reactions of the participants according to the six stages mentioned above, not only because of the choice itself, but mainly according to the reasons given for the choice. In this manner, he assigned the participants' responses to levels of morality, and thus, he determined the moral level of each person on the scale (Kohlberg, 1969).

Kohlberg's work is, without a doubt, a trail-blazing work in the field of moral theory and research. Nevertheless, it has drawn much criticism. The main criticism focuses on the argument that there is not always a connection between the measures of moral discretion, thinking or principles, and the behavior in practice at the time of a test. People may answer moral dilemmas in a certain way under laboratory conditions, but it is impossible to know how they will actually react in real-life conditions. This loose connection also leads to the argument that the very meaning of the developmental hierarchy of moral thinking as presented by Kohlberg needs further investigation (Rest, 1983). Another criticism concerns the artificial nature of moral dilemmas in research is that it represents only a vague connection to the moral dilemma scenarios in reality (Christensen et al., 2014).

1.3 Morality in psychology research

1.3.1 Modern research on moral dilemmas

As we have seen, the research of moral issues is based on moral dilemmas. It was Piaget (1965/1932) who laid the foundations for research on moral thinking, and it was Kohlberg (1969) who developed Piaget's research and created the main theory explaining the development of moral thinking. He also added a qualitative dimension, positioning different levels of moral thinking and judgment not only along an axis of development but also along an axis of quality.

Indeed, the research of moral dilemmas offers fascinating possibilities to study the grounding of psychological principles of human moral cognition, thinking and behavior. This possibility has attracted an increasing number of researchers to this subject, and although there has been a significant development and progress in the study of moral issues and dilemmas, it has been accompanied by criticisms concerning methodology used in these studies (McGuire, Langdon, Coltheart, & Mackenzie, 2009).

Modern science and research in moral psychology have focused on two challenges to the long dominant cognitive development paradigm conceived by Piaget and nurtured by Kohlberg (Piaget, 1965/1932; Kohlberg, 1969). The first cognitive developmental researchers assumed that moral judgment is the product of conscious, effortful reasoning and focused on the deliberate application of explicit moral theories and principles to particular cases (Kohlberg, 1969; Piaget,

1965; Turiel, 1983, 2005). The first challenge to this approach claimed that moral judgment takes the form of intuition, accomplished by rapid, automatic and unconscious psychological processes (Damasio, 1994; Haidt, 2001; Hauser, 2006; Schweder & Haidt, 1993;). A central motivation for this challenge comes from studies demonstrating people's inability to articulate a rational basis for many strongly held moral convictions (Bjorklund, Haidt, & Murphy, 2000; Cushman, Young, & Hauser, 2006; Hauser, Cushman, Young, Jin, & Mikhail, 2007). The second challenge claims that moral judgment is driven primarily by affective (emotional) responses (Blair, 1995; Damasio, 1994; Greene & Haidt, 2002; Schweder & Haidt, 1993). Evidence for the role of affective responses is largely neuro-scientific (Ciaramelli, Muccioli, Ladavas, & di Pellegrino 2007; Damasio, 1994; Greene, Nystrom, Engell, Darley, & Cohen, 2004; Greene, Sommerville, Nystrom, Darley & Cohen 2001; Koenigs et al., 2007; Mendez, Anderson, & Shapira, 2005). In addition, other modern researchers have conducted behavioral studies of moral judgment using affective manipulations. Yet, although there is strong evidence that moral judgment is driven largely by intuitive, emotional responses, it does not follow from this that emotional intuition is the only factor involved (Valdesolo & DeSteno, 2006; Wheatley & Haidt, 2005).

Other recent studies show that while people cannot offer justifications for some of their moral judgments, they are quite able to do so for others (Cushman, Young, & Hauser (2006). People also alter some moral judgments when asked to engage in conscious reasoning (Pizarro, Uhlmann, & Bloom, 2003). Others studies implicate reasoning processes in moral judgment using brain imaging and reaction time data (Greene et al., 2004). Together, these studies seem to capture an important and relatively common experience, which is the deliberation about right and wrong, informed by an awareness of one's explicit moral commitments. Reconciling these apparent alternatives 'intuitive' versus 'rational', and 'affective' versus 'cognitive', has therefore become a focal point of research (Cushman, & Greene, 2010). As part of this debate, Cushman, & Greene (2010) argued that moral judgment is the product of interaction and competition between distinct psychological systems. In their article: "Our multi-system moral psychology: Towards a consensus view" they claim that:

"Most successful attempts share a common insight: moral judgment is accomplished by multiple systems. Here, we pursue a dual-process approach in which moral judgment is the product of both intuitive and rational psychological processes, and it is the product of what are conventionally thought of as "affective" and "cognitive" mechanisms... A dual-process model of moral judgment can explain features of the data that unitary models cannot" (Cushman & Greene 2010, pp-2-3).

They also suggested that cognitive/affective and conscious/intuitive processes, in fact, reflect the same underlying structure within the moral mind. Finally, they concluded that the dual-process model should be understood as part of a larger constellation of psychological systems that enable the human capacity for moral judgment (Cushman & Greene, 2010).

Other interesting results and conclusions in the moral domain have been demonstrated by various researchers as follow: In his innovating work, Foot (1967) claimed that when facing a dilemma involving causing harm to another person or persons, it is considered more morally permissible to cause harm to some of the people in order to save more.

Following these ideas, Greene et al. (2001, 2004) suggested that complex moral judgment processes involve combined cognitive and affective moral components. They claimed that the cognitive component is more conscious while the affective component is actually unconscious.

Cushman, Young and Hauser, (2006), related to the dimension of intention in moral judgment. They suggested that the intentional nature of any moral action is significant, whether the individual is on the strong or the weak side. In additional studies it was also found that people will prefer (if they must) to cause harm to other people unintentionally rather than intentionally (Moore, Clark, & Kane, 2008).

1.3.2 Emotions and moral thinking

The connection between emotions and other aspects of moral thinking and moral decision making has been increasingly studied in cognitive psychology and neuroscience in the time that has passed since the early work of Kohlberg and especially over the last decade (Cushman & Greene, 2012). Contemporary approaches have begun to appreciate and study the complex interplay and the connections between affective reactions and cognitive reasoning in moral decision-making (Greene, 2011). Research has revealed that emotions are involved in socio-moral concerns and dilemmas that involve conflict between socio-moral norms. The study of such dilemmas has provided researchers with an excellent testing ground for the role of emotions in moral decision-making (Cushman & Greene, 2012). Contemporary research also points out that social norms usually oppose harmful actions against other people and it has been suggested that an emotional aversion to harming others may have evolved as part of humans' decision-making (Haidt, 2007). Recent studies support the natural assumption that when the individual is exposed to the experience of harming other people, it triggers strong emotional reactions that are also expressed in cognitive and physiological levels, especially if the harmful action involves physical force like intentional killing (Cushman, Young, & Hauser, 2006; Greene, Morelli, Lowenberg, Nystrom & Cohen, 2007),

Greene et al., (2001, 2004) indicated that situations in which harming another person is justified are usually and normally accepted for the purpose of social welfare, mainly in extreme conditions. Several lines of evidence indicate that emotions play a significant role in moral decision making. Early functional neuroimaging studies showed that responding to H2S ("harm to save") moral dilemmas (where one must decide whether to kill another person in order to save more lives) involves activity in brain areas associated with emotional reactivity, emotion regulation and social cognition. . There are two possible courses of action in these dilemmas: refusing to harm another person, despite all possible consequences or saving as many people as possible even at the cost of harming one person, known as the 'utilitarian', H2S decision (Koenigs et al., 2007).

Experimental stress conditions induced in healthy volunteers reduce the proportion of utilitarian choices in moral dilemmas (Starcke, Ludwig, & Brand, 2012; Youssef et al., 2012). These landmark results suggest that emotional experience might promote the choice of deontological decisions in moral dilemmas, and overcoming this bias would involve emotion regulation.

Greene's dual-process theory (Greene, 2008) championed these ideas by arguing that H2S moral dilemmas involve tension between automatic affective processes related to harming another person and controlled reasoning processes that favor maximal utility. However, Greene asserted that in these kinds of dilemmas, utilitarian responses would override the affective reactions. Moll & de Oliveira-Souza (2007) and Tassy et al. (2012) suggested that rather than having mutually competing roles, emotions and reasoning jointly contribute to moral decision-making. Whether competitive or collaborative, the interactions between emotions and cognition in moral dilemmas may be influenced by individual differences in emotion regulation (Pizarro, 2000; Talmi & Frith, 2007).

It has recently become clear that abstract judgment and personal choice of action in moral dilemmas rely on distinct psychological and neural processes. When participants have to judge the moral acceptability of a utilitarian course of action in a moral dilemma and then report their own choice of action, they make more deontological judgments, but also more utilitarian choices (Tassy, Oullier, Mancini, & Wicker 2013).

In addition, variations of the affective proximity between participants and the potential victim, for example, a family relative, have been described as influencing moral choice, but not moral judgment (Tassy et al., 2013). It was also suggested in recent studies that in addition to prospective thinking and social emotions, which probably contribute to moral decision–making in general; moral choice may also involve increased self-focused emotions relating to moral judgment

(Tassy et al., 2012). These findings raise the question of whether emotion regulation influences moral choice.

Research conducted by Szekely & Miu (2014) investigated the relations between emotional reactivity, emotion regulation and moral choice in H2S dilemmas. The researchers focused on moral choice rather than moral judgment because they assumed that possible self-projection in moral dilemma situations and in deciding which course of action to follow, could be more emotionally salient and more readily uncover emotional biases on decision-making. In addition, they based their decision to focus on moral choice on former research showing that in comparison to moral judgment, moral choice might involve increased self-relevant emotions (Moll & de Oliveira-Souza, 2007; Tassy et al., 2012). This research (Szekely & Miu 2014) , used a subset of the moral dilemmas battery developed by Greene et al. (2004). The dilemmas used were classified as "high-conflict", and may be more sensitive to individual variation in emotional reactivity (Koenigs et al., 2007). All the dilemmas described threatening situations, such as war, a terrorist attack, speeding train and global epidemic, in which physically hurting or killing one person would save several others. In those studies (Koenigs et al., 2007), emotional reactivity to these moral dilemmas was assessed by distinct emotion and other dimensional measures (i.e. emotional arousal and valence). In the discussion of this research using H2S moral dilemmas, Szekely & Miu (2014) presented three main findings:

1. A wide spectrum of emotions was experienced during these moral dilemmas, with self-focused emotions such as fear and sadness being the most common.
2. There was a positive relation between emotional arousal during deliberation concerning moral dilemmas and deontological choices.
3. Individual differences in reappraisal, but not in other emotion regulation strategies such as acceptance, and rumination, are negatively associated with deontological choices and this effect is carried through emotional arousal.

Christensen et al. (2014) tried to look for the variables known to influence moral judgment in order to find out which of them matters most, and how they interact. One main result of their work is that, when dilemmas are validated, a more complex pattern appears and it is revealed that moral judgments are reached by a combination of deliberation deontological thinking and arousal of emotions.

1.3.3 Guilt feelings and moral judgment

Some observations about moral judgment relate to a hierarchy of judgment making processes. This is relevant to judgment of the morality of particular acts, our own or those of others. People normally do not consider a person as responsible for outcomes that he was unable to anticipate, which means that foreseeability is commonly accepted as a requirement for responsible moral decision-making (Shaver 1985). Hamilton (1978) claims that people are blamed only for negative outcomes that they were obligated to prevent. Finally, Weiner (1995) observed that such obligation is meaningful only if the outcome was controllable by the person, that is, if he or she could have intentionally prevented it. Thus, guilt feelings arise when a person thinks that he/she should have and could have prevented harmful action if he/she had made a moral decision (Malle, Moses, & Baldwin, 2010).

Of course, things are not always so clear-cut and extraneous variables can alter moral judgment beyond rational rules (assuming that such rules actually exist) and operate in many instances (Alicke, 2000). One of the most important rules governing guilt feelings relates to intentional moral transgressions when a person intentionally performs an immoral action and consequently suffers amplified feelings of guilt (Cushman, 2008; Heider, 1958; Ohtsubo, 2007; Shaver, 1985). Delineating the steps involved in moral judgments of intentionality can help us to understand the dynamics of judgments of blame. Schematically, a person looks at the negative event (decision) to see if it was intentional? If the answer is yes, then the next step is to examine the actual intention or goal of the actor. If the answer was no, then the next step would be to examine whether the actor had an obligation and the ability to prevent the harm, examining foreseeability and controllability (Guglielmo, Monroe, & Malle, 2009). In contrast, Knobe (2003a,

2003b) challenged this fundamental order and proposed instead that the evil character or blameworthiness of an action can influence people's judgments of intentionality. The same behavior that is seen as unintentional when performed without moral implications, for example, killing an insect, may, in fact, be seen as intentional when performed with moral implications, for example, killing another person.

A study conducted by Guglielmo and Malle (2010) showed that when an action (such as killing) is performed unskillfully, people are far less likely to view the killing as intentional. They demonstrated that judgments of intentionality, even those relating to immoral actions, are guided by information concerning the individual's skills and for that reason, even difficult actions are less often judged to be intentional.

1.3.4 Gender differences in moral dilemmas

In psychological research the moral domain is considered to be one of the most complex aspects of the human mind. Substantial evidence confirming gender-related neurobiological and behavioral differences between men and women suggests gender specificities in moral development and behavior (Aleman & Swart 2008).

Similarities and differences between men and women have been investigated in many disciplines including the study of moral attitudes and dilemmas, but evidence regarding gender differences in moral reasoning is mixed (Jaffee & Hyde, 2000). The dual-process model proposed by Greene et al. (2007) suggests that men and women may not differ in terms of their cognitive evaluations of outcomes and thus show equal levels of utilitarian judgments. Nevertheless, women may experience stronger affective responses to harm than men, leading to systematic gender differences in deontological judgments.

Fumagalli et al. (2010) investigated the role of gender, education and religious belief on moral choices of women and men with a moral judgment task. They found no differences between the two genders in utilitarian responses to non-moral dilemmas and to impersonal moral dilemmas. They did find that men gave significantly more utilitarian answers to personal moral (PM) dilemmas than women (PM dilemmas involve highly emotional decisions). Cultural factors such as education and religion had no effect on performance in the moral judgment task.

Friesdorf, Gawronski & Conway (2014) found that gender differences in affective processing are common and robust. For example: women tend to experience stronger emotional responses than men (Brody & Hall, 2000; Cross & Madson, 1997; Fischer & Manstead, 2000; Gross & John, 1998), they are more persuaded by messages appealing to emotion (Meyer & Tormala, 2010) and score higher on measures of empathic concern (Eisenberg & Lennon, 1983). In addition, women are more adept at identifying with other's emotional states (Bullis & Horn, 1995; Hall & Schmid Mast, 2008). A study that directly examined the role of gender in moral dilemma judgments was conducted by Fumagalli and colleagues (2010). They found that men showed a stronger preference for utilitarian over deontological judgments than women, particularly on 'personal' moral dilemmas where harm requires physical force. However, the question remains whether in the process of moral judgments men are more utilitarian than women or women are more deontological than men. According to the dual-process model (Greene et al., 2001), deontological and utilitarian judgments stem from two independent psychological processes: deontological inclinations are affective and utilitarian inclinations are cognitive. This means that the two moral inclinations are opposite implying a negative relationship between them. Thus, for empirical evidence whether men are more utilitarian than women, or women are more deontological than men, it is necessary to measure deontological and utilitarian inclinations independently.

Research performed by Conway & Gawronski (2013) relied on the notion that deontology assumes that the morality of an action depends on its consistency with moral norms, while the principle of utilitarianism implies that the morality of an action depends on its consequences. They suggested that deontological judgments are shaped by affective processes, whereas utilitarian judgments are guided by cognitive processes. Research conducted by Friesdorf, Gawronski & Conway (2014) employed process dissociation to independently assess deontological and utilitarian inclinations in women and men. They performed a "meta-analytic reanalysis" of 40 studies with 6,100 participants. Results indicated that men showed a stronger preference for utilitarian over deontological judgments than women when the two principles implied conflicting decisions. The findings suggest that:

"gender differences in moral dilemma judgments are due to differences in affective responses to harm rather than cognitive evaluations of outcomes" (Friesdorf, Gawronski & Conway, 2014 pp-11).

1.3.5 Summary

1. *General consideration*

This sub-chapter is dedicated to the research of the moral dilemmas domain. As observed, traditional theories of moral development emphasize the role of controlled cognition in mature moral judgment, while a more recent trend emphasizes intuitive and emotional processes. In the course of time a dual-process theory synthesizing these perspectives was also developed. This theory associates utilitarian moral judgment (approving harmful actions that maximize good consequences) with controlled cognitive processes and associates non-utilitarian moral judgment with automatic emotional responses. The theory suggests that a cognitive load manipulation selectively interferes with utilitarian judgment. This interference effect provides direct evidence for the influence of controlled cognitive processes in moral judgment, and more specifically, in utilitarian moral judgment (Greene et al., 2007).

1. *Critique of these theories*

Criticism of early moral theories and especially Kohlberg's (1969) early theories principally revolved around the examination of considerations of moral thinking, and these were used to form a hierarchy of levels of moral thinking, but were less concerned with the moral decisions themselves. Moreover, Kohlberg's dilemmas were imaginary – meaning that they were not based on real events and did not consider the emotional facet as a factor influencing thinking and especially the decision, nor did they consider the intuitive (non-rational) dimension of moral decisions (Haidt, 2001).

3. A synthesis of modern research findings

Later and contemporary studies have tried to cope with the disadvantages of previous research in this field. As an interim summary of these studies, several main points should be noted:

- Emotions have a significant, if not decisive influence on thinking and especially on moral decisions concerning moral dilemmas (Guglielmo, Monroe & Molle, 2009).
- Insofar as the dilemma is more realistic and clearer, the examinee's ability to make a decision will increase. This is also expressed in the speed of decision-making (Moll & de Oliveira-Sousa, 2007).
- Insofar as the examinee is more emotionally involved in the dilemma, the examinee's ability to make clearer moral decisions increases, although, of course, they are more influenced by the emotional pan (Greene, 2011).
- There may be a substantial difference between the moral consideration and a moral decision. There are cases in which examinees will think in one direction but make a decision in another direction. This is primarily influenced by the balance between the personal utilitarian factors versus the principled moral factor (Greene & Haidt, 2002).
- The development of examinees' guilt feelings depends on the results of their moral decisions – insofar as the decision is more extreme or causes a higher price involving injury to a person's life, guilt feelings will grow (Alicke, 2000).
- Insofar as the extremity of the situation becomes more serious, and insofar as the circumstances are more severe and the risk more concrete, then positive accepted moral behavior will decrease, although consciousness of it remains in force. In other words, people will make decisions, which are not moral in order to survive, although they are well aware of the lack of morality of their acts (Christensen et al., 2014).
- Intuition is an important factor in moral decision-making,

although it is possible that later, when explaining the cognitive considerations for the making of the decision, actors will not provide sufficient consideration for this element (Haidt & Joseph, 2007).

- Personal states and specific circumstances will have significant influence both on moral judgment and also on moral decision-making (Aquino & Reed, 2002).
- Dilemmas relating to physical injury and especially killing of humans are more meaningful and arouse stronger emotional reactions (Gillath, McCall, Shaver & Blascovich, 2008).

1.4 Jewish moral dilemmas during and after Jewish Holocaust

Introduction

In this sub-chapter we attempt to describe a wider perspective on the moral issues, dilemmas and decisions of the Jews during and after the Holocaust. Of course, the paper is too short to relate to and describe all the complex moral dilemmas that Jews were forced to face during that time. Due to this limitation, we have chosen seven main dilemmas noted in Holocaust historical literature from the Holocaust period 1939-1945 and another seven dilemmas from the period following the Holocaust, i.e. 1945-2016. We gave each dilemma a specific name and concise wording. These 14 dilemmas are presented in the following pages. The order of their presentation is chronological, according to the sequence of historical events.

Before we begin to describe these moral dilemmas, it is important to try to understand the unimaginable reality that the Jews were forced to face:

"In the reality of the Holocaust the normal order of life was completely undermined and the main acute daily thought focused on the question of whether to be "moral" and die or to be "immoral" and survive" (Goldhagen, 1998, pp. 12-13).

This was described most succinctly by Roman Frister, a survivor of different "work" camps and the "death march":

"The way to liberation from destructive desperation was strewn with the bodies of noble souls". (Frister, 1993, p. 11).

Another chilling and accurate description of the delusional reality of the Holocaust was provided by Viktor Frankl, a survivor of the Auschwitz extermination camp:

"There was neither time nor desire to consider moral or ethical issues. Every man was controlled by one thought only: to keep himself alive for the family waiting for him at home, and to save his friends. With no hesitation, therefore, he would arrange for another prisoner, another "number," to take his place in the transport". (Frankl, 1981, pp. 14-15).

1.4.1. Jewish moral dilemmas during the Holocaust (1939 – 1945)

The "Judenratt" dilemma

Haim Romoskovski, Head of the "Judenratt" (The Jewish council appointed by the Nazi regime) in the Lodz Ghetto in Poland believed in "rescue through work", meaning that if the Jews would work for the Nazis they would not be harmed because they were involved in production, especially manufacture for the Nazi war machine. He decided to respond to the Nazis' demand to receive a list of Jews, who would be transported from the ghetto to extermination. He feared that if he refused, the Nazis would take more Jews and would do this indiscriminately. Of course, he did not know and moreover did not believe that the real intention of the Nazis was to murder all the Jews sooner or later (Zuckerman, 2009). Before the first transportation of Jews to Chelmno death camp in January 1942, he turned to the mothers asking them to deliver their children to send for extermination according to the Nazi demand. According to the concept of "rescue through work" he explained:

"Since we were not guided by the question how many would be lost, but rather how many could be saved, we (the Judenratt) came to the conclusion that however difficult this would be, we would have to accept and undertake performance of the stipulation (sending the children to extermination) ... I must amputate limbs in order to save the body, I must take the children, and if not, they may God forbid take

others ...at the time of the edict we had to consider and measure who had to be saved, who could be saved, and who it was permitted to save. Intelligence demands that those should be saved who could be saved and who have a chance to be saved and not those who in any case it was impossible to save". (Farabstein, 2002, p. 193).

The "Judenratt" was a council of Jews appointed by the Germans in the "ghettoes" to supervise the performance of their orders concerning Jews' everyday life in the "ghetto". The "ghetto" was a very small part of each city – only a few streets but the Nazis forced all of the Jews in each city and its surroundings to enter the "ghetto" and remain imprisoned there behind walls with a very meager food supply, in conditions of overcrowding, hunger, disease and death (Czerniakow, 1968).

Alongside the Judenratt, worked the Jewish police; a sort of operational arm inside the Judenratt carrying out the Judenratt's instructions for the Jewish population. The chairman of the Judenratt held full responsibility and dominion over the Judenratt's operations (Nasmith, 1983). The heads of the Judenratt performed their roles despite their total and continuous desire to resist the Nazis and did all they could to save as many Jews as possible. The reason for their cooperation with the Nazis was pinned in the perception that in this way it would be possible to save most or at least some of the Jews. They were forced without any alternative to perform acts of cooperation with the Nazis, acts which they despised and opposed. In particular, as noted above, from time to time according to the Nazis' demand, they had to transmit lists of Jewish residents of the ghetto to the Nazis, who were then assigned for transportation to the death camps. The heads of the Judenratt hoped each time anew that the current transportation would be the last (Gutman, 1979b). ***The main dilemma*** that they faced was whether, as the heads of the Judenratt they should prepare and transmit the lists to the Germans or not? The reason for saying yes to this question was their hope that this would save the Jews that were not on the list. The reason for saying no was refusal to cooperate with Nazi oppression and acts of murder. The heads of the Judenratt knew very well that their refusal to cooperate in this manner would lead to their deaths. Most often under compulsion of the threat to their life they decided to collaborate with Nazi demands (Katz, Ben Ami & Ilan, 2005).

The "little smuggler" dilemma

"Parents would stay home all day, wringing their hands nervously and waiting for their breadwinners to come home. With tears they would swallow the food that their children had brought them at the risk of their lives" (Kaplan, 1961, p. 77).

In the ghettoes, the Jews endured hunger imposed intentionally by the Nazis, and many died of starvation. In these extreme conditions, there were parents who accepted that their small children (who usually volunteered by themselves) would have to smuggle food from the "Aryan", or non-Jewish side of the ghetto wall of the city to the families imprisoned in the ghetto (Kaplan, 1961). They knew well that they were certainly endangering the lives of the young smugglers, who were usually killed when, as often happened, they were caught during the smuggling action. Only small and nimble children could crawl under the fence or through the narrow gaps in the wall to bring food. Adults could not perform this work (Kermish, 1966, 1989).

The main dilemma was a parental dilemma since the children's dilemma was different – whether to risk their own lives for themselves and for their families or not. The parents' moral consideration that allowed them to agree was the lack of an alternative, knowing that if the child did not bring food for the family, they would all die anyway from starvation. The moral consideration that would prevent the parents from agreeing was the desire to prevent the more immediate risk to the child's life (Heberer, 2011, Efrat & Baban, 2015).

Giving children away dilemma

"In Poland and Lithuania, even under the conditions of the ghetto and gnawing starvation, there was no widespread transfer of Jewish children to Christian families until the end of 1941 and beginning of 1942, when the extermination began ...when the transportations to the extermination camps began and all hope was extinguished, there were some who wanted to save their children in this manner until the madness would pass. This process also occurred in parallel in Western

Europe in the same circumstances, meaning [it was used] as the last alternative, when the only possibility that remained was to hide among gentiles in the Christian world" (Farabstein, 2002, p. 201).

During the Holocaust there were Jewish parents who gave their small children to Christian religious institutions mainly monasteries or to individual gentiles, so that they could raise them and thus perhaps save their lives (Blady Szwaiger, 2000). These parents gave up their children, sometimes, but not always, leaving payment for their keep (Bogner, 2000). ***The main dilemma*** for the parents was whether to give their children up and transfer the control of their fate to non-Jews who might do with them as they wished, including conversion to Christianity, abandonment or even extradition to the Nazis. The motivation for the transfer of the children was the slim chance that this might save the child's life, when there was no other alternative. The consideration against this action was that it was necessary to part from the child and leave his fate in the hands of others (Freiberg, 1988). Other fears for the parents were that even if the child was saved, he would not be raised as a Jew and that it might be impossible to find him again after the war (Levine, 2002). Moreover, the very fact of separation from the child in such an extreme situation of certain risk of death was a terrible emotional burden on the parents' conscience and mental state (Radlich, 1983). The brave gentile women and men, who risked their own lives, and sometimes the lives of their families, in order to save Jewish children, were later awarded the status of "Righteous among the Nations" by the State of Israel (Evers-Emden, 2000).

The crying baby dilemma

... "and at a time when the evil Nazis were conducting searches to find those miserable people, a baby among those who were hidden burst out crying and could not be silenced ... one of them went up to the baby and put a cushion over its mouth... later when they removed the cushion, they saw that the child had suffocated" (Farabstein, 2002, p. 176).

· · ·

One of the strategies used by the Jews to survive the Holocaust was to hide from the Nazis in any possible hiding place: in lofts, in cellars, behind double walls, in cemeteries, in caves, in barns and any other place where it was possible to hide (Aharonson, 1992). The Nazis incessantly searched for the Jews and when they found them the consequence was death. In such cases, when it was impossible to silence them, parents were sometimes forced to shut their baby's mouth, suffocating them to death because they continually cried and the sound of crying, if not being stopped immediately, would expose all of those hidden (Neistatt, 1944). The parents did this in order to save the rest of the group in hiding from being discovered and murdered (Kaplan, 1961). *The dilemma* was should the parent kill their own child in order to save other people or not. The moral consideration in favor of this killing was that the life of the majority was more important than the life of the single child. In contrast, the opposing moral consideration argued that the sanctity of an individual life is no less than that of a group of others (Levine, 2002). Of course, beyond these moral considerations there was the extraordinary mental capability that the parent needed to be able to take the life of their own child (Nimsovitch, 1968).

The thief's dilemma

"The rule of life in the camp specified: "eat your bread and if you can, eat the bread of your neighbor too" (Levi, 2011, p. 173).

In the ghettoes, in the concentration and extermination camps and in other places, the Nazis administered a regime of terror and fear in order to break the spirit of the Jews and weaken them physically and mentally. Often when they needed the cooperation of Jews, they tried to attain this by a combination of deception, terror and promises of different benefits. The Jews lived in a very extreme and unimaginable reality, in which they usually did not know what reactions to expect from the Nazis and in which their lives were always hanging on a thread (Kermish, 1989).

Almost every day the Jews were forced to make risky and sometimes fatal decisions, without knowing which decision would lead to which outcome. In the slave labor, concentration and extermination camps, the Nazis would punish the most minor crimes with death. In these conditions, there were phenomena of Jewish collaboration such as informing, serving in the Jewish police, stealing things, avoiding giving help to others, exploiting benefits at the expense of others etc. (Lubotkin, 1979). ***The main dilemma*** *was* whether to be "moral" and certainly risk my life or to be "immoral" / "utilitarian" to save my life. This difficult decision-making is represented by the "Dilemma of the hat". If a prisoner in the death camp lost his hat and had to turn up at roll call without it, they were liable to be punished with immediate execution. In such a situation, the prisoner had to deliberate whether to try to steal another prisoner's hat or not. If he did not steal it, he would die; if he did steal it and use it, the other prisoner would die (Yerushalmi, 1995).

The "Sonderkommando" dilemma

"At first we saw nothing special and then they brought us to the closed door of the gas chamber. When the door opened, they shouted at us: "come here, take the bodies and throw them into the ovens" (from the evidence of a Sonderkommando man, Josef Sackar) (Greif, 1999, p. 112).

The "Sonderkommando" was the name given to the Jewish prisoners forced to perform special functions and tasks in the extermination camps by the Nazis. The Sonderkommando units were composed of Jewish prisoners and operated in the area of the slaughter houses – next to the gas chambers and incinerators in the Auschwitz-Birkenau and other extermination camps (Bar, 1978). The "Sonderkommando" were forced by the Nazis to perform the most terrible work involved in operating the slaughter houses, such as: helping the Jews to undress before entering the gas chambers, taking the bodies out of the gas chambers after death, extracting teeth from those murdered, burning bodies in ovens and grinding the bones of the dead. They did all those terrible actions knowing that eventually the Nazis would kill them too, when they no longer needed them anymore. On 7th October, 1944, the Sonderkommando in Auschwitz-Birkenau rose up against the Nazis and during the rebellion almost all of the rebels were slaughtered on the same day (Greif et al., 1983). ***The main dilemma*** facing the men of the Sonderkommando was whether to agree to serve in this unit or to refuse and risk immediate execution. The reason to agree and cooperate was the desire to stay alive and the hope that they might be rescued. The reason not to agree to serve in the Sonderkommando was that in this way they could avoid assisting the Nazis' slaughter of their Jewish brothers (Greif, 1998, 1999).

The rebels' dilemma

"Any escape – and certainly injury to the guards – would endanger those who remained there, who had no strength or daring to escape. Was it permissible to save themselves by endangering others?" (Farabstein, 2002, p. 196).

These words of one of the heads of the Jews in "Kunin" labor camp in Poland, relate to a discussion that took place in the camp in 1943 concerning the possibility of rebelling against the Nazis and escaping from the camp.

In ghettoes, labor camps, concentration camps, extermination camps and in additional places, there were groups of young Jews (relatively very few for the size of the entire population), who rose up in organized armed rebellion against the Nazis. Sometimes there were also individual initiatives to attack the Nazis, but they did not have much effect (Baltman, 2002). This resistance was simultaneously heroic and hopeless, but the very fact that it existed is a testimony of honor for the Jewish people since they rose up against a much greater force that persecuted and tried to annihilate them (Freiberg, 1988). The problem was that those young Jews man and woman who chose armed struggle did not ask and did not receive the permission of other Jews for their armed rebellion, although their actions endangered the lives of all Jews in the ghettos. Furthermore, most of Jewish population feared the reaction of the Nazis to armed resistance and the leadership of the ghetto – the "Judenratt" - opposed such action for the same reason (Weinrab, 1984). Everyone knew that the Nazis would take revenge against all or most of the Jews, even those who did not rebel (Heskel, 2012). ***The main dilemma*** facing the rebels was, therefore, whether there was moral justification for armed struggle against the Nazis without the support of other Jews. In certain cases, Jews did avoid rebellion for this reason, but the predominant view among the rebels was that the Nazis would anyway murder all the Jews sooner or later and this supported the principle that it was better to rebel and achieve some revenge for the massacre (Holevski, 2001).

1.4.2 Summary of psychological reactions to Holocaust moral dilemmas

To sum up, this part, drawing on the above literature review, we tried to explain the Jewish moral reaction during the Holocaust. It is based on the model developed by Kohlberg which explains moral thinking and action developmental (Kohlberg 1969). It describes the different moral reactions of the Jews in the Holocaust – a time of continuously altering conditions in a state of war and terror; a time of total chaos when regular life and social patterns were completely undermined and disrupted (Farberstein, 2002).

First, the definitions of the different moral attitudes are explained with examples from the Holocaust:

Deontological Morality is the expected normal behavior acording to the law and accepted norms and values of a particular society (Waller, 2005; Beauchamp, 1991; Kamm, 1996). *An example* of this kind of moral behavior is making room for another Jewish family in your own tiny apartment in the "Ghetto" (Gutman, 1990B). *Another example* would be parents who would not allow their children to smuggle food into the "Ghetto" out of parental responsibility and fear for the risk to their children's lives (Kermish, 1989).

Utilitarian Morality is a behavior which the individual believes will produce an expected benefit (Bredeson, 2011; Gay, 2002). It can and often does contredict Deontological Morality. *An example* of this kind of moral behavior is profiteering on the black market that some Jews conducted in the "Ghettoes", while exploiting the state of their brothers in order to enrich themselves (Gutman, 1990b).

Survival Morality - has an "instinctive" character and serves the basic human drive for survival (Koenigs et al., 2007). It is a "special kind" of utilitarian morality and will always contradict deontological morality. *An example* for this kind of moral behavior is the forced consent of Jewish prisoners to serve in the "Sonderkommando" unit in the extermination camps in order to save their lives (Greif, 1999).

Superior Morality – is a deontological moral behavior that overcomes the instinct to make a survival decision in a life-threatening situation. It includes independent moral consideration of universal humanistic values that are even superior to the instinctive human drive for survival in the face of concrete risk to life . *An example* for this kind of moral behavior was exhibited by Jews or gentiles who risked their own lives to save other Jews from extermination (Bogner, 2000).

The main principle in the solution of moral dilemmas is that insofar as the situation is more critical – then the moral deliberation is harder. The moral decision that a person would take is based on his basic moral attitude, but it is also influenced by the situation. This means that even though a person holds a certain kind of moral attitude, nevertheless, in reality, he may act in a contradictory way. In the reality of the Holocaust there was always a conflict or tension between different and often contradicting moral attitudes. Because the Holocaust did not occur in one day, but it was an ongoing process which became more severe over time, the need to take different moral decisions also changed. At the beginning of the Holocaust when there was not yet a concrete danger to life, there was nevertheless a lot of existential distress and strong fear. Moral deliberation or tension arose at this stage between Deontological morality versus Utilitarian morality. Then when the actual mass murder began, tension arose between Deontological morality and Survival morality, or between Superior morality and Survival morality. Naturally, most people will take a survival moral decision in order to survive and only a very few will take a superior moral decision. According to Greif (1999), this is what happened in the Holocaust.

The figure below describes the **extent of difficulty** involved in reacting to a moral dilemma at three different levels, where 1 is the easiest level and 3 is the most difficult level. According to the model - in a normal situation of ordinary daily life, most people will perform deontological moral behavior. In a stressful situation, but still not faced with a direct threat to their life, most people will act according to utilitarian morality. In crisis situations, when there is a concrete threat to their life, most people will act in line with survival morality and very few will choose superior morality. The following figure illustrates these three levels:

Level 1 - the moral deliberation is *Deontological versus Utilitarian morality*.

Level 2 - the moral deliberation is *Deontological versus Survival morality*.

Level 3 - the moral deliberation is *Superior versus Survival morality*

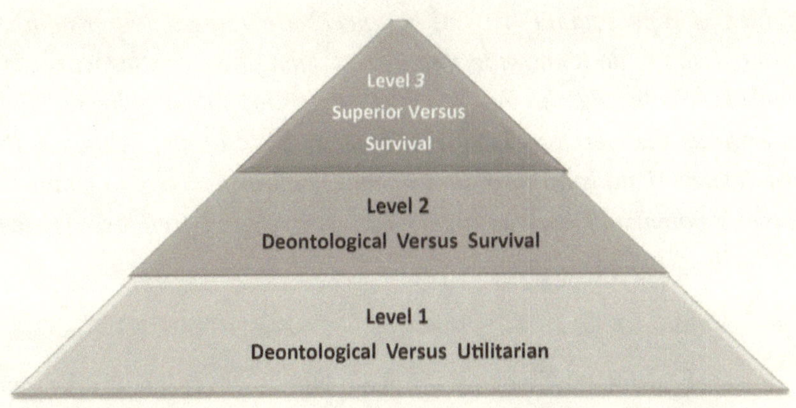

Figure 1.2- Levels of reaction to Holocaust moral dilemmas

1.4.3 Jewish moral dilemmas after the Holocaust (1945 – 2015)
Introduction

"The Holocaust was not just an attack on millions of Jews as individuals rather it was also an attack on the very existence of the Jewish people...The knowledge that the danger of complete extermination hovered over them then definitely influenced every Jew everywhere during the Holocaust and still does today" (Goldhagen, 1998, p. 17).

Although the Holocaust ended on 8th May 1945 with the surrender of Nazi Germany, in the mind of Holocaust survivors it continued to influence them and their families each and every day. Strong feelings burned in the survivors, especially shame and pangs of conscience due to various events that they underwent and actions that they performed, and also a desire for revenge (Gampel, 2005). An example was the story of a 16-year-old youth, a survivor of "Dachau" concentration camp in Germany.

"He appealed to a Jewish rabbi, Meir Birenbaum, one of the officers of the British army who liberated the camp and told him about a "terrible crime" that he had committed: The German soldiers forced him to tighten a rope around his father's neck. He refused but his father ordered him to do it knowing that if he did not, the Germans would kill him too. So he did this out of "respect for his father". Immediately afterwards the Germans hung his father in front of him. Although the youth knew that his life was saved because of his decision to honor his father's command, he was haunted by heavy guilt feelings". (Farabstein, 2002, p. 533).

Out of the historical literature we have chosen seven main dilemmas from the Post-Holocaust period 1945-2015. We gave each dilemma a specific name and concise wording. The seven dilemmas are presented here according to chronological order.

The revengers' dilemma

The words of Rabbi Moshe Friedman in the undressing room in the crematorium in Auschwitz death camp to the Nazi commander a few minutes before his death:

"You terrible and despised murderers of the world don't imagine that you can eliminate all of the Jewish people. The Jewish people will exist for ever and will not disappear from the stage of history. But you, contemptible murderers will pay a high price. For each innocent Jew you will pay tenfold, you will disappear forever. The day of reckoning

is approaching; our spilt blood – will be demanded from you and you will find no refuge, until its burning rage will be spent upon you and annihilate your living blood!" (Bar, 1978, p. 220).

When the war ended, Holocaust survivors felt a strong desire for revenge against the Nazi persecutors. This revenge was mainly expressed by the very fact that they survived and could now go on with their lives, marry, have children and immigrate to the new Jewish state – Israel (Bar-Zohar, 1991). Most survivors tended to suppress their impulse for actual revenge and the desire to spontaneously injure the murderers and simply asked for just punishment for the criminals through legal channels. Nevertheless, some of the expressions of the desire for revenge and the need to see that justice was attained were expressed in different actions (Carmi, 1961). However, there were not many survivors who translated their instincts into action and performed private or organized acts of vengeance by killing former Nazis suspected of murdering Jews during the Holocaust. These acts were not preceded by any official investigation or legal trial (Segev, 1991). ***The main dilemma*** for those who wanted to perpetrate these acts of vengeance was whether it was permissible or forbidden to kill Germans suspected of having murdered Jews during the Holocaust without any process of investigation and official legal proceedings? ***The moral justification*** for such vengeance was the recognition that these were loathsome murderers and that revenge should be imposed upon them in accordance with the implied will of those who were murdered. In contrast stood the opinion that such actions are illegal and might involve mistaken identity and the killing of innocents (Wiesenthal, 2012).

The "Kapo" dilemma

"It is well known that with the help of a small marginal pain, remaining strengths can be enlisted to overcome a fiercer pain. The "Capos" also know that. Although some of them do indeed hit us simply out of bestial violence, there are some who almost hit us out of love, when they feel that soon we will succumb under the weight of the

*burden and suffering. With the blows, they give us words of encourage-
ment and reinforcement, like the wagoner speaking to horses pulling
the load".* (Levi, 2011, p. 71).

With the end of the war the survivors naturally had strong feelings for revenge against Jews who had been forced to work under the Nazis during the Holocaust. These included members of the Judenratt, Jewish police and those who held positions such as the "Kapo" - foreman - in the camps, etc. In Israel various survivors claimed to have identified Jews in Israeli streets, who, despite being Holocaust survivors themselves, had also acted as "Nazi collaborators". They demanded the arrest of these Jews by the police. For example, ex-"Kapos" were accused of physically and mentally abusing Jewish prisoners in the camps. These complaints led to more than 30 court cases against Jews accused of collaboration with the Nazis at the end of the 1940s and in the early 1950s. The verdicts ranged from acquittal to a death sentence pronounced against Yehezkhal Ingster, who was found guilty of being responsible for the killing of Jewish prisoners in "Gross-Rosen" camp. However, Ingster's sentence was later commuted to two years and Ingster died soon after the re-sentencing.

These trials were not widely reported in the press at that time and most of the witnesses in the trials were Holocaust survivors (Levine, 2015). The police demanded the legislation of a "Law against Jewish War Criminals" in order to address these complaints, but this demand was rejected until Mordechai Nurik, a Member of "Knesset" (the Israeli parliament), proposed the "Law to bring Justice against Nazis and their Assistants" on 27th March, 1950. During the discussion on this bill in the Knesset, the speakers emphasized the need to exact vengeance against the Nazis and to enforce the full arm of the law against them. There was also mention of the responsibility of the entire generation in Germany that had cooperated actively or remained silent and thus assisted the massacre (Hausner, 1988). There was much said about the need to remember that the world forgave and pardoned post-Nazi Germany after the war at the expense of the victims and that the

State of Israel should act in all manners to prevent a new Holocaust. The issue of the Jewish collaborators was one of the main issues that were discussed in the Knesset session during the first years of Israel existence. Later, in discussion in the Committee for Law and Constitution and its sub-committee, this issue became the main and most contentious issue. Eventually, these discussions led to the legislation of the "Law to bring Justice against Nazis and their Assistants" in 1950 (Weitz, 1997). The main dilemma that faced the legislators in every legal case was whether it was morally possible to judge Holocaust survivors who perform crimes, despite the fact that they acted in most extreme conditions in ghettos, concentration and extermination camps or to accept their behavior (Levine, 2015; Yablonka, 1996, 2000).

They *"went like lambs to the slaughter" dilemma*

We (the Jewish people) should not go like lambs to the slaughter! This was the main message of Abba Kovner (Kovner, 1981); one of the leaders of the Jewish Partisans to the residents of the "Vilna" ghetto in Lithuania. This message or maybe a kind of "command" became the post-Holocaust model for the "desired" resistance of Jews against the Nazis. The silence of the Jews and the submissive way in which most Jews went to their deaths without protest, was considered by at least part of the Israeli public opinion in the first years after Holocaust as "evidence" of their unwillingness to resist. "Went like lambs to the slaughter" is the metaphor that is used to describe those who were led to their death and did not resist by trying to rebel. The expression sounds like and is often interpreted in Israel as an accusation against the passive behavior of the Jewish masses who were slaughtered during the Holocaust (Kovner, 1981, 2002). This expression had become a focal point in the memory of the Holocaust in Israel since the early days of the state's establishment, when Holocaust victims were seen by the Israelis who did not experience the Holocaust, as going passively to their deaths. Instead, they wanted to emphasize the commemoration of the ghetto resistance and partisans who fought against the Nazis. This phrase is sometimes used until today (Farber, 2007). **The main dilemma here** is whether it is morally possible to define the Jewish victims and survivors of the Holocaust as those "who went like lambs to the slaughter", meaning that because they acted in a cowardly manner in the face of Nazis aggression, failing to resist them or even passively aiding their own slaughter, they should be scorned (Weitzberg, 1996).

The restitution payments dilemma

"This government, which will engage in negotiations with the murderers who annihilated our people, will be a malicious government that will base its dominion on bayonets and grenades". (From the words of Menahem Begin, head of the opposition during the demonstration against the Reparations Agreement between Israel and West Germany, 7th January, 1952, in Weitz, 2005, p. 40).

From 1953, West Germany paid large financial restitution payments to the State of Israel (which at that time was very poor) and also paid compensation to the Holocaust survivors individually. The restitution payments were compensation for the damage caused by Nazi crimes against Jews during the Holocaust (Feldman, 1984).

The "Reparations Agreement" or the "Luxembourg Agreement" that defined the restitution payments was signed between the State of Israel and the Federal Republic of Western Germany on 10th September, 1952 in Luxembourg. Under its terms, West Germany transferred a sum of 3 billion West German Marks, between 1953 and 1965, as compensation for the suffering and material damage endured by the Jews during the Holocaust. The West German government also committed itself to paying "renta" – a pension - to Holocaust survivors. These are regular monthly payments to cover medical expenses that the survivors require, as compensation for their suffering in the concentration and death camps and as restitution for the loss of basic rights such as the right to education for those survivors who were children during the Holocaust, etc. The amount of the payments is determined according to criteria that assess the extent of the damage caused to the survivor (Ofer, 2007). Some of the restitution payments for the property of the Jewish communities in Germany itself, such as the synagogues and public buildings that were confiscated, have been given to the communities that remain in Western Germany. The Reparations Agreement was signed on 10th September 1952 in Luxemburg, when affidavits were exchanged by the governments of West Germany and Israel (Levracht, 1973). In Israel, there were people who argued that it was morally impossible to accept money from the Germans and objected to the payments, claiming that, in fact, they indicated absolution for the Nazi murderers and disrespect for the memory of the Holocaust victims. They emphasized that the German people should never be forgiven (Sagi, 1986). ***The main dilemma here*** was, in light of this dispute, whether to make a rational-utilitarian decision and accept the reparations or to make an affective-intuitive decision and reject them given the fear that their acceptance would symbolize forgiveness for the Nazis and for their homeland - Germany (Katz, 2009).

The Kasztner dilemma

"The tragedy of Kasztner is the tragedy of a man who was murdered twice". (Weitz, 1995, p. 3).

Weitz's words indicate that Kasztner was murdered mentally and publicly for the first time when he was judged and found guilty of collaboration with the Nazis and again a second time when he was murdered by an assailant following his trial.

Dr. Israel Kasztner, one of the leaders of Hungarian Jewry during the Holocaust, was a member of the Budapest "Aid and Rescue Committee" and organized different rescue operations, the most famous of which was the "Kasztner train". Kasztner negotiated with senior Nazi officers in Hungary during the Holocaust to save Jews in return for bribes or other benefits. In this manner he succeeded in saving at least 1, 685 Jews towards the end of 1944 in what was known as the "Kasztner train". Instead of being transported for extermination to Auschwitz-Birkenau death camp, the passengers of this train were deported to freedom and sanctuary in neutral Switzerland (Gutman, 1990a).

In 1954, against the background of the debate raging during those years in Israel regarding Holocaust survivors who had collaborated in different ways with the Nazis, Kastner was tried in court. He was described in the trial by the judge Benjamin Halevi as one who had "sold his soul to the devil" because of the character of his relations with the Nazis that indicated that he had cooperated closely with them

(Hatis-Rolf, 1998). The main suspicion was that he had conducted inappropriate relations with Nazi officers derived from the fact that he gave testimony after the war supporting the conduct of one of the Nazis officials in Budapest, Kurt Becher in the Nuremberg trials. In the first "Kasztner trial" in Jerusalem, Kasztner was found guilty of collaborating with the Nazis, but he was later acquitted on appeal to the High Court of Justice. Sadly, he was murdered by a Jewish assailant influenced by public incitement to hatred against Kasztner after his acquittal (Weitz, 1995). ***The main dilemma*** for Israeli society with regard to this issue was whether it was moral to define Kasztner as a collaborator with the Nazis and to punish him as such when he actually did this in order to save Jews (Yablonka, 2000; Brand & Brand, 1960).

The resistance dilemma

This dilemma is succinctly expressed in the words of the poet Haim Guri:

"Those who stole a loaf of bread resisted

Those who taught in secret resisted

Those who wrote and published warnings and destroyed illusions resisted

Those who hid sacred scrolls resisted

Those who forged certificates resisted

Those who smuggled people from state to state resisted

Those who wrote records of the events and hid them resisted

Those who offered assistance resisted

Those who connected the besieged and smuggled in orders and weapons resisted

Those who conducted armed warfare in city roads and forests and mountains resisted

Those who arose in rebellion in the camps resisted

Those who rebelled in the ghettoes behind the crumbling walls, in the most desperate revolt resisted"

(Lurie, 2015, p. 1)

.   .   .

In Israeli literature and public debate on the Holocaust, continuous controversy ensues with regard to the question: what should be highlighted more – active "resistance" against the Nazis meaning rebellion and armed resistance or "passive" resistance that included: escape, hiding, hard labor for the Nazis, bribery etc.? (Bauer, 1983) **The main dilemma** is whether to emphasize "active" or "passive" resistance. The argument in favor of emphasizing "passive" resistance is that most of the Jews were saved by "passive" means (Laor, 2009). This argument appears more forceful from a historical viewpoint since most of those who survived were engaged in forced labor under the Nazis, and because they were used for work until the last moment their lives were saved (Machman, 1998). In contrast, there is no doubt that "active" armed resistance was more heroic, requiring more initiative and daring and from a national-education viewpoint, this is the "right" way of reacting against an attack that the Israeli state would like to inculcate in the younger generation. This is because active armed resistance emphasizes the value of resistance against those who aim to destroy the Jewish people and the State of Israel (Tal, 2000).

Holocaust comparison dilemma

"While the Holocaust, or the Jewish Holocaust, is engraved in the Jewish-Israeli collective consciousness and forgetting it is unimaginable, the State of Israel still does not recognize the Armenian genocide ... it is therefore not unsurprising that for most of the students and even for many adult citizens in Israel, the "Armenian Holocaust" is at the most a recognized concept, with a rather unclear content" (Amnesty International, 2015).

In Israel and the Jewish world in general, there is an ongoing debate questioning whether the Jewish Holocaust was such a unique, one-time phenomenon that it is impossible to compare it to any other historical phenomenon or if it is one of a series of similar historical events. Such similar events could be the genocide of the Armenians by the Turks during the 1st World War in 1914, the genocide in Ruanda in 1994, etc. (Moras, 1972). **The main dilemma** here is whether it is possible to compare the Holocaust to these other historical events. The main argument in favor of such a comparison is that all genocides in human history have the same striking characteristics, so that it is correct and desirable to compare the Holocaust to these similar events (Neuberger, 1994). The argument against such a comparison claims that the Holocaust is so unique in its extent and force and the scope of its horrors that it would be incorrect to compare it with any other event. This dispute also has implications for the way in which the world perceives current actions of Israel and the way in which Israel perceives its own actions and behavior, especially in the context of the Arab-Israeli conflict (Oron, 1995b, 2003, 2005, 2006).

1.4.4 Summary

This sub-chapter describes some of the main moral dilemmas faced by the Jews during and after the Jewish Holocaust. As we have seen, Holocaust survivors were saved thanks to four main strategies: The first three well-known factors are personal ingenuity, repeated luck and the help of other people – Jews or non-Jews. The fourth lesser known factor is the adoption of utilitarian morality or, in other words, survival morality. This morality contradicts "accepted" morality, but it was essential for survival. The moral dilemmas are a very important part of the Holocaust story but have somehow been neglected by public interest and study in Israel. The next sub-chapter describes how the Holocaust is taught in Israel.

1.5 Jewish Holocaust in Israeli education

"There can be no doubt that the Holocaust shaped and still continues to shape our collective memory and has become part of our national identity and we therefore have an obligation to teach children about the Holocaust in the education system. We should continuously deal with questions about the messages of the Holocaust" (Kolett, 2014 pp-16).

Introduction

The following pages focus on formal Holocaust studies in Israeli high schools and the students' journeys to Poland. This stage is considered the most significant stage for the transmission of the legacy of the Holocaust to Israeli youth and the shaping of Holocaust memory. There are several main educational-social-cultural stages, which children in Israel undergo with regard to the Holocaust: (a) from childhood until high school: during this period the main learning occurs on memorial days when general information is given in school. (b) In high school: Holocaust studies are part of the curriculum for the matriculation exams and there is an organized guided journey to Holocaust extermination sights in Poland for those choosing to travel. (c), during compulsory military service in the army soldiers are given lectures about the Holocaust. For army officers there is also an organized guided journey to the Holocaust extermination sights in Poland (d), Holocaust studies are offered in universities and colleges for those who wish to study this subject. It is noted that there is also a very broad phenomenon of journeys for organized groups of adults to the sites of the Holocaust and its commemoration in Poland (Lev, 2007).

1.5.1 Formal Learning of the Holocaust

"The Holocaust can remind us that Israel is also the means to protect against any future attempt to obliterate the Jewish people in its entirety. The Holocaust can teach us that there are sane people and developed cultures who are liable to enlist to perform genocide and that allowing the slaughter of those distant from them will eventually allow the slaughter of their own relatives. The Holocaust will teach us the power of strength of resistance exists in the soul of the normal person, a power that they themselves could not imagine. We must learn not only in order that they should know, we should learn despite the pain. That pain is less large than the suffering that may be the fate of the Jewish people and humanity if we forget". (Barnea, 2014, p. 27).

From the early days of the State of Israel, the Holocaust was seen as a fundamental event that defined Israeli society at different levels and consequently influenced the Israeli education system, although its appearance and content altered over the years (Machman, 1998).

Machman (ibid., p. 687) notes:

"It is impossible for the subject of the Holocaust not to be mentioned at one stage or another of the education process".

Israeli researchers and institutions were the pioneers in the field of Holocaust studies; they were the ones who provided most of the initial learning materials and those who began to deal with public commemoration and recognition of the Holocaust (Aharonson, 1999). Initial official actions in the State of Israel regarding the teaching of the Holocaust were most meaningful. The first was a decision by the "Knesset" (Israeli Parliament) to establish an official day of remembrance for the Holocaust and resistance against the Nazis, to be known as "Holocaust Remembrance and Heroism Day". This day was first organized in 1951 and officially certified by the Knesset in 1953. This law also constituted the basis for the establishment of "Yad Vashem", a national institution for the research, education and commemoration of the Holocaust (Cohen, 2004).

Israeli schools and the Ministry of Education began to deal with the issue of the Holocaust in the early 1950s. In the middle of the 1950s and until the beginning of the 1960s, the Ministry of Education and the "Ghetto Fighters' Museum" published several textbooks concerning the Holocaust, testimonies and memories of Holocaust survivors and guidebooks for teachers and education counselors. These books constituted an important contribution since there were very few teaching materials available for classroom use (Schatzker, 1973). At that time learning materials that dealt with the Nazi period and the Holocaust began to appear in the Ministry of Education learning programs for the disciplines of history and literature. Nevertheless, teaching the Holocaust was not yet widely established and many schools did not teach it or only did so randomly (Keren, 1985). In most cases, schools held memorial ceremonies and informal activities, especially on Holocaust Day, and most of the teaching of the Holocaust in

Israel during that period was Zionist-nationalist in character (Keren, 1998).

Following the Eichman trial in 1961, awareness and interest in the Holocaust increased significantly in the Israeli public and especially among Israeli youth. The Ministry of Education, therefore, established a public committee on the issue of teaching the Holocaust in schools and published several new textbooks on the Holocaust. In addition to Ministry of Education learning materials, various works were published by other institutions such as the "Ghetto Fighters Museum" and "Yad Vashem". In comparison to previous decades, the educational programs began to give greater emphasis to the heroism of European Jews during the Holocaust and even to identify with them. This trend was strengthened after the "Six Days War" in 1967 and the "Yom Kippur (Day of Atonement) War" in 1973. The Ministry of Education published a more comprehensive yet optional learning program for secondary schools on anti-Semitism and the Holocaust called "From the Holocaust to Revival".

In 1979, the Ministry of Education decided to make the Holocaust a compulsory subject of the high school learning program and in 1981 a new learning program containing 30 hours of learning and materials was published. This new program constituted part of the studies for the Matriculation exam in history. The new learning program created an urgent need for appropriate training for teachers. In addition to the universities and colleges, independent institutions offered special training courses for teachers, learning programs and educational mate-rials and thus became an essential part of Holocaust teaching in Israel (Gutman, 1990b). While the Israeli public was continually divided on political, social and religious issues, the subject of the Holocaust was seen as a unifying element, important for all parts of the society as a subject of national consensus (Gottwein, 1998).

From the early 1980s, experiential and informal learning of the Holocaust had also developed. Schools began to invite Holocaust survivors to tell their personal stories to students and the number of educational trips to museums and institutions relating to the Holocaust increased. The most significant change occurred with the launch of the program for organized journeys to Poland, which was facilitated officially after the fall of the communist regime in Poland in 1988. For more than 30 years now (the first official journey to Poland was in 1983) the journeys have played an important role in Holocaust learning (Keren, 1987).

Over the years, systematic continuous and large scope efforts have been invested to broaden and improve Holocaust teaching in Israel's school system. The goals of Holocaust teaching have become more complex and more sophisticated. If in earlier years the main goal was to commemorate the victims and historical learning, today the goals have become broader and also include educational messages relating to Jewish and Israeli identity, democracy, values, and ideology (Lev, 2007; Lev, Shadmi & Ben-Ezra 2006). The tools, activities and techniques for Holocaust teaching were also widened and became far more complex, integrating the Holocaust with other subjects and using cognitive and experiential teaching methods based on experiential learning principles (Andresen, Boud & Cohen, 2000; Kolb, 1984). At the end of the 1970s and the beginning of the 1980s, new thinking was introduced concerning the learning contents and the subject of the Holocaust. It was defined as one of 26 elective subjects from which the history teacher could choose three as distinct from compulsory subjects that were to be taught in greater depth. Following this decision, a public debate ensued along two main axes concerning the goals of Holocaust teaching: Whether Holocaust studies should emphasize the Holocaust as a historical event, or whether they could also be used as a tool for the transmission of educational-national messages (Schatzker, 1980, 1998, 1999).

In 1979, the Pedagogical Committee of the Ministry of Education and the superintendent of history studies decided to allot a third of a history learning unit to Holocaust studies. The other two-thirds are devoted to 20th century general history and the history of recent generations of the people of Israel. A year later in 1980 the "Knesset" (Israeli Parliament) decided to amend the "National Education Law" and added a new goal for education in Israel – education for "Awareness of the Holocaust and Heroism" (Shapira, 1997).

Since the 1980s, two main trends have developed: The first depicts the Holocaust according to the Zionist narrative. This trend emphasizes the emotional-experiential dimension of the Holocaust, while positioning the Zionist and Jewish story at its core. It appeals to the emotions through different means, the most important of which is the journey to extermination sites in Poland. The goal is to present the Holocaust at the center of Jewish historical discussion and to develop the students' deep affinity with the victims of the Holocaust. The second approach is an academic trend, a more universal viewpoint with an academic foundation that focuses more on universal implications of the Holocaust. These trends influence formal and informal Holocaust public discussion and studies in Israel.

Over recent years the Ministry of Education has presented the Holocaust according to the Zionist narrative. It emphasizes the experiential and emotional aspects of the Holocaust, while positioning the Jewish and Zionist story at the center. This approach appeals to the students' emotions through different means, especially the journey to Poland. The goal is to create the students' deep identification with the Holocaust and its victims. In contrast, as noted above, there is another growing trend that takes a universal approach founded on academic research that sees the Holocaust as a universal historical event (Cohen, 2010). Until 2014 the Ministry of Education program for the matriculation exam in Holocaust studies included chapters dealing with the causes for the rise of Nazi Germany, Nazi ideology, the Holocaust and the Second World War. This formal education focused on regular academic studies based mostly on textbooks and taught in history lessons during school studies for matriculation exams in Grades 11-12 (Ministry of Education, 2015a).

In December 2014 as a result of the appointment of a new Minister of Education, Shai Peron a change was instituted. The Ministry of Education published a revised learning program on the subject of the Holocaust, known as "In the paths of memory" (Ministry of Education, 2015a). This is an organized set learning program from nursery to Grade 12 that came into operation from the school year 2014-2015. This is the first time that the Ministry of Education determined a learning program that obliges the teaching of the Holocaust heritage for the entire education system and all age groups under its jurisdiction. The program was influenced by the ministry's perception that students should be guided to "significant learning", which is actually another definition for "experiential learning" (Ministry of Education, General Manager's Directive, 2014). The purposes of the program were defined as follows:

"General goals: (a) familiarity with the events of the Holocaust; (b) familiarity with the lost (before the Holocaust) *Jewish world; (c) creating empathy towards Holocaust victims; (d) highlighting revelations of human spirit during the Holocaust and its expression in areas of creativity, culture, philosophy and the arts; (e) empowering a sense of self-efficacy through cognitive and emotional tools to cope with the story of the Holocaust.*

Goals relating to values: (a) reinforcement of Jewish values and international humanistic values; (b) reinforcement of democratic values and tolerance and fostering the aspiration to found an exemplary society; (c) fostering human sensitivity; (d) commitment to the continued existence of the Jewish people; (e) commitment to the fight against racism; (e) commitment to the existence of a Jewish and democratic state" (Ministry of Education, General Manager's Directive, 2014, p. 3).

The motto for the program is "a better future for humanity is embodied not in a particular social regime but in a better human" (In the paths of memory, (Ministry of Education, 2015a, p.1). This is a quotation from the work of the famous Jewish author and educator, who was murdered during the Holocaust, Dr. Janusz Korczak.

The program includes four main subjects that are delivered according to age group: (a) The Jewish world in all its hues and communities before the Holocaust (b) The human story during the Holocaust including: Jews coping with the Holocaust period, Righteous Gentiles among the Nations (non-Jewish people who risked their lives and often their families' lives in order to save Jews during the Holocaust), and those who stood by the side and the Nazis and those who assisted them; (c) Liberation and the return to life (d) Fundamental concepts of the Holocaust.

The main alterations in this program in contrast to the past programs are: (a) An official instruction was given to teach the subject of the Holocaust from the nursery through all age groups (b) Personal research of Grade 12 students on the subject of the Holocaust replaced the former matriculation exam. This research constitutes 30% of the general grade for the subject of history as previously expressed by the exam (In the paths of memory, (Ministry of Education, 2015a).

The program aroused public criticism from two aspects: (1) the claim that it is too early to start to teach the subject of the Holocaust in nursery. (2) Replacing the matriculation exam with personal research work which bears a grade. It is argued that due to this change the teachers will teach less on the subject of the Holocaust and the students, despite their deeper work on the specific subject that they research, will in total receive only a restricted and partial picture of the subject of the Holocaust. Since the program only began to operate in the school year 2014-2015, it is still in its infancy and there has been no study of the influence of these changes.

1.5.2 The journeys to Poland

In the last 25 years, the journeys to Poland have become the most important component of the Holocaust teaching program and the visits to the Holocaust sites in Poland have become a sort of "pilgrimage" for many of Israel's youth who participate in these journeys. Teachers, parents and students feel that the journey to Poland is very important and invest serious efforts so that the students can participate in the journeys. The organized journeys began in 1983, the 40th anniversary of the Warsaw Ghetto Uprising. They have increased over the years and hundreds of thousands of Israeli students from state high schools have travelled to Poland within the frame of journeys organized by the Ministry of Education (Worgen, 2008). The journeys to Poland are actually the direct or the logical continuation of the experiential learning that characterizes part of Holocaust studies in their broadest sense. The journeys to Poland are the peak of the experiential learning program that includes commemorative ceremonies, theater performances, documentary films, cinema films, trips to the memorial and commemoration centers in Israel, direct meetings with Holocaust survivors or viewing them through televised clips etc. The journey to Poland includes visits to historical sites – ghettoes, extermination camps, memorials, synagogues and additional sites (Lindenstrauss, 2012).

The Ministry of Education encourages, initiates, certifies and subsidizes the school journeys under its organization and responsibility through the school systems with the assistance of the Ministry of Tourism. The journeys organized by the Ministry of Education follow a regular defined route through several central sites, including ceremonies and educational-learning activities at the different sites. The journey to Poland is the culmination of an educational and academic process, which lasts a full academic year and consists of several stages:

1. Preparation: academic studies, meetings with survivors/witnesses, visiting Holocaust museums and watching documentary and epic Holocaust films.
2. A guided group journey to Poland, usually lasting eight days.
3. Educational processing of the emotional and learning experiences throughout the journey and afterward.
4. Sharing experiences and reflections arising from the journey with the community (Bitts, 2004; Bar Natan, 2004).

The goals of the journey are to learn about: 1. Jewish life in Poland before the Second World War. 2. The ideological principles of the Nazis and the conditions that led to their rise. 3. History of the Holocaust. 4. Jewish resistance during the Holocaust. 5. Relations between Jews and non-Jews. 6. Moral and universal - humanist values focusing especially on the "Righteous among the Nations" – those non-Jews who saved Jews during the Holocaust. The perception is that this experiential learning allows the student to understand the destruction and loss of the Jews of Europe, the moral corruption of the Nazis, the importance of Jews' resistance to the Nazis and the enormous dimensions of the horror and catastrophe that the Jewish people endured (Soen & Davidovich, 2011).

Criticism of the Journeys

"I do not dare to speak in the name of the dead, and in the name of the survivors I am not qualified to speak. I shall only write in my own name, a graduate of Auschwitz: stop using the Holocaust for political needs and especially stop what is known as "the March of the Living". That very name is outrageous. On soil that is drenched in death there is no place for marches. It is only permissible to tread here with humility, without demonstrativeness, without any waving of national flags ... we must cope with the past, but first we must take care for the future. Arrogant nationalism, lack of tolerance for others and their language, violence under the guise of patriotism, imperviousness regarding the distress of those seeking refuge, hatred towards Arabs and education for supremacy do not signify assimilation of the meaning of the massacre: that evil and cruelty may exist among those who have culture, irrespective of how developed they may be from a scientific and economic point of view" (Bondi, 2014 p.28),

Over the years, there has been growing debate about the justification for the journeys to Poland focusing on several main issues:

1. The high cost of the journeys, averaging approximately NIS 6,000 ($1,520) per traveler today, which leads many parents to avoid sending their children on such a journey. This leads to a situation where the journey becomes a journey "only for the rich" although the Ministry of Education and other entities provide partial subsidies for the journey according to individual parents' requests.
2. Doubts regarding the educational value of the journey – some of the teachers and educators are worried that the students see the journey as an enjoyable trip with their friends and do not relate seriously to its educational aspects.
3. "The business" revolving around the journeys including an

entire department in the Ministry of Education that deals with the journeys, the secret service that protects the journeys, the tourist offices and air transport companies et cetera. In addition, the tourist companies in Poland also profit from the journeys. It is therefore questioned whether this does not constitute a "commercialization" of the Holocaust and creates a moral mistake.

4. The students' behavior on the journeys has often been extreme and even rude, angering the Poles and damaging the image of Israel (Rama, 2011).

5. The journey to Poland emphasizes a nationalist message at the expense of universal values (Maltz, 2016).

6. The journey to Poland causes emotional trauma inflicted on teenagers, imposes high cost on parents, emphasizes national-utilitarian values and ignores the universal values. Furthermore, it strengthens nationalism and a centralist approach that grasps the world as a hostile place for the Jewish people and the State of Israel (Starkman & Dattel, 2016).

In contrast to this, those who defend the journeys claim that although there are some defects, there is still no good alternative that is better than the experience of the journey and the deep experiential learning that it affords (Shalem, 2008).

1.5.3 Research on the journeys to Poland

Research on Holocaust studies over the years has found that the most effective means for this study are the journey to Poland and listening to testimony of survivors as part of the preparation for the journey in Israel or on the journey itself. This, together with the establishment of the "tradition" of the journeys, has reinforced the trend to continue to take the students to Poland (Mimouni-Bloch, Rostami & Bloch, 2012). Cohen (2010) found that most of the students graded the journey and also the testimony of the survivors as very significant and important. These findings support the effectiveness of experiential learning as an efficient and most meaningful type of learning, as previous studies on experiential learning revealed (Kolb, 1984; Fink, 2010).

Research on Holocaust studies indicates that at the one extreme of the journeys, there are universal models, those that see the Holocaust as a disaster for humanity as a whole (Davidovich, Soen & Haber, 2014). This type of disaster should be studied in affinity with democratic values: the value of life, human dignity, tolerance, acceptance of those who are different and other, determined confrontation against malicious authoritarian forces, etc. At the other extreme are ethnocentric-particular models that see the Holocaust first and foremost and primarily as a tragedy for the Jewish people. This perspective sees the instilling of national and Jewish values as the supreme goal of Holocaust experiential learning. This approach is expressed in the contents of the journey that especially emphasize the Jewish aspects of the Holocaust and its affinity to the establishment of the State of Israel (Davidovich, Soen & Haber, 2014).

Many studies have been conducted on the journeys to Poland over the years. Some were studies initiated by the Ministry of Education and many others by private institutions, universities, etc. The following is a chronological review of the principal findings of these studies:

- The main influences of the journey are an increase in the student's knowledge of the Holocaust and reinforcement of their commitment to the memory of the Holocaust: participation in the journey increases the tendency to see the Holocaust as a tragedy for humanity as a whole and also reinforces Jewish identity and strengthens respect for democratic values (Feldman, 2001).
- Students who participated in the journey to Poland had more knowledge about the Holocaust in comparison to those who did not travel there and the experience of the journey had an influence on the students' sensitivity towards the Holocaust (Romi & Lev, 2003).
- The journey to Poland reinforced participants' Jewish and Zionist self-identity (Fisherman & Kaniel, 2004).

- The journey to Poland strengthened the participants' ability to study under mental stress and strengthened understanding of universal and democratic values. It also improved knowledge about the Holocaust and reinforced the perception that the Holocaust had universal meaning and not only Jewish meaning (Mayseless & Solomon, 2005).
- The most significant difference between high school students who participated in the journeys to Poland and those who did not, was that those who did not travel to Poland were found to have less knowledge of the Holocaust than the participants in the journeys acquired (Romi & Lev, 2007).
- The journeys lead to acquisition of national and less universal understanding since they focus on the reinforcement of national pride and the importance of the existence of the Jewish state. It was also shown that the journey tends to strengthen existing attitudes towards Judaism, Zionism and the Holocaust and not to alter them. There was an enhancement of understanding concerning moral issues and reinforcement of emotion towards the Holocaust (Rama, 2011).
- The journey to Poland led young people to strengthen their Israeli identity, and have identify more strongly with Zionist values but also radicalized their feelings towards Arabs as the factor endangering the security of Israel. No difference was found between participants who had a family connection to Holocaust victims or survivors and those who did not have such a connection (Kimchi, 2011).
- The journey to Poland did not significantly improve the young people's consideration toward the Polish people. Most of the students revealed negative consideration of the Poles and saw them as anti-Semitic and collaborators with the Nazis in relation to the Jews during the Holocaust (Davidovich & Hazan, 2011).
- Students returning from the journey to Poland were found

to be more emotionally mature, evaluate more the importance of family and society and feel more secure in their state (Berger, 2012).

- The journey led to an increase in the Jewish components of students' identities. There was an evident sense of increased identification with the victims and also with Liberal values alongside increased understanding of the existential threat towards Israel (Mimouni-Bloch, Rostami & Bloch, 2012).

Gurani (2015) summarized the various research studies and models concerning the journeys to Poland from three different angles: 1. the universal message of the Holocaust, which sees the Holocaust as parallel to other cases of genocide. 2. The Jewish-national meaning of the Holocaust that sees the Holocaust as a unique event for the Jewish people and refuses to assign the term "holocaust" to other cases of genocide. 3. A synthesis of both previous angles.

1.5.4 Holocaust education in the Israel Defense Force (IDF)

As a continuation of the Ministry of Education educational-learning program, Israel Defense Forces (IDF) soldiers learn about Holocaust during their military service. The main message to the soldiers is that a powerful Israeli army with the ability to act independently is essential to prevent the repetition of another Holocaust. The slogan for this is "never again". IDF soldiers routinely visit the "Yad Vashem" museum in Jerusalem and those studying in officers' courses visit the "Beit Wohlin museum" at Givataim near Tel Aviv as part of their course. Since 1955, the "Flower for a Survivor" army project has encouraged the development of a special connection between IDF soldiers and Holocaust survivors. In this project the soldiers visit the survivors and assist them (Lomski-Feder, 1997).

The main program that the IDF operates is the "Witnesses in Uniform" program, in which groups of officers and other army commanders are sent to Poland and other countries together with Holocaust survivor witnesses to visit the sites of the Holocaust and trace the events of the Holocaust. The purpose of these missions is to increase the soldiers' direct personal connection to the events that occurred during the Holocaust. The program was initiated by an IDF officer, Elazar Stern, the son of Holocaust survivors, after a visit together with his parents to Auschwitz death camp. Standing proudly with an Israeli flag and in uniform at the sites of the slaughter of the Jewish people is often described as a central experience in these journeys. In September 2003, there was a flyover by fighter aircrafts of the Israeli air force over Auschwitz death camp in parallel with a ceremony of "Witnesses in Uniform" on the ground at the site. The flyover was initiated by a pilot (an ex-Commander of the Israeli Air Force) Major-General Amir Eshel, himself a Holocaust survivor (Guterman, Yablonka & Shalev, 2008). A study conducted by Ganor (2006) found that knowledge of the Holocaust increased significantly in response to Holocaust studies in the IDF. In addition to the emphasis on national messages, universal conclusions are deduced as well.

Occupation with moral questions from the period of the Holocaust has constituted the foundation for work on contemporary moral questions in the IDF, and Holocaust events serve as a means to learn national and universal humanist lessons. In other words, the memory of the Holocaust is used in the IDF to deliver both national and universal messages. It transpires that the IDF has demonstrated much more sensitivity for injury to Arab citizens as an outcome of Holocaust learning (Ganor 2006). According to this research, IDF soldiers and officers report that the trauma of the Holocaust does not allow them to be insensitive to enemy civilian populations and this influences their discretion and decisions in their operational activities and in warfare. This research also found that IDF soldiers who are second generation Holocaust survivors are those who have brought about the change in the IDF's attitude towards the Holocaust. They have influenced its perception to the extent that the Holocaust has an influence on the military code of ethics, reinforcing humanist values. Soldiers who had a personal link to the Holocaust were found to hold more universal viewpoints. Contrastingly, soldiers who did not have such a personal link to the Holocaust were found to have stronger national viewpoints (Ibid).

In another study by Davidovich, Amir and Heskel (2011) concerning the journeys of the IDF soldiers to Poland as part of the

"Witnesses in Uniform" program, it was found that universal values were strengthened among the soldiers. In contrast, particular values such as Jewish-Zionist identity, national pride and the significance of Jewish symbols were not developed as a result of these journeys. The participants in the journey noted that it had strong significance for them as soldiers, officers and as human beings.

1.5.5 Summary of Holocaust memory and conceptions over time

Drawing on the above literature review, we can now summarize the conceptualization of Holocaust memory over time, and suggest a better understanding of the "mutual" recovery process from Holocaust trauma. We would call this a "mutual" process because for the Jews, this actually involves recovery from both a national trauma and a private trauma at the same time. A few kinds of "mutuality" can be noticed: (a) Holocaust survivor together with their descendants. (b) Holocaust survivor and their descendants together with the rest of Israeli society. (c) Jewish people in the worldwide diaspora together with the State of Israel.

Our perception is that the Holocaust was a national trauma for the Jewish people, which need to be healed. Let us explain this process. After the Holocaust Jews all over the world and mostly in Israel (where most of Holocaust survivors arrived) needed to cope with the national trauma. Individuals and the nation underwent a national psychosocial recovery process from the trauma. The different aspects of this process are presented in Table 1.3 below:

Table 1.3 - Summary of the mutual social - psychosocial recovery process

Generations and years	Reaction of survivors	Reaction of the Israeli society	Expression in legislation and law	Expression in education
First generation: Holocaust survivors	Shock, shame, repression of feelings and memories	Shock, shame, rejection of survivor's stories, Recognition of moral responsibility to memory	The Law to exact Justice against the Nazis and their Collaborators And The Memorial Day low (both legislated in 1951)	Disorderly holocaust studies in some of the schools
Second generation: The children of Holocaust survivors	A sense of legitimacy for their feelings from society and opening up to tell the story	Understanding and acceptance of survivor's actions and experiences during the Holocaust	In 1961, Eichman trial in Jerusalem, In 1980, the law of compulsory Holocaust studies in schools was legislated	In 1981, Holocaust studies became part of the Matriculation exams
Third generation: The grandchildren of Holocaust survivors	Increased efforts to tell about the Holocaust and leave testimony for the younger generation	Identification with the survivors, desire to know and understand more	In 2015, State directive for compulsory Holocaust studies also in primary schools and kindergartens	In 1999, the mass journeys to Poland under the Ministry of Education began. A search for new ways to teach the Holocaust, the debate about the journeys to Poland
Fourth generation The great-grandchildren of Holocaust survivors	Second generation continues to tell their parents' story?	Processing and deepening understanding, drawing conclusions ?	State directive to learn about other genocides?	New Holocaust learning program?

After describing the recovery process, we can now suggest a structure that can explain this process, which we name "*Time and Action Creating Mutual Recovery from Holocaust Trauma*".

This structure describes four time intervals in which parallel processes of recovery from the Holocaust trauma evolve. The principle is that distancing in time together with appropriate action enables both the individual and the nation to gradually access the Holocaust trauma, and to touch upon its experiences in order to understand its complex meanings. This strategy engenders a multi-generational psycho-social healing process from the Holocaust trauma for Holocaust survivors, their descendants and for Jewish-Israeli society as a whole. Three essential conditions are needed in order to ensure the effective operation of this strategy: motivation to cope with the Holocaust trauma, a decision to do so and the ability to do so over time. The main stages of this process are now described here:

Time interval 1: 1941 – 1961: 8th May 1945 was the end of the Holocaust; survivors began their journey to a new life, mostly in Israel. As an outcome of the tremendous loss and trauma, the Holocaust was conceived by Jewish society as something that should not be dealt with if they did not have to. Survivors bore pain, shame, pangs of conscience and anger. *The main psychological reaction of society was rejection followed by repression.*

Time interval 2: 1961 – 1990: 1961 - Eichmann trial, Holocaust survivors began to talk about what had happened. As an outcome of the testimonies given by survivors in the Eichmann trial (1961), the Holocaust is conceived in society as a legitimate and important event whose memory should be perpetuated. *The main psychological reactions of society are: understanding followed by recognition.*

Time interval 3: 1990 – 2015: 1990 - Beginning of government organized journeys to Poland; Holocaust studies become a national goal. As an outcome of the journeys to Poland, the perpetuation of Holocaust memory is conceived in society as a national educational goal. *The main psychological reactions of society are empathy followed by identification.*

Time interval 4: 2015 + Growing debate about the justification, necessity and benefits of the journeys being conducted continuously. We predict that the next step will be "*Acceptance followed by Reconciliation*". This reaction is based on efforts to cope with Holocaust memory not only from the emotional aspect but also from academic universal perspective. New conclusions can be drawn, producing multiple lessons for the future. The process is illustrated in Table 1.4 below.

Table 1.4: "Time and Action Creating Mutual Recovery from Holocaust Trauma"

Time interval	Main emotional reaction of the society towards the Holocaust	Main initiator of change
1941-1961	Rejection followed by Repression	Eichman trial in 1961
1961-1990	Understanding followed by Recognition.	In 1990, the beginning of government organized journeys to Poland
1990-2015	Empathy followed by Identification	From 2010 on, growing debate over the justification of the journeys to Poland
2015+	Acceptance followed by Reconciliation (expected)	Changing Holocaust learning program (expected)

1.5.6 Gap in knowledge

Undoubtedly the Holocaust was a terrible tragedy and national trauma for the Jewish people that will influence it for many generations to come. Although 70 years have passed since the end of World War II and The Holocaust, it is still, without doubt, the most important field of much interest for Jews and other people all around the world. Nevertheless, the main Jewish attention concerning this topic is usually focused on the issue of the mass murder of the Jews who were the victims of the Nazis. Public and academic discourse in Israel usually tends to ignore ethical issues and dilemmas relating to the Jews' behavior, mostly during but also after the Holocaust (Weinrab, 1984). This is not surprising since dealing with issues such as these can be considered as picking at a very deep, still open wound; it is easier to remain within the secure boundaries of the area of public consensus, including the following core conceptions, which represent the contents that Jews and Israelis usually learn and are "expected" to remember about the Holocaust:

- The Holocaust is a unique and exceptional event in human history and as such it is impossible to compare it or analogize it to any other similar events.
- During the Holocaust, there were murderers – the Nazi Germans and their accomplices from other nations, and there were the murdered – the Jews and other "selected" groups who were innocent victims of Nazi crimes.
- Jewish fighting and resistance to the Nazis was a broad phenomenon that characterized Jewish efforts to survive during the Holocaust, a characteristic recognized in the phrases "The Holocaust and Heroism"/ "The Holocaust and the Rebellion".
- The Holocaust should never be forgotten so that it will not reoccur.
- A strong Israel will prevent another Holocaust.

These concepts shape Jewish memory of the Holocaust from the national viewpoint. They also form the axes of Israeli and Jewish thinking about the Holocaust and necessitate Holocaust learning and organized journeys of Israeli high school students to Poland to visit the sites of extermination and rebellion. They influence Holocaust research and autobiographic and other types of literature on this topic; however, little consideration is given to the issue of the Jews' moral behavior (Blady Szwaiger, 2000). On the basis of this conceptualization the main educational emphases in Holocaust studies today are:

- In formal class learning for the matriculation exams, the aim is to learn the framework story - the facts of what happened in the Holocaust.
- In the experiential learning during the journeys to Poland, the aim is to feel the pain of the Holocaust and to

experience the survivor's stories in person on the sites of
extermination in Poland (Ministry of Education, 2015c).

So, when we want to define the gap in knowledge, two main points
can be mentioned:

1. A gap in knowledge in the field of Jewish Holocaust moral
dilemmas from a retrospective point of view – what do Israeli high
school students who are learning about the Holocaust think about the
ways in which Jews coped with the moral dilemmas of the Holocaust?

2. A gap in knowledge regarding the effect of the present Holocaust
learning program in high school on the students' perceptions of Holocaust moral dilemmas.

The next chapter describes the original and innovative research
conducted on the moral dilemmas of the Holocaust that is the subject
of this thesis.

CHAPTER 2- METHODOLOGY

2.1 Introduction

As already explained in Chapter 1, public and academic discourse and also school learning in Israel usually tend to ignore moral issues and more specifically, they do not mention moral dilemmas relating to the Jews' behavior during and after the Holocaust (Weinrab, 1984; Aharonson, 1999). There has therefore been no academic research investigating school students' attitudes towards such dilemmas. The present research attempts to close this gap in knowledge by investigating the moral attitudes of Israeli students who participate in the high school Holocaust Learning Program (HLP) towards these moral dilemmas. It is an exploratory research that deals with a new research question regarding the Jewish Holocaust – how do young Jews living in Israel (the fourth generation after the Holocaust) understand the Holocaust from the moral aspect. More specifically, the **main aim** of this research is to explore the attitudes of Israeli youth towards the way Jews coped with the moral dilemmas of the Holocaust. An **exploratory approach** was chosen because the research subject has not been yet investigated and clearly defined in previous research. The research is a **longitudinal survey** combining **mixed methods** data-gathering and analysis, which was conducted from January 2015 until January 2016 over a period of two academic years, from the middle of Grade 11 until the middle of Grade 12. The following aims constitute the main axes of this research.

2.2 Research aims

1. To identify the level of agreement or disagreement with the different moral behaviors of the Jews during and after the Holocaust among Israeli high school students who participated in a Holocaust Learning Program.
2. To test whether the Holocaust Learning Program generated changes in the participant's moral attitudes.
3. To test whether changes in the participant's moral attitudes during their Holocaust Learning Program is moderated by gender, having Holocaust victims as relatives and participation in the journey to Holocaust memorial sites in Poland.
4. To identify whether and how social and educational factors are perceived by participants as influencing their moral attitudes.
5. To identify the moral lessons that the students perceived they had learned from the Holocaust Learning Program.
6. To examine whether moral attitudes are associated with perceived moral lessons from the Holocaust Learning Program.
7. To understand the meanings constructed through stories by participants in relation to their experiences of Holocaust Learning Program.

2.3 Research methods

2.3.1 Research paradigm

As noted above, the research was an exploratory research (Stebbins, 2001; Shields & Rangarajan, 2013), chosen because it was mostly fitting for the investigation of a field of knowledge that has not yet been clearly defined, in this case the field of Jewish Holocaust moral dilemmas. A mixed-methods research was conducted in order to collect the data (Greene, 2007a; Creswell & Clark, 2011). The quantitative part employed statistically measurable closed-ended questionnaires. The qualitative part employed individual in-depth interviews (Sabar Ben-Yehoshua, 2002; Morgan, 1988). A comprehensive literature review was used to compare the research results concerning moral dilemmas with other results from the academic literature, even if they came from other domains of moral investigation.

2.3.2 Sampling method

The population sample selected for this study is an intentional sample (De Souza, et al., 2012. p.189). The reason for selecting this type of sample is that this method of selection provides a sample that accurately and significantly represents the population from which it was selected to clarify the studied phenomenon (Mason, 1996).

2.3.3 Research population

The research participants were 102 Israeli high school students, boys and girls, from three public schools in northern Israel. They were aged 17-18 and studying in Grade 11 when the research began in January 2015, All of them volunteered to participate in this research. Their political attitudes were not examined in this study because they had not yet reached voting age for Israeli parliamentary elections. With regard to the students' religious-cultural status, they all defined themselves as Israeli Jews. Most of the participants had a personal-family connection to the Holocaust. This meant that they were the third or fourth generation after the Holocaust period and had a grandparent or great-grandparent or other close family relative who had experienced and survived the Holocaust in some way or another. Most of the participants also took part in the heritage journey to see Holocaust memorial sites in Poland. Table 2.1 describes the research population's main characteristics.

Table 2.1: Research population's main characteristics

Category	Characteristic	N	%
School	"Einot Yarden"	6	5.88%
	"Har Vagay"	62	60.78%
	"Emek Hahula"	34	33.33%
	Total	**102**	**100.00%**
Participants' gender	Male	36	35.29%
	Female	66	64.71%
	Total	**102**	**100.00%**
Participants' age	17	90	88.24%
	18	12	11.76%
	Total	**102**	**100.00%**
Participants' religion	Jewish	**102**	**100.00%**
Participants' citizenship	Israeli	**102**	**100.00%**
Whether participant has or had family members who were Holocaust victims or survivors	Yes	62	60.40%
	No	40	39.60%
	Total	**102**	**100.00%**
Whether the participant participated in the journey to Poland	Yes	71	69.61%
	No	31	30.39%
	Total	**102**	**100.00%**

Research field

The research field consisted of three high schools in the north of Israel. These schools belong to the state public school system. The student population came from a variety of small towns and rural settlements. In the three schools, students are taught about the Jewish Holocaust as part of their history course for the matriculation exams, in line with the Israeli Ministry of Education program. The program includes the story of the rise of the Nazis to power in Germany, the Nazi Racial Theory and central events of the Holocaust (Ministry of Education,

Education and Learning Program on the subject of the Holocaust, 2015b). The schools also participate in the Ministry of Education program for a journey to the Holocaust sites in Poland, based on experiential learning (Kolb, 1984). The preparation for the journey to Poland includes meetings with Holocaust survivors, visits to the Holocaust museums, watching films and plays and participating in workshops. Some of these workshops are conducted by the students themselves who serve as investigator-learners. The experiential learning process for the journey to Poland includes three stages: the preparation before the journey, the journey itself and the summary shortly after the return from the journey. Participation in the program is not obligatory and depends on a significant financial payment, approximately NIS 6,000 (about 1,500 Euro) and the appropriate behavior of the students (Ministry of Education, *Journeys to Poland*, 2015c). Organized Israeli Youth Heritage Expeditions (journeys) to Poland began in 1983, on the 40th anniversary of the Warsaw Ghetto Uprising. During the early 1990s, the journeys were placed under the supervision of the Israeli Ministry of Education. As mentioned, many Israeli youths in Grades 11 and 12 (aged 16-18) have participated in these journeys. The journey's main goal is to study the Holocaust and enhance the students' connection to the Jewish people and Jewish heritage (Lindenstrauss, 2012; Worgen, 2008). Each school conducts the learning programs for the journey to Poland according to the Ministry of Education program, but schools also have a certain extent of autonomy with regard to the points that they choose to emphasize. The school is assisted by professional guides during the preparation and during the journey itself. Each school chooses the educational institute that they prefer from a list of institutions recognized by the Ministry of Education, and these institutions supply the guides. This creates certain differences between the schools' programs (Lindenstrauss, 2012). It should be noted that some of the participants in this research also participated in the journey to Poland and some did not.

2.3.4 Research tools

The research employed two kinds of research tools - Closed-ended questionnaires and in-depth interviews. The questionnaire was composed of three parts:

(1) The Demographic Questionnaire

The demographic questionnaire examined the socio-demographic characteristics of the students who participated in the research, including their age, gender, and school, place of residence, religion and whether or not they had a family connection to a Holocaust survivor or victim of the Holocaust. It is actually the first part of the questionnaire investigating moral attitudes towards the Holocaust administered to the students at Measurement Point 1. The full questionnaire appears in Appendix I.

(2) The Moral Attitudes Questionnaire

The main research tool used in this study is a specially developed closed-ended questionnaire investigating the participant's moral attitudes towards Holocaust moral dilemmas. The questionnaire is based on the pioneering work of Kohlberg (1973) and many of his followers, for example: Foot (1967), Hsee (1996); Hsee et al.,(1999), Graham et al. (2011) and Lotto, Manfrinti & Sario (2013). It presents seven main moral dilemmas that faced Jews during the Holocaust (1939-1945) and seven more main dilemmas that faced Jews after the Holocaust and up until the present time (1945-1915). These fourteen dilemmas were chosen because of the fact that they stand out after a comprehensive review of the relevant literature regarding the Holocaust and post-Holocaust eras. Table 2.2 below demonstrates the fourteen Holocaust and post-Holocaust moral dilemmas. Each dilemma is followed by two alternative solutions - deontological moral based solution as opposed to survival moral based solution. Participants are asked to choose one or both of the solutions. All of the dilemmas and all the solutions provided are historically authentic. The fourteen dilemmas are listed in Table 2.2 below and are presented in detail in Chapter 1.

Table 2.2– Holocaust and post-Holocaust moral dilemmas

Holocaust era dilemmas (1939-1945)	Post-Holocaust era dilemmas (1945-1915)
1. The Judenratt dilemma	1. Went like lambs to slaughter dilemma
2. The Sonderkommando dilemma	2. The Capo dilemma
3. The Rebels dilemma	3. The Kastner dilemma
4. The thief's dilemma	4. The Resistance dilemma
5. The crying baby dilemma	5. The Revengers dilemma
6. The Little Smuggler dilemma	6. The Restitution payments dilemma
7. The Giving away children dilemma	7.The Comparison of the Holocaust dilemma

Participants were requested to indicate their personal attitude concerning the two suggested different solutions, A or B, for each dilemma on a 5-point Likert scale where 1 = strongly disagree, and 5= strongly agree. They could choose to relate to one solution (A or B), or to both solutions, A+B. Alternatively, they could mark the response "I have no opinion" or write a solution of their own. The full questionnaire appears in Appendix I.

(3) The Perceived Influences and Lessons Learned Questionnaire

The Perceived Influences and Lessons Learned Questionnaire was specially developed for this research and based on former questionnaires used, for example, by Cohen (2010); Kimchi, (2011); Mimouni-Bloch, Rostami & Bloch, (2012) and Berger (2012). It is a closed-ended questionnaire investigating the factors that participants perceived as influences on their moral attitudes and their attitudes towards given moral lessons that might be derived from their learning. The purpose of the questionnaire is to obtain feedback from the participants with regard to factors that they perceived as influences, which affected the development of their moral attitudes and possible perceived lessons which were learned during Holocaust Learning Program process.

It included two parts: The first part comprised a list of factors that might be perceived as affecting the development and shaping of the participants' moral attitudes. These perceived influential factors are derived from major domains in the participant's life. Participants are asked to mark the extent of each factor's influence on their moral attitudes on a 5-point Likert scale where 1= no influence and 5= strong influence. They can also add another factor/factors.

In the second part of the questionnaire there is a list of possible different moral lessons that were given to the participants and might be derived from their studies of the Holocaust. These lessons are part of Jewish-Israeli discourse over the Holocaust and can be found in literature, newspapers, television, movies and mainly in school learning. The lessons are presented as statements to which they were asked to express their agreement or disagreement on a scale of 1-5 point Likert scale where 1 = not at all agree and 5 = very much agree. They can alternatively write a lesson/lessons of their own. The full questionnaire appears in Appendix 2.

(4) The individual in-depth interviews

Thirteen of the 102 student participants, who answered the questionnaires, also volunteered to participate in the in-depth interviews and were interviewed at Measurement Point 3 (January 2016). Four of the students were boys - Boaz, Elad, Asaf and Ronen. Nine of the interviewees were girls - Yonat, Pazit, Noa, Lily, Rachel, Miriam, Sarah, Aia and Dina. Elad, Asaf and Sarah did not participate in the journey to Poland. Ronen, Boaz, Aia, Miriam and Lily do not have family relatives that are Holocaust victims or survivors. All the other interviewees did have such a connection; usually a grandmother or grandfather that was still alive, and they had heard about their experiences in the Holocaust at different levels of scope and detail. They are actually the third or fourth generation following Holocaust survivors. The average age of the students was 17.3 when the interviews took place and they were in the middle of their last year in high school. Interviewees were asked questions that touched upon their family connection to the Holocaust, the decision to participate or not to participate in the journey to Poland, their experiences regarding Holocaust learning, their views towards the moral dilemmas, the moral lessons they learned (from the Holocaust Learning Program including the journey) and their experience of participation in the study itself. Results from the interviews appear in Chapter 3. In the presentation of the results, all the students' names are fictitious. The guidelines for the interviews and interviewees' characteristics appear in Appendices 3 and 4.

2.3.5 Research procedure

The research took place over a period of two academic years: It began in January 2015 when the students were in the middle of Grade 11and ended in January 2016 when they were in the middle of Grade 12. The research process included three points of measurement at three points in time during this period: **Measurement Point 1** took place when the students were in the middle of Grade 11 in January 2015. At this time, they began their formal learning process for matriculation exams in Jewish Holocaust history and the preparation for the journey to visit Holocaust memorial sites in Poland. **Measurement Point 2** took place after the students returned from the journey to Poland in September 2015 at the beginning of Grade 12. **Measurement Point 3** took place in January 2016 in the middle of Grade 12. At this time, students completed their matriculation exams on the Holocaust studies. It was also a significant period of time after the second measurement. At these three measurements points, 102 participants filled in the Moral Attitudes Questionnaire which included a demographic section followed by 14 moral dilemmas. Thirteen of the participants were also interviewed when Measurement point 3 took place in January 2016. Additionally, at Measurement point 3 (towards the end of the research), all participants answered one more questionnaire - the "Perceived Influences and Lessons Learned Questionnaire". The questionnaires were administered by the teachers in the classrooms and were filled out manually. Table 2.3 provides a summary of the research procedure

Table 2.3: Summary of research procedure

Time	Tools
Measurement Point 1- Jan 2015, Grade 11, Beginning of Holocaust learning at school	A. Demographic Questionnaire B. Moral Attitudes Questionnaire
Measurement Point 2 - Sep 2015, Grade 12, Middle of learning and after returning from the journey to Poland	A. Moral Attitudes Questionnaire
Measurement Point 3 - Jan 2016, Grade 12, Matriculations exams of Holocaust studies which remark the end of learning	A. Moral Attitudes Questionnaire B. Perceived Influence and Lessons Learned Questionnaire C. Individual In-depth Interview

2.3.6 Data-analysis

Organization of data analysis of research studies

Data was collected and organized in five studies according to the different aims. Quantitative data from the questionnaires were analyzed using IBM SPSS Statistics Version 23 64-bit edition software and included descriptive statistical analysis (percentage, means SD) and inferential statistical analysis (ANOVA tests and Bonferroni t-tests). Data collected from the in-depth interviews underwent qualitative thematic analysis. The research studies and aims are presented in table 2.4 below.

Table 2.4 – Studies and Aims

Subject studied	Aims
Study 1- Students' initial moral attitudes at the beginning of learning	1. To identify the level of agreement or disagreement with the different moral behaviors of the Jews during and after the Holocaust among Israeli high school students who began to participate in a Holocaust Learning Program.
Study 2- The evolution of the students' moral attitudes	2. To test whether the Holocaust Learning Program generated changes in the participant's moral attitudes. 3. To test whether changes in the participant's moral attitudes during their Holocaust Learning Program were moderated by Gender, having Holocaust victims as their relatives and/or their participation in the journey to Holocaust memorial sites in Poland.
Study 3- Perceived influences and lessons learned	4. To identify whether and how social and educational factors are perceived by participants as influencing their moral attitudes. 5. To identify the perceived moral lessons emerged from Holocaust Learning Program.
Study 4- The associations between moral attitudes and moral lessons	6. To examine whether moral attitudes are associated with perceived lessons from the Holocaust Learning Program.
Study 5- The experiences of Holocaust learning	7. To understand the meanings constructed through participants' stories regarding their experiences in the Holocaust Learning Program.

Quantitative data from the questionnaires were analyzed using IBM SPSS Statistics Version 23 64-bit edition software. Data collected from the in-depth interviews underwent qualitative thematic analysis. All analysis was performed in line with the research aims.

The structure of the moral attitude categories for statistical data analysis

The classification of the moral dilemmas and their moral solutions in categories as presented here was used for the statistical analyses in Studies 1, 2 and 4.

The literature review presented in Chapter 1 leads to the conclusion that all Holocaust era dilemmas relate to survival, meaning that the solution could lead to life or death. In these dilemmas, **moral deliberation** exists between solutions based on "deontological morality" versus solutions based on "survival morality". "Deontological morality" is a morality based on state and religious laws together with the values of the particular culture and society. It is accepted as normal in a specific society or societies and characterizes moral decisions in standard daily situations (Waller, 2005; Beauchamp, 1991; Kamm, 1996). The opposite is "Utilitarian morality". This is a morality that grasps moral action as one that should maximize the benefit for the person who carries out a certain action. As such, this kind of moral behavior could contradict deontological morality (Bredeson, 2011; Gay, 2002) and in another expression: "Survival morality" is actually "Utilitarian morality's little brother. Koenigs et al., (2007) noted that in extreme moral situations facing the danger of death the "utilitarian" morality decision can be saving a life. The meaning is that "Survival morality" involves decision-making based on a kind of utilitarian morality where the "utility" is simply survival. "Survival morality" therefore completely contradicts the substance of deontological morality. It is a kind of morality, whose only goal is to preserve lives in the face of great danger. This morality often characterized Jews' behavior during the Holocaust. Holocaust survivors would usually not have survived if they had acted otherwise (Greif, 1989; Wiesenthal, 2012). However, a closer observation of Holocaust era dilemmas demands a wider classification of the dilemmas posed to Jews during that period. The seven Holocaust era dilemmas were classified in three different categories according to similar characteristics and moral deliberation. Each category has its own specific characteristics and moral deliberation or "tension".

Category 1 – *"The collaboration dilemmas"*, including the 'Judenratt dilemma', the 'Sonderkommando dilemma' and the 'Rebels dilemma'. The main common characteristics of this category are: A. The question is whether or not to collaborate with the Nazis in order to survive. B. The influence of the individual's decision on the wider circle of his community.

Category 2 – *"The acute dilemmas"*, including the 'Crying baby dilemma' and the 'Thief's dilemma'. The main common characteristics of this category are: A. the acute nature of the dilemma – the need to make a rapid decision with no way back. B. the direct influence of the individual's decision on a specific other individual in a very close social circle – his family or a small group of hiding Jews in the 'crying baby dilemma' and the group of prisoners in the extermination camp in the 'thief's dilemma'.

Category 3 –*"The parental dilemmas"*, including the 'Little Smuggler dilemma' and the 'Giving children away dilemma'. The main common characteristic of this category is the direct influence of the individual – the influence of the parent's decision on the fate of his child.

In all these categories, moral tension exists between deontological morality and survival morality. The above classification of dilemmas' categories was used for the statistical analysis.

Post-Holocaust era dilemmas are different from Holocaust era dilemmas mainly because of the fact that the ever-present risk of death no longer exists. These dilemmas are expressions of the continuous Jewish struggle to cope with the memory, the consequences and the effects of the Holocaust. These dilemmas generate moral tension between moral solutions that varies according to the nature of the dilemma. As in Holocaust era dilemmas, a closer observation of the post - Holocaust era dilemmas reveals a wider classification. The seven post-Holocaust era dilemmas were classified in three different categories according to similar characteristics and moral deliberation. Each category had its own specific characteristics and moral deliberation or "tension" is created between different contradicting moral solutions.

Category 4 – *"The perception of Jewish behavior towards the Nazis dilemmas"*, including the 'Like Lambs to the Slaughter dilemma', the 'Kapo dilemma', The 'Kastner dilemma' and the 'Resistance dilemma'. The main common characteristic of this category is the attempt to understand and evaluate the way that Jews behaved towards the Nazis from different angles. In this category, **moral deliberation** exists between "judgmental" versus "accepting" attitudes (Yablonka, 1996, 2000).

Category 5 – *"Consideration of revenge and compromise dilemmas"*, this category includes the 'Revengers dilemma' and the 'Restitution Payments dilemma'. The main common characteristic of this category is Jewish thinking and decisions concerning the way to treat former Nazis' crimes in the post-Holocaust era. In this category, **moral deliberation** exists between "affective-intuitive" versus "rational-utilitarian" attitudes (Katz, 2009).

Category 6 –*"The perception of the Holocaust as a historical event"*, this category includes only one dilemma – 'the Comparison of the Holocaust dilemma'. The essence of the dilemma is whether or not to compare the Jewish Holocaust to other genocides in history. In this dilemma, **moral deliberation** exists between "universal" versus "Jewish-particular" moral solutions. A "universal" moral solution is envisaged when the Holocaust is apprehended by the Jews as a universal event with universal implications while a "Jewish-particular" moral solution is envisaged when the Holocaust is apprehended as something which is a solely "Jewish" event which is unique and stands out due to its dimensions and character with no relation to the genocides of other nations or peoples in history. Therefore, the conclusion is that it cannot be compared to any other similar events (Oron, 1995b).

The above described categories are presented in Table 2.5 and Figure 2.1 below:

Table 2.5: Categories of Holocaust and Post-Holocaust Moral Dilemmas and solutions

The Categories of Holocaust Moral Dilemmas and solutions			
Dilemmas Categories	**Mutual Main Characteristics**	**Categories of Moral deliberation Between solutions**	**Point of View**
1. "Collaboration dilemmas": The 'Judenratt dilemma'+ 'Sonderkommando dilemma'+ 'Rebels dilemma'	Influences a wide social circle, collaboration dilemmas	Deontological **versus** Survival	Retrospective- Jews perception toward Jews behavior
2. "Acute dilemmas": The 'Crying Baby dilemma'+ 'The Thief's dilemma'	Influences a close social circle, acute dilemmes	Deontological **versus** Survival	Retrospective- Jews perception toward Jews behavior
3. "Parental dilemmas": The 'Little Smuggler dilemma'+ 'Giving Children Away dilemma'	Direct inter-personal influence, Parental dilemmas	Deontological **versus** Survival	Retrospective- Jews perception toward Jews behavior
The Categories of Post-Holocaust Moral Dilemmas and solutions			
4. "The perception of Jewish behavior towards the Nazis": The 'Like Lambs to the Slaughter dilemma'+ 'Capo dilemma'+ 'Kastner dilemma'+ 'Resistance dilemma'	Different evaluations of Jewish behavior towards the Nazis	"Judgmental" **versus** "Acceptance"	Retrospective- Jews perception toward Jews behavior
5. "Consideration of revenge and compromise": The 'Revengers dilemma'+ 'Restitution Payments dilemma'	Deliberation about Jewish Post-Holocaust actions towards Nazis' crimes	"Affective-Intuitive" **versus** "Rational-Utilitarian"	Retrospective- Jews toward Nazis
6. "The perception of the Holocaust as a historical event", The 'Comparison of the Holocaust dilemma'	Different perceptions of the Holocaust as a historical event	"Universal" **versus** "Jewish-Particular"	Backward Forward-Perspective-Jews toward the world

Figure 2.1 - Moral Dilemmas classification

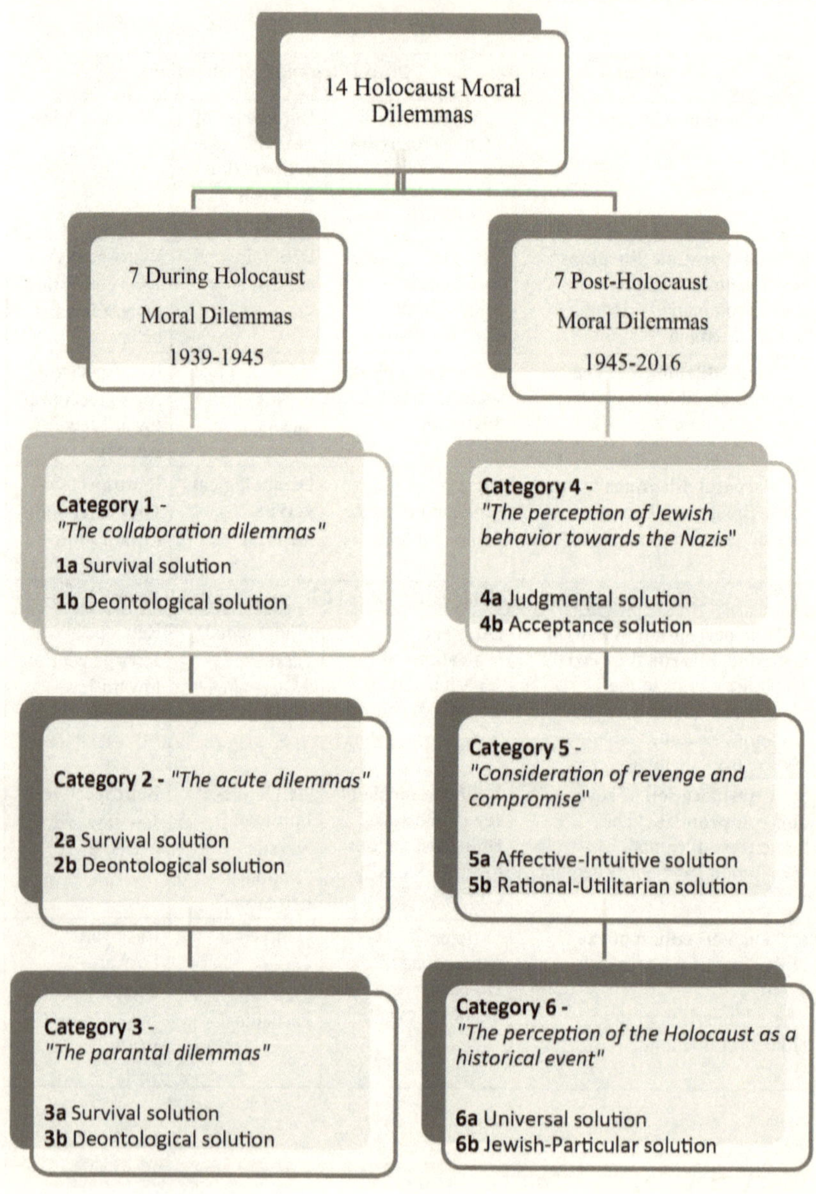

The structure of perceived influences and lessons learned categories for statistical data analysis:

The classification of perceived influences and lessons learned categories presented here was used for the statistical analysis in Study 3. The different influences and lessons were first analyzed separately by items and then sorted into categories according to similar characteristics in order to create a higher level of analysis. The influential factors and their classification into categories are presented in Table 2.6:

Table 2.6 - Categories of perceived influences

A. Socio-Cultural influences	B. Educational-Learning influences
1. The Nuclear Family 2. Close friends 3. Prior knowledge and experiences until Grade 11	1. Learning for the matriculation in Holocaust Studies 2. Participation in this research

The lessons and their classification according to categories are presented in Table 2.7:

Table 2.7 - Categories of perceived moral lessons

A. Humanist-Liberal moral lessons	B. Nationalist- Utilitarian moral lessons
1. "The strong must avoid harming the weak" 2. "If we lose our morals, we may become like the Nazis". 3. "It is important to learn about Holocaust moral dilemmas"	1. "Moral dilemmas are not relevant in war situations" 2. "Since the Nazis harmed us, we can harm others"

It should be noted that "Humanist-liberal lessons" relate to humanist-liberal moral values, while "Nationalist- Utilitarian" lessons relate to nationalist-utilitarian moral values. Moral values create moral attitudes (Soen & Davidovich, 2011; Rama, 2011).

2.4 Ethics

The purpose of research ethics is to defend the personal rights of those who participate in the research (Dushenik & Sabar Ben-Yehoshua, 2002). With regard to compliance with ethical requirements in the present research, several ethical issues arose:

Investigating the moral behavior of the victims was a central ethical issue. It arose especially at the beginning of the research during a meeting with students before filling in the questionnaires. Is it at all morally possible to judge the way that Holocaust victims acted in the face of moral dilemmas in such an extreme and extraordinary reality, when all the laws and norms were shattered? This question worried some of the student participants and also worried the researcher, both as a researcher and as a Jew. The solution to this difficulty was found by presenting the research work on this topic as a sort of mental psychological-educational exercise intended to broaden our knowledge and understanding of the Holocaust. In the conversations with the students that preceded the first administration of the questionnaire, it was emphasized that there was actually no real possibility of judging the Jews' behavior at that time.

Care was needed in the construction of the dilemmas and solutions to avoid composition of the dilemmas and their solutions in a manner that might direct the students to a particular option. The ethical principle to resolve this issue was to construct the dilemmas and solutions in as objective a manner as possible using "dry" language. The text was drafted in a way that would reduce emotional expression and descriptions of the horrors and thus reduce any deviation in the responses. To cope with this constriction we consulted academic colleagues and Holocaust historians.

It was necessary to avoid taking a stance with regard to the moral dilemmas and their solutions at the meetings where the questionnaire was explained to the students and also during the interviews.

Consent to participate in the research: Before the beginning of the research the students received an explanation regarding the purposes of the research and were asked to give their signed consent to their participation in the research on a personal consent form. This was preceded by obtaining similar consent from the parents and from the school. At no stage was any pressure exerted on the students to volunteer to participate in the research, nor were they given any incentive, material or other for their participation. The different consent forms appear in Appendices 5 and 6.

To sum up the methodology chapter a summarizing table (Table 2.8) is presented below.

Table 2.8: Summary of the methodology

Approach	Exploratory research
Paradigm	Mixed-methods research
Method	Longitudinal survey research
Research Procedure	Measurement Point 1: Jan 2015: At the beginning of Holocaust learning Measurement Point 2: Sep 2015: At the middle of learning and after visiting memorial Holocaust sites in Poland Measurement Point 3: Jan 2016: Matriculation exams and end of Holocaust learning
Population	102 Israeli high school students
Research Tools	A. Demographic questionnaire B. Holocaust moral attitudes questionnaire C. Individual In-depth interview D. Perceived influence factors and lessons learned questionnaire
Data Analysis	A. Qualitative inductive thematic analysis B. Quantitative descriptive and deductive statistics analyses
Ethical Considerations	Anonymity, parents' consent, participants' informed consent.

In this chapter, the methodology of the research has been presented in detail. The next chapter presents the research results from the five different studies conducted in the research.

CHAPTER 3- RESULTS

This chapter presents results, discussion and preliminary conclusions of the five studies

- ***Study 1* - Students' *initial moral attitudes at the beginning of learning***
- ***Study 2 - The evolution of the moral attitudes***
- ***Study 3- Perceived influences and lessons learned***
- ***Study 4 –The* associations *between moral attitudes and moral lessons***
- ***Study 5 - The experiences of Holocaust learning***

3.1 Study 1: Students' initial moral attitudes at the beginning of The Holocaust Learning Program

Introduction

Study 1 aimed to identify the level of agreement or disagreement with the different moral behaviors of the Jews during and after the Holocaust of Israeli high school students who participated in Holocaust Learning Program.

It is an innovative initiative since no such research has ever been attempted before. This is not surprising, since dealing with Jewish moral dilemmas can perhaps be considered as picking at a very deep, still open wound; therefore, public and academic discourse in Israel usually tends to ignore ethical issues and dilemmas relating to the Jews' behavior during and after the Holocaust (Weinrab, 1984). Naturally it is easier to remain within the secure boundaries of the area of public consensus in which the Holocaust is considered to be a unique and exceptional event in human history, in which the Nazis murdered the Jews because of their ideology of racism and anti-Semitism, the Jews resisted the Nazis in order to survive and the world was indifferent to the Jewish tragedy (Blady Szwaiger, 2000). Due to the fact that dealing with Holocaust moral dilemmas was a new experience for the participating students more questions were raised: Would participants cooperate with the research? Could they formulate and consolidate moral attitudes towards such a complicated and rather unknown subject? Which moral attitudes would hopefully emerge? In the following pages, we try to answer these interesting questions.

Method

This study presents a statistical analysis of the responses to the Moral Attitudes Questionnaire which was filled in by 102 participants in January 2015, when they were in the middle of Grade 11 soon after they began the Holocaust Learning Program. The Moral Attitude Questionnaire describes dilemmas faced by the Jews during and after the Holocaust and students were asked to respond by choosing possible solutions to the dilemmas. Data analysis related to the responses for each one of the moral dilemmas. Analysis was performed with the tool of descriptive statistics, presenting the distribution of the responses in percentages, the central tendency index – mean, and the deviant tendency index – SD.

Each dilemma was analyzed independently in order to examine the specific choice of solution, which indicated the participant's moral attitudes towards each dilemma. The aim at this stage was to identify the students' initial attitudes at the beginning of the Holocaust learning process and the start of the research. The results are presented in two parts – Holocaust era dilemmas followed by post-Holocaust era dilemmas. It should be noted that the students could choose to mark their agreement or disagreement with either or both of the two solutions given for each dilemma. Therefore, the total number of responses may exceed102, which is the total number of participants.

Results

3.1.1 - Students' initial moral attitudes towards Holocaust-era dilemmas (1939-1945)

All the Holocaust era dilemmas relate to survival, meaning that the solution could lead to life or death. In these dilemmas, there is moral tension between solutions based on "deontological morality" versus solutions based on "survival morality".

Following the presentation of the detailed results in each table for each dilemma, results were sorted into three major categories: ***"disagreement", "uncertainty" and "agreement".*** In all tables: (Mean<3 = disagreement; Mean>3 = agreement; Mean>4 = strong agreement). Individual results for each dilemma and some general results are now presented:

Category 1 – ***"The collaboration dilemmas",*** including the 'Judenratt dilemma', the 'Sonderkommando dilemma' and the 'Rebels dilemma'. The main common characteristics of this category are: A. The question of whether or not to cooperate with the Nazis in order to survive. B. The influence of the individual's decision on the wide circle of his community.

1. *The "Judenratt" (Jewish council) dilemma*

The essence of the dilemma is the choice between Jewish leadership collaboration with the Nazis in the "Ghetto" (A closed, exclusively Jewish area) versus resistance. The outcome of resistance to Nazis orders for the leaders of the Jews was death. The Nazis demanded that the head of the "Judenratt" must prepare lists of Jews, who transport to extermination in death camps.

Solution A - the survival moral solution is: "I would prepare the list".

Solution B - The deontological moral solution is: "I would not prepare the list".

Table 3.1.1: Responses to "the Judenratt" dilemma

Time	Solution	Strong disagree 1	Disagree 2	Uncertain 3	Agree 4	Strong agree 5	%	N	Mean	SD
1	A	5.49%	5.49%	35.16%	50.55%	3.30%	100	91	3.41	.87
	B	8.16%	26.53%	34.69%	22.45%	8.16%	100	49	2.96	1.08

'No opinion' for Solution A, N =2; for Solution B, N =1; for 'Other Solution', N = 7

The distribution of the responses reveals that Solution **A**- the survival solution was awarded responses in the following proportions: 11% - disagreement, 35% - uncertainty and 54% - agreement. Solution **B**- the deontological solution received: 35% - disagreement, 35% - uncertainty and 31% - agreement. *This means that participants agreed more with the survival solution.*

2. *The "Sonderkommando" (special Jewish forced labor group) dilemma*

The essence of the dilemma for the Jewish prisoner is whether to work in forced labor for the Nazis death machine in the death camps versus refusal to do so, which would lead to the prisoner's death.

Solution A – The survival moral solution is: "I would work in the Sonderkommando".

Solution B – The deontological moral solution is: "I would refuse to work in the Sonderkommando".

Table 3.1.2: Responses to "the Sonderkommando" dilemma

Time	Solution	Strong disagree 1	Disagree 2	Uncertain 3	Agree 4	Strong agree 5	%	N	Mean	SD
1	A	2.53%	13.92%	22.78%	40.51%	20.25%	100	79	3.62	1.04
	B	7.94%	15.87%	20.63%	36.51%	19.05%	100	63	3.43	1.20

'No opinion' for Solution A: N=3; for Solution B: N=2, for 'Other Solution' N = 3

The distribution of responses reveals that Solution **A**- the survival solution was awarded responses in the following proportions: 17% - disagreement, 23% - uncertainty and 61% - agreement. Solution **B**- the deontological solution was awarded: 24% -disagreement, 21% - uncertainty and 56% - agreement. *This means that participants agreed more with the survival solution.* However, the close results demonstrate the deliberation in this dilemma.

3. *The "Rebels dilemma"*

The essence of the dilemma is whether to participate in armed rebellion against the Nazis without the wide support of all the Jewish community or, on the other hand, to avoid its rebellion and continue to cooperate with the Nazis. Rebellion could mean sometimes a tiny chance of escaping from the "Ghetto" but the Nazis would probably murder the entire population instantly as a punishment.

Solution A – The deontological moral solution is: "I would not join the rebellion without the support of the community".

Solution B –The survival moral solution is: "I would join the rebellion in any case".

Table 3.1.3: Responses to "The rebels" dilemma

Time	Solution	Strong disagree 1	Disagree 2	Uncertain 3	Agree 4	Strong agree 5	%	N	Mean	SD
1	A	8.20%	13.11%	21.31%	37.70%	19.67%	100	61	3.48	1.19
	B	7.04%	14.08%	19.72%	42.25%	16.90%	100	71	3.48	1.14

'No opinion' for Solution A: N=5; for Solution B: N=3, for 'Other Solution': N=19

The distribution of the responses reveals that Solution **A**- the deontological solution was awarded responses in the following proportions: 21% - disagreement, 21% - uncertainty and 68% - agreement. Solution **B**- the survival solution was awarded: 21% - disagreement, 20% - uncertainty and 59% - agreement. *This means that participants agreed more with the deontological solution.*

Summary for Category 1 - *"the collaboration dilemmas"*: In two out of the three dilemmas, survival solutions were awarded more agreement than the deontological solutions. However, there was always a high level of deliberation between the two contradicting options.

Category 2 – *"The acute dilemmas"*, includes the 'Crying baby dilemma' and the 'Thief's dilemma'. The main common characteristics of this category are: A. the acute nature of the dilemma – the need to make a rapid decision with no way back. B. the direct influence of the individual's decision on a specific other individual within a very close social circle – his family or a small group of hiding Jews in the 'crying baby dilemma' and the group of prisoners in the extermination camp in the 'thief's dilemma'.

4. *"The thief's dilemma"*

The essence of the dilemma for a Jewish prisoner in death camp is whether to steal food, a shoe, or hat etc. in order to survive or to die if he did not steal the object.

Solution A – The deontological moral solution is: "I would not steal a hat from another prisoner".

Solution B – The survival moral solution is: "I would steal a hat from another prisoner because if I don't have a hat the Nazis will shoot me".

Table 3.1.4: Responses to "The thief's' dilemma"

Time	Solution	Strong disagree 1	Disagree 2	Uncertain 3	Agree 4	Strong agree 5	%	N	Mean	SD
1	A	1.33%	4.00%	32.00%	44.00%	18.67%	100	75	3.75	.86
	B	15.52%	25.86%	32.76%	24.14%	1.72%	100	58	2.71	1.06

'No opinion' for Solution A: N=8; for Solution B: N=5, for 'Other Solution': N=12

The distribution of the responses reveals that Solution **A**- the deontological solution was awarded responses in the following proportions: 5% - disagreement, 32% - uncertainty and 63% - agreement. Solution **B**- the survival solution was awarded: 41% - disagreement, 33% - uncertainty and 26% - agreement. *This means that participants agreed more with the deontological solution.*

5. *The "Crying baby" dilemma*

The essence of the dilemma is whether a parent or another person should kill the crying baby, whose incessant crying threatens to expose the group of Jews in the hiding place to the Nazis, who would kill them.

Solution A – The survival moral solution is: "I would kill the baby".

Solution B – The deontological moral solution is: "I would not kill the baby".

 SHAY EFRAT

Table 3.1.5: Responses to "The crying baby" dilemma

Time	Solution	Strong disagree 1	Disagree 2	Uncertain 3	Agree 4	Strong agree 5	%	N	Mean	SD
1	A	22.81%	15.79%	24.56%	33.33%	3.51%	100	57	2.79	1.24
	B	1.56%	4.69%	17.19%	53.13%	23.44%	100	64	3.92	.86

'No opinion' for Solution A: N=10; for Solution B: N=8, for 'Other Solution': N=15

The distribution of responses reveals that Solution **A**- the survival solution was awarded responses in the following proportions: 37% - disagreement, 25% - uncertainty and 38% - agreement. Solution **B**- the deontological solution was awarded: 6% - disagreement, 17% - uncertainty and 77% - agreement. *This means that participants agreed more with the deontological solution.*

Summary for Category 2: "The acute dilemmas," in both dilemmas the deontological solutions were awarded more agreement than the survival solutions.

Category 3 –*"The parental dilemmas",* including the 'Little Smuggler dilemma' and the 'Giving children away dilemma'. The main common characteristic of this category is the direct influence of the individual – the parent's decision – on his child's fate.

6. *The "Little Smuggler dilemma"*

The essence of the dilemma is whether to allow the child to smuggle food for the starving family into the "Ghetto" (a tiny enclosed Jewish region of the town) or to protect him from the risk of death by stopping him from doing so, thus perhaps risking death by starvation for the entire family.

Solution A – The survival moral solution is: "I would allow the child to smuggle".

Solution B – The deontological moral solution is: "I would not allow the child to smuggle".

Table 3.1.6: Responses to "The little smuggler" dilemma

Time	Solution	Strong disagree 1	Disagree 2	Uncertain 3	Agree 4	Strong agree 5	%	N	Mean	SD
1	A		11.25%	22.50%	57.50%	8.75%	100	80	3.64	.80
	B	1.75%	8.77%	43.86%	38.60%	7.02%	100	57	3.40	.82

'No opinion' for Solution A: N=1; for Solution B: N=0, for 'Other Solution': N=8

The distribution of the responses reveals that Solution **A**- the survival solution was awarded responses in the following proportions: 11% - disagreement, 23% - uncertainty and 66% - agreement. Solution **B**- the deontological solution was awarded: 11% - disagreement, 44% - uncertainty and 45% - agreement. *This means that participants agreed more with the survival solution.*

7. *The "Giving away children dilemma"*

The essence of the dilemma is whether parents should trust particular gentiles and give their small children to them in order to save their lives, or not to trust them and avoid giving their children away.

Solution A – The survival moral solution is: "I would give my child away".

Solution B – The deontological moral solution is: "I would not give my child away".

Table 3.1.7: Responses to "The giving away children" dilemma

Time	Solution	Strong disagree 1	Disagree 2	Uncertain 3	Agree 4	Strong agree 5	%	N	Mean	SD
1	A	5.38%	1.08%	9.68%	43.01%	40.86%	100	93	4.13	1.01
	B	14.58%	25.00%	31.25%	14.58%	14.58%	100	48	2.90	1.26

'No opinion' for Solution A: N=1; for Solution B: N=0, for 'Other Solution': N=7

The distribution of responses reveals that Solution **A**- the survival solution was awarded responses in the following proportions: 6% - disagreement, 10% - uncertainty and 84% - agreement. Solution **B**- the deontological solution was awarded: 40% - disagreement, 30% - uncertainty and 30% - agreement. *This means that participants agreed more with the survival solution.*

Summary for dilemmas category 3: "The parental dilemmas". It seems that for both dilemmas the survival moral solutions were awarded more agreement than the deontological solutions.

3.1.2 The initial moral attitudes towards Post-Holocaust-era dilemmas (1945-2016)

Post-Holocaust era dilemmas differ from Holocaust dilemmas mainly because of the fact that there is no longer an ever-present threat of death. These dilemmas are expressions of the continuous Jewish struggle to cope with the memory, the consequences and the effects of the Holocaust. In these dilemmas, moral tension between moral solutions varies according to the nature of the dilemma. As in Holocaust era dilemmas a closer look at post-Holocaust era dilemmas revealed a wider classification. The seven post-Holocaust dilemmas were sorted into three categories according to similar characteristics. Each category has its own specific characteristics and its own moral tension between the two contradicting moral solutions. Individual results for each dilemma and some general results are now presented.

Following the presentation of the detailed results in each table for each dilemma, results were sorted into three major categories: ***"disagreement", "uncertainty" and "agreement".*** In all tables: Mean<3 = disagreement; Mean>3 = agreement; Mean>4 = strong agreement. The individual results for each dilemma and some general results are present:

Category 4 – *"Dilemmas relating to the perception of Jewish behavior towards the Nazis"*, included the 'Like Lambs to the Slaughter dilemma', the 'Kapo dilemma', The 'Kastner dilemma' and the 'Resistance dilemma'. The main common characteristic of this category is the attempt to understand and evaluate the way that Jews behaved towards the Nazis from different angles. **Moral deliberation** for this category exists between "judgmental" versus "acceptance" attitudes.

8. *"They went like lambs to the slaughter dilemma"*

The essence of the dilemma is how to relate to what was seen by Israeli society in the first years after the Holocaust as the Jews' "passive" reaction to the extermination.

Solution A – The judgmental moral solution is: "We should blame them for their 'passive' reaction".

Solution B – The acceptance moral solution is: We should not blame them".

Table 3.1.8: Responses to "They went like lambs to the slaughter" dilemma

Time	Solution	Strong disagree 1	Disagree 2	Uncertain 3	Agree 4	Strong agree 5	%	N	Mean	SD
1	A	58.82%	23.53%	9.80%	7.84%		100	51	1.67	.95
	B		1.20%	9.64%	50.60%	38.55%	100	83	4.27	.68

'No opinion' for Solution A: N=4; for Solution B: N=0, for 'Other Solution': N=17

The distribution of the responses reveals that Solution **A**- the judgmental solution was awarded responses in the following proportions: 59% - disagreement, 10% - uncertainty and 8% - agreement. Solution **B**- the acceptance solution was awarded: 1% - disagreement, 10% - uncertainty and 90% - agreement. *This means that participants agreed more with the acceptance solution.*

9. *The "Kapo" (foreman) dilemma*

The essence of the dilemma is whether to take action for criminal prosecution against Jews who served under the Nazis in the concentration and death camps as those who directed special prisoners' working units ("Commandos") or prisoner's residences ("Blocks"). Those people were often blamed by survivors for wicked unnecessarily abusive acts against the prisoners.

Solution A – The judgmental moral solution is: "We should judge them".

Solution B – The acceptance moral solution is: "We should not judge them".

Table 3.1.9: Responses to "The Kapo" dilemma

Time	Solution	Strong disagree 1	Disagree 2	Uncertain 3	Agree 4	Strong agree 5	%	N	Mean	SD
1	A	8.43%	2.41%	21.69%	46.99%	20.48%	100	83	**3.69**	1.09
	B	20.00%	21.82%	34.55%	14.55%	9.09%	100	55	**2.71**	1.21

'No opinion' for Solution A: N=3; for Solution B: N=1, for 'Other Solution': N=14

The distribution of the responses reveals that Solution **A**- the judgmental solution was awarded responses in the following proportions: 11% - disagreement, 22% - uncertainty and 67% - agreement. Solution **B**- the acceptance solution was awarded 42% - disagreement, 35% - uncertainty and 24% - agreement. *This means that participants agreed more with the judgmental solution.*

10. *The Kastner dilemma*

The essence of the dilemma is whether to accuse Dr. Israel Kastner who was the head of The 'Jewish Rescue Committee' in Budapest for betrayal of his people. This was because in order to save Jews he made financial deals with Nazi officers.

Solution A – The acceptance moral solution is: "We cannot accuse him of betrayal because he made deals with the Nazis in order to save Jews".

Solution B –The judgmental moral solution is: "We should accuse him of betrayal because he made deals with the Nazis, who murdered our people".

Table 3.1.10: Responses to "The Kastner dilemma"

Time	Solution	Strong disagree 1	Disagree 2	Uncertain 3	Agree 4	Strong agree 5	%	N	Mean	SD
1	A		1.14%	11.36%	47.73%	39.77%	100	88	**4.26**	.70
	B	33.33%	33.33%	11.90%	9.52%	11.90%	100	42	**2.33**	1.36

'No opinion' for Solution A: N=6; for Solution B: N=1, for 'Other Solution': N = 8

The distribution of the responses reveals that Solution **A**- the acceptance solution was awarded responses in the following proportions: 1% - disagreement, 11% - uncertainty and 88% - agreement. Solution **B**- the judgmental solution was awarded 67% - disagreement, 12% - uncertainty and 21% - agreement. *This means that participants agreed more with the acceptance solution.*

11. *The Resistance dilemma*

The essence of the dilemma is whether to emphasize Jewish armed resistance ("active resistance") against the Nazis on one hand or to emphasize unarmed resistance ("passive" resistance") on the other.

Solution A – The acceptance moral solution is: "Passive resistance should be emphasized" because this is how most Jews were saved.

Solution B - The judgmental moral solution is: "Active resistance should be emphasized to educate new generations to actively resist oppression.

Table 3.1.11: Responses to "The resistance" dilemma

Time	Solution	Strong disagree 1	Disagree 2	Uncertain 3	Agree 4	Strong agree 5	%	N	Mean	SD
1	A	1.89%	3.77%	33.96%	47.17%	13.21%	100	53	**3.66**	.83
	B	4.44%	15.56%	37.78%	33.33%	8.89%	100	45	**3.27**	.99

'No opinion' for Solution A: N=5; for Solution B: N=4, for 'Other Solution': N=28

Looking at the distribution of answers reveals that Solution **A**- the acceptance solution awarded 6% of disagreement, 34% of uncertainty and 60% of agreement. Solution **B**- the judgmental solution awarded 20% of disagreement, 38% of uncertainty and 42% of agreement. *The meaning is that participants agreed more with the acceptance solution.* Moreover, the multiplicity of "Other solutions" given for this dilemma (28) which all advocated a lack of emphasis for neither of the attitudes, actually increase the agreement with the acceptance moral solution.

Summary for dilemmas category 4: *"The Perception of Jewish behavior towards the Nazis".* In three out of four dilemmas, the acceptance moral solutions were awarded more agreement than the judgmental solutions.

Category 5 – *"Consideration of revenge and compromise",* included the 'Revengers dilemma' and the 'Restitution Payments dilemma'. The main common characteristic of this category was Jewish thinking and decisions concerning how to treat former Nazis crimes in post-Holocaust era. **Moral deliberation** for this category exists between "affective-intuitive" versus "rational-utilitarian" attitudes.

12. *The Revengers dilemma*

The essence of the dilemma is whether it is morally right to kill Nazis who were involved in the murder of Jews in Europe during the Holocaust.

Solution A - The affective- intuitive moral solution is: "We should exact revenge against those who murdered our people and families".

Solution B - The rational-utilitarian moral solution is: "We should not exact revenge by killing people, because we are not murderers".

Table 3.1.12: Responses to "The revengers" dilemma

Time	Solution	Strong disagree 1	Disagree 2	Uncertain 3	Agree 4	Strong agree 5	%	N	Mean	SD
1	A	6.06%	19.70%	24.24%	28.79%	21.21%	100	66	**3.39**	1.20
	B	7.69%	4.62%	24.62%	43.08%	20.00%	100	65	**3.63**	1.10

'No opinion' for Solution A: N=5; for Solution B: N=3, for 'Other Solution': N = 8

The distribution of the responses reveals that Solution **A**- the affective- intuitive solution was awarded responses in the following proportions: 26% - disagreement, 24% - uncertainty and 50% - agreement. Solution **B**- the rational-utilitarian solution was awarded 12% - disagreement, 25% - uncertainty and 63% - agreement. *This means that participants agreed more with the rational-utilitarian solution.*

13. *The Restitution payments dilemma*

The essence of the dilemma is whether it is morally justified for Holocaust survivors as individuals, and Israel as a state, to receive payments from Germany as restitution for Nazi crimes during Holocaust.

Solution A - The rational-utilitarian moral solution is: "We should accept the restitution payments because we need them to rehabilitate our lives".

Solution B - The affective- intuitive moral solution is: "We should not accept the restitution payments because it constitutes a kind of forgiveness for those who murdered our people".

Table 3.1.13: Responses to "The restitution payments" dilemma

Time	Solution	Strong disagree 1	Disagree 2	Uncertain 3	Agree 4	Strong agree 5	%	N	Mean	SD
1	A	1.08%	2.15%	4.30%	51.61%	40.86%	100	93	4.29	.75
	B	19.05%	30.95%	21.43%	16.67%	11.90%	100	42	2.71	1.29

'No opinion' for Solution A: N=1; for Solution B: N=1, for 'Other Solution': N=18

The distribution of the responses reveals that Solution **A**- the rational-utilitarian solution was awarded responses in the following proportions: 3% - disagreement, 4% - uncertainty and 93% - agreement. Solution **B**- the affective-intuitive solution was awarded 50% - disagreement, 21% - uncertainty and 29% - agreement. *This means that participants agreed more with the rational-utilitarian solution.*

Summary for dilemmas category 5: *"Consideration of revenge and compromise".* It seems that for all dilemmas in this category, the rational-utilitarian moral solutions were awarded more agreement than the rational-utilitarian solutions.

Category 6 - *"The perception of the Holocaust as a historical event",* included only one dilemma - 'the Comparison of the Holocaust dilemma'. The essence of the dilemma is whether or not to compare the Jewish Holocaust with other genocides in history. **Moral deliberation** for this dilemma exists between "universal" versus "Jewish-particular" moral solutions. A "universal" moral solution would be found when the Holocaust is perceived by the Jews as a universal event similar to other genocides with universal implications while "Jewish-particular" moral solution means that the Holocaust is apprehended as "Jewish only" event which is not really attached or connected to other nations or people history. Therefore, the conclusion is that it cannot be compared to any other events.

14. *The Comparison of the Holocaust dilemma*

The essence of the dilemma is the deliberation between two options: 1. to learn about the Jewish Holocaust from a particular point of view which emphasizes the Jewish tragedy without mentioning other similar genocides during World War II or in other historical periods. 2. To learn about the Jewish Holocaust from a universal point of view; an approach that emphasizes the connection between genocides of other ethnic and national groups and the Jewish Holocaust.

Solution A - The universal moral solution is: "The Holocaust can and should be compared to other genocides".

Solution B - The Jewish particular moral solution is: "The Holocaust cannot be compared to other genocides, because it was unique".

Table 3.1.14 – Responses to "The comparison of the Holocaust" dilemma

Time	Solution	Strong disagree 1	Disagree 2	Uncertain 3	Agree 4	Strong agree 5	%	N	Mean	SD
1	A	16.67%	4.55%	31.82%	37.88%	9.09%	100	66	**3.18**	1.20
	B	2.82%	7.04%	21.13%	32.39%	36.62%	100	71	**3.93**	1.06

'No opinion' for Solution A: N=4; for Solution B: N=2, for 'Other Solution': N = 22

The distribution of the responses reveals that Solution **A**- the universal solution was awarded responses in the following proportions: 21% - disagreement, 32% - uncertainty and 47% - agreement. Solution **B**- the Jewish particular solution was awarded 10% - disagreement, 21% - uncertainty and 69% - agreement. *This means that participants agreed more with the* Jewish particular *solution.*

3.1.3 Discussion and conclusions

Discussion concerning the students' initial moral attitudes towards Holocaust era dilemmas:

Study 1 aimed to identify the level of agreement or disagreement with the different moral behaviors of the Jews during and after the Holocaust among Israeli high school students who participated in a Holocaust Learning Program.

Observation of the results for the different dilemmas indicates that there was much variance between the proportions of responses for the survival and the deontological solutions, according to the nature of each dilemma. In order to evaluate the moral attitudes expressed by the students towards the dilemmas it is also helpful to look for common characteristics between them in order to create categories that will enable more profound understanding. This, therefore, will be the nature of our discussion. All Holocaust era dilemmas can be classified as "high-conflict" dilemmas; such dilemmas appear in threatening situations, such as war, a terrorist attack or natural disasters. As such, they are more sensitive to individual variation and emotional reactivity (Koenigs et al., 2007). Holocaust dilemmas are also "harm to save" (H2S) moral dilemmas in which one must decide whether to kill another person in order to save more lives (ibid.). It should also be remembered that dilemmas relating to physical injury and especially killing of humans (such as Holocaust dilemmas) are more meaningful and arouse stronger emotional reactions (Gillath, McCall, Shaver & Blascovich, 2008). Therefore, it is understandable to assume that there will be some similarities as well as some differences between the responses to different dilemmas. The discussion now focuses separately on each category of dilemmas.

Category 1: ***"The collaboration dilemmas"***. This category includes the 'Judenratt dilemma', the 'Sonderkommando dilemma' and the 'Rebels dilemma'. The main common characteristic of these dilemmas is the influence of the individual's decision on the wide circle of his community. Results reveal that in two dilemmas out of three in this category the survival morality solutions were awarded more agreement than the deontological morality solutions with a high level of deliberation between the two contradicting options. Participants' agreement with the deontological morality demonstrated in the differences between the results for the *'Judenratt dilemma'* and the *'Sonderkommando dilemma'* (Efrat & Baban, 2016a). In the first dilemma, the action of causing harm (making a list of people who will be transferred to be exterminated) is a foreseen but unintended action performed in order to do achieve a better good - to save yourself, your family and hopefully the rest of the Jews in the 'Ghetto'. This is the reason why participants supported the survival and not the deontological solution. In the 'Sonderkommando dilemma' the action of causing harm (working to assist the Nazis in the process of extermination of the Jews) is less unintentional because the action is performed in a direct manner – however, it is, of course, fundamentally unintended but forced. Furthermore, you cannot save anyone if you make a deontological decision and refuse to work, you will just die and someone else will take your place. This is the reason why both survival and deontological contradict solutions were awarded support in this dilemma with a little advantage for the survival solution. In the *'Rebel's dilemma'*, the main question is whether to participate in armed rebellion against the Nazis without the wide support of Jewish community and Jewish leadership in the "Ghetto" (the Judenratt"), which forced to work under the Nazi regime. In this case, the action of rebellion is not coerced by a greater force, it is a voluntary, intentional act and the result is expected to be the death of many Jewish people by the Nazis as retaliation for the rebellion. This is the reason that in this dilemma the deontological moral attitude was awarded more support. **The conclusion** is that in this category participants overall felt and thought that it was better to find solutions according to survival morality since the effect of such a decision on a large group of people would perhaps allow some chance of rescue for at least some of the people. When the moral decision affects a smaller number of people, with less or no chances of survival the deliberation is greater regardless of whether the moral action is intentional or not. Consequently, in this category, participants eventually gave more support for the survival moral solutions despite great difficulty and much deliberation that they experienced when deciding to support what for them is usually an unacceptable moral behavior.

Category 2: *"The acute dilemmas"*. This category includes the 'Crying baby dilemma' and the 'Thieves dilemma'. The main common characteristic of these dilemmas is the direct influence of the individual's decisions on a specific other individual in a very close social circle. In the "crying baby dilemma" it is the family or a small group of hiding Jews. In the 'thief's dilemma' it is the group of prisoners in the camp. The dilemmas in this category (like all Holocaust dilemmas) are "harm to save" (H2S) moral dilemmas in which one must decide whether to kill another person in order to save more or other lives (Koenigs et al., 2007). In the terrible daily reality of the Holocaust, most of the time "more lives" included your own life. There are two possible courses of action in these dilemmas: refusing to harm another person despite all possible consequences or saving as many people as possible even at the cost of harming one person, which is known as the 'utilitarian' H2S decision (Koenigs et al., 2007). In both the dilemmas in this category the deontological solutions were awarded more agreement than the survival solutions. These results contradict Greene's (2008) dual-process theory regarding H2S (harm to save) moral dilemmas. According to this theory in H2S moral dilemmas, utilitarian responses will override affective reactions and reduce deontological choices (Greene, 2008). On the other hand, our results are supported by the findings of Starcke, Ludwig and Brand (2012), which indicated that experimental stress conditions in research with healthy volunteers reduce the proportion of utilitarian choices in moral dilemmas. His results suggested that emotional experience might promote deontological decisions in moral dilemmas (Starcke, Ludwig, & Brand, 2012; Youssef et al., 2012). **The conclusion** is that the great emotional challenge involving strong feelings and difficulty in grasping the kind of horrors undergone in the Holocaust can explain this tendency towards deontological solutions which seem to be more "rational" or "sane" or "appropriate" at this stage when the students had just begun the Holocaust Learning Program.

. . .

Category 3: *"The parental dilemmas"*. This category included the 'Little Smuggler dilemma' and the 'Giving children away dilemma'. The main common characteristic of these dilemmas is the direct influence of the parent's decision on his children. In both dilemmas of this category the survival morality solutions were awarded more agreement than the deontological solutions. This means that participants showed more support for survival solutions, although there was an obvious risk to the child's life, in contrast to the parent's natural instinct tendency – not to risk their child's life. Choosing the survival solution was significantly clearer in the "Giving children away dilemma" than in the "Little Smuggler dilemma" probably because of the higher risk to the child's life and guilt feelings that the latter dilemma arouses. Our results are supported by Alicke (2000) who found that the development of examinees' guilt feelings depends on the results of their moral decisions: insofar as the decision is more extreme or causes a higher price involving injury to a person's life, then guilt feelings will grow more. Our results are also supported by the findings of Tassy et al. (2013), who noted that variation of the affective proximity between participants and the potential victim (for example, a family relative), has been described as influencing moral choice but not moral judgment. **The conclusion** is that participants preferred to support solutions based on survival morality - to take a risk regarding the life of a single child in order to improve the chances of survival for the child or other family members. They did so, although they recognized that this was not the "right" (deontological) moral decision.

Discussion on the students' initial moral attitudes towards Post-Holocaust era dilemmas:

Post-Holocaust era dilemmas differ from Holocaust dilemmas mainly because there is no longer a constant threat of imminent death. These dilemmas are expressions of the Jewish people's continuous struggle to cope with the memory, the consequences and the effects of the Holocaust. In these dilemmas the tension that exists between the different moral solutions varies according to the nature of the dilemma. As for Holocaust dilemmas, the Post-Holocaust dilemmas were sorted into categories according to common characteristics. Each category is now discussed separately:

Category 4: ***"The Perception of Jewish behavior towards the Nazis"***. This category includes the 'Like Lambs to the Slaughter dilemma', the 'Kapo" dilemma', the 'Kastner dilemma' and the 'Resistance dilemma'. In three out of the four dilemmas the "acceptance" moral solutions were awarded more agreement than the "judgmental" solutions. It was only for the 'Kapo" dilemma' that the participants agreed more with the judgmental solution. The results indicate that participants usually supported the solution that represented understanding and acceptance for the "passive" behavior of the Jews during the Holocaust. Moreover, there was a lack of willingness to reproach them for not rising up in armed rebellion against the Nazis.

These results testify that the participants distanced themselves from attitudes that were strongly represented and to some extent are still held in Israeli society towards the "cowardly" behavior of the Jews during the Holocaust (Farber, 2007: Weitzberg, 1996). The acceptance moral attitude adopted by the participants resembles what is nowadays the prevalent view in Israeli society. This view sees the Holocaust as a national disaster in which the reality was so difficult, cruel and different to an exceptional and unique extent that the behavior of the Jews cannot be judged (Moras, 1972; Neuberger, 1994). In general, the participants adopted the attitude that it is impossible to retroactively judge those who experienced this reality in person. This attitude demonstrates moral thinking that complies with the highest level on Kohlberg's scale of moral development – "hierarchy of principles orientation". At this stage of development, the individual weighs evaluative-moral considerations that are in substance both complex and universal (Kohlberg, 1969). So what may be the reason that in the 'Kapo dilemma' the picture is reversed? A possible explanation is the power that the term or the expression "Kapo" carries in Jewish-Israeli memory. "Kapo" was the "title" given to a Jewish foreman in the extermination camps, and it became a synonym for a cruel Jewish collaborator with the Nazis, who intentionally hurt Jewish prisoners in the camps (Levine, 2015). Our explanation is supported by the findings of Guglielmo and Malle (2010). They indicated that when a person intentionally and skillfully injures or kills another person, then people are far less likely to view their action as morally justified, even when the circumstances are complex. In the reality of the Holocaust the students' responses to the 'Kapo dilemma' correspond exactly with this explanation. **The conclusion is** that the participant usually agreed with what is now the more accepted view in Israeli discourse concerning Jewish behavior during the Holocaust: it cannot be judged retrospectively.

Category 5: *"Consideration of revenge and compromise"*. This category includes the 'Revengers dilemma' and the 'Restitution Payments dilemma'. In both dilemmas the rational-utilitarian moral solutions were awarded more agreement than the rational-utilitarian solutions. This picture was prominent in the 'Restitution payments dilemma' but was present also in the 'Revengers dilemma'. It seems that the difference between the results in category **5** derives from the acceptance of the perception that 'Restitution payments' are definitely useful and needed and for those reasons, acceptance of these payments is justified. On the other hand, killing Nazis war criminals, who murdered Jews seems to be less justified or moral because of the illegal and violent nature of this kind of act. These assumptions are in line with other research findings indicating that social norms usually oppose harmful actions against other people and that emotional aversion to harming others may have evolved as part of humans' decision-making (Haidt, 2007). Our results also correlate with recent studies that support the natural assumption that when an individual is exposed to the experience of harming other people, it triggers strong emotional reactions that are expressed both at cognitive and physiological levels, especially if the harmful action involves physical force such as killing and intention as in murder (Cushman, Young, & Hauser, 2006; Greene et al., 2007). **The first conclusion** is that our participants actually followed social, moral norms, which reject the possibility of taking the law into one's own hands and carrying out personal justice. **The second conclusion** is that even now, 70 years after the end of the Holocaust, the issue of revenge against Nazis war criminals still burns in the soul of Israeli youth, although they are already the third or fourth generation after the Holocaust victims or survivors.

Category 6: ***"The perception of the Holocaust as a historical event".*** This category includes only one dilemma - 'the Comparison of the Holocaust dilemma'. The results indicated that participants agreed more with the 'Jewish particular' solution. These results are not surprising because there is a very strong perception of the Holocaust as a "solely Jewish" historical event, which cannot be compared to other genocides in Israeli society and education (Oron, 2006). Still many of the participants choose to support the universal attitude which grasps the Holocaust as a common human historical event with worldwide implications (Gurani, 2015). **The conclusion** is that at the beginning of their Holocaust Learning Program, the participants had serious deliberations regarding the "traditional" accepted perception of the Holocaust as a historical event. Perhaps, in some way, they felt intuitively that this perception was too narrow. Maybe they had formerly held moral attitudes or values that favored more liberal views that could be defined as a 'universal moral attitude'.

Discussion on the maturation, motivation and development of moral thinking:

Due to the fact that dealing with Holocaust moral dilemmas was a new experience for the participating students, various questions arose at the beginning of the research: Would participants cooperate with the research? Could they formulate and consolidate moral attitudes towards such a complicated and rather unknown subject? Which moral attitudes would emerge? Our results reveal that the participants responded willingly and seriously to the moral dilemmas which they were asked to consider. These results are appropriate for teenagers' stage of mental and moral developmental at ages 16-18, according to Elliott & Feldman (1990). Most of the participants chose to support one of the two solutions provided for the dilemmas (in the questionnaire), so there were not many responses of the type "I have no opinion". Thus, it seems that the issue of the Holocaust moral dilemmas was interesting, important and meaningful for the participants and that they were highly motivated to deal with it despite the emotional and intellectual difficulty that the issue of Holocaust always arouses, as indicated by Weitz (1997). It seems that the participants had an emotional and cognitive need to express their opinions since they not only marked the suggested solutions on the questionnaire but also, in many cases, added their own wording, often using the "other solution" option in order to explain their choices. A minority of these "other solutions" provided unrealistic solutions to the actual Holocaust situations and this can be explained by the fact that the participant's knowledge was still limited at the beginning of the Holocaust Learning Program when they filled out the questionnaire for the first time. Another possible explanation is the emotional difficulty that the dilemmas aroused. When we try to assess the participant's ability to cope with the task of defining moral attitudes, it seems that they had not only the ability but also the emotional and cognitive need to express their moral opinions.

This type of functioning characterizes late adolescence (16-18) when the development of the self reaches a point that permits the creation of a consolidated personal identity (Harter 1990). This personal identity includes principles of social behavior, attitudes concerning religion, nationality, a political approach, gender identity together with moral values and conceptions (Harter 1990). The results regarding the participants' ability and need for self-definition of moral values is also supported by the "personal identity development" theory created by Erikson (1968). The stage that interests us in Ericson's model is Stage 5 "Who am?": "Identity versus confusion". The goal at this stage is to consolidate identity or to consolidate different identities such as sexual identity, social identity and later also political and moral identity (Erikson, 1987). In relation to the present research, the participants demonstrated both the need and the desire to state their own moral attitudes. The ability that the participants demonstrated to adopt moral attitudes is also in line with the theory of thinking development presented by Piaget (1965). Piaget described the formation of moral attitudes as depending on the individual's cognitive ability to perform high level moral thinking. He also defined moral discretion as a process of thinking and judgment that leads to the performance of an act perceived as correct in a given situation. This ability depends on the individual's ability to reach a formal level of thinking including moral thinking in late adolescence (age 16-18). At this time the teenager recognizes the possibility of the existence of different attitudes concerning moral questions and no longer perceives moral rules as absolute but rather as connected with changeable social norms and values (Piaget & Inhelder 1973). This provides a plausible explanation for the present research results indicating that the students did indeed demonstrate mature moral thinking and perception, matching Piaget's description of this stage of development of moral thinking. **One conclusion** is that as a result of their interest in the Holocaust, their motivation to participate in the research and the development of their social and cognitive ability our participants succeeded in forming moral attitudes towards Holocaust dilemmas. **Another conclusion** is that the age of 16-18 is a suitable time to learn and understand complex moral issues, including Holocaust moral dilemmas.

The third question for Study 1 was: which moral attitudes would emerge? The large amount of deliberation between the two attitudes - the survival moral attitude as opposed to the deontological moral attitude testifies to the serious difficulty involved in coping with these dilemmas at this stage when the participants were at the beginning of their Holocaust learning. The participants actually had to deliberate between supporting or opposing the Jews' actual behaviors during the Holocaust in situations in which moral decisions often demanded the cost of the life of another person or persons in order to save your own life. As described by Kermish (1989), Lubotkin (1979), Weissmandel (1960) and Yerushalmi (1995), Jews usually choose survival moral solutions in order to survive. This may explain the emotional and intellectual difficulty that the dilemmas aroused among the participants which was manifested in the deliberation between solutions. The moral thinking that leads to the survival solution complies with stage 1.1 in Kohlberg's moral thinking hierarchy – "Obedience and punishment orientation" (Snarey, Kohlberg & Noam, 1983)

At this stage, good behavior is a result of the child's desire to avoid punishment that could be imposed by an external authority (such as parents) if the behavior contradicts the desire of that authority. Thus, the extreme situation of continuous risk to life under a regime of terror during the Holocaust lowers and reduces moral thinking and moral attitudes or at least moral decisions to a level of moral thinking that characterizes young children confronting authority. This insight is in line with the findings of Cristofari & Guitton (2014) that people will make decisions which they do not consider to be "moral" in order to survive, although they are well aware of the lack of "morality" of their acts. With regard to the present research, the participants vacillated between attitudes that they considered "moral" and those that they considered as "not-moral". They did this in light of their current understanding of the dilemmas and had to make decisions that were not necessarily their first choices.

On the one hand, there was the possibility of moral thinking that leads to a deontological solution, which complies with stage 2.2 in Kohlberg's moral thinking hierarchy - "Social conventions or law and order orientation" (Kohlberg & Gilligan, 1972). At this stage, moral decision is based on the young adolescent's concern to fulfill their duty as determined by the laws of society to their best understanding. The thinking is directed towards others, taking care of their welfare and treating them with respect. In line with this theory, it is natural that the young participants aged 16-18, who participated in this research will support the deontological approach. Nevertheless, the unique nature of Holocaust dilemmas and the participants' traditional, social and emotional connection to the Holocaust cause serious deliberation and create support also for the utilitarian or in this case - the survival solution for the dilemmas. This complex moral thinking complies with stage 3.2 - "hierarchy of principles orientation" the highest level on Kohlberg's scale of moral development (Kohlberg, 1969). At this stage of development, the individual weighs evaluative-moral considerations that are in substance both complex and universal. The goal is to make the moral decision or to perform moral judgment according to the highest relevant moral principles. **The last conclusion**, therefore, is that dealing with Holocaust moral dilemmas developed and increased our participants' moral thinking.

So far, we have described and discussed the students' initial moral attitudes. However, these attitudes represent only the initial stage of the participant's moral thinking at the beginning of their Holocaust Learning Program. In Study 2 we present the evolution and changes of the students' moral attitudes over the three different research stages.

3.2 Study 2- The evolution of moral attitudes

Introduction

Having identified the participants' initial fundamental moral attitudes in Study 1, we shall now look for possible evolution and changes in these attitudes through the three different research stages (Measuring Points 1, 2 and 3) which were performed in parallel to the Holocaust Learning Program. This study, therefore, has two aims: The first is to test whether the Holocaust Learning Program generates changes in the participant's moral attitudes. The second is to test whether changes in the participant's moral attitudes during their Holocaust Learning Program are moderated by their gender, having relatives who are Holocaust victims or survivors and participation in the journey to Holocaust memorial sites in Poland. The first and second parts of the study present the evolution of the participants' moral attitudes towards Holocaust-era and Post-Holocaust era dilemmas. Then we move to the third part, where we present analysis of the effect of several moderators: gender, having relatives, who are Holocaust victims' and participation in the journey to Poland. In the fourth and last part we shall present the evolution of the participants' choice of the options: "Other solutions" and "No opinion" for moral dilemmas as they were used by the participants in the Moral Attitude Questionnaires during the three research stages.

Method

This study presents a statistical analysis of the responses to the moral attitudes questionnaire which was filled in by 102 participants three times: first in January 2015 when they were in the middle of Grade 11, soon after the Holocaust Learning Program began, secondly in September 2015 after the journey to Poland and at the beginning of

Grade 12, and thirdly in January 2016 in the middle of Grade 12 when the Holocaust Learning Program ended.

In the first part- *"the evolution of Holocaust-era moral attitudes"* and **the second part** – *"the evolution of Post-Holocaust era moral attitudes"*, data analysis for the entire population of participants was performed by "Repeated Measures" deductive statistical analysis using ANOVA tests and Bonferroni t-tests. This type of analysis was used in order to examine whether there was a significant statistical difference in the evolution of the moral attitudes between one point of time and the next. The measurements were conducted at the three points in time for each participant's attitudes towards each moral dilemma, so that a comparison could be performed between the measurements of each and every one of the participants. Initially, a comparison was drawn between the measurements at Measurement Points 1 and 2. This was followed by presenting the evolution of the results between Measurement Points 1- the beginning of the process, and 3- the end of the process, using descriptive statistical analysis to calculate the difference in mean results.

In the third part – *"Moderators of change in moral attitudes"* deductive statistics were calculated for responses to the Moral Attitudes Questionnaire by "Profile Analysis". This is one of the types of tests that can be conducted to analyze the difference resulting from the "Repetitive Measures" analysis. The purpose of this analysis was to test whether different Moderators produce statistically significant differences in the participants' profiles. ANOVA tests and Bonferroni t-tests were used for deductive statistical analysis. This type of analysis was used in this study to examine whether there was a significant statistical difference in the evolution of the moral attitudes between one point of time and the next for several pairs of moderators: boys in comparison to girls; participants who have or had family members who were Holocaust victims or survivors in comparison to those who did not have such relatives; participants in the research who also took part in the journey to Poland in comparison to those participants who did not take part in the journey. The mean results of each such moderator were tested along the stages of data-collection in order to see whether there were significant differences in influence between the different pairs at the different research stages. At first, we present the mean results showing the evolution of participants' attitudes, using deductive statistics including repeated measures profile analysis. A two-way ANOVA model was used to test each analysis, in which the first factor was the intervention and the second factor was the moderator. The statistical indicator in each analysis is denoted as F regarding the interaction between the intervention and the moderator. A statistically significant F for the interaction means that the two pairs of moderators that are compared evolved in a significantly different manner from one measurement point to another. This kind of result suggests a moderation effect, which would then be further investigated by targeted comparisons using the t- test and the effect size indicator (d). This is followed by the presentation of the evolution of the results between Measuring Point 1- the beginning of the process, and Measuring Point 3- the end of the process, using descriptive statistical analysis to calculate the difference of mean results. N- refers to the number of participants in a specific section, who chose the given solution at all three measurements times. It is noted that the findings presented here only relate to the main statistically significant results.

In the fourth part *"the evolution of 'Other solutions' and 'No opinion' options"* - descriptive statistics analysis was used to present the evolution of the participant's choices for those options along the different research stages.

Results

3.2.1 The evolution of Holocaust era moral attitudes

For the further analysis of this part the seven Holocaust era dilemmas were sorted into three categories according to similar characteristics. The extent of the participant's agreement or disagreement with the different moral solutions is expressed here for all categories: (Mean<3 = disagreement; Mean>3 = agreement; Mean>4 = strong agreement)

Category 1 – "The collaboration dilemmas": including the 'Judenratt dilemma', the 'Sonderkommando dilemma' and the 'Rebels dilemma'. Moral deliberation exists between deontological and survival moral solutions. The main common characteristic of this category is the influence of the individual's decision on the wide circle of his community. These are *"Collaboration" dilemmas"* because the question, whether to collaborate with the Nazis or not, is the core of the different dilemmas in this category.

Table 3.2.1: Mean results for category 1- "The collaboration dilemmas"

1a - Survival moral solution				1b - Deontological moral solution			
Time	N	Mean	SD	Time	N	Mean	SD
1	98	3.48	.83	1	73	3.51	.84
2	98	3.484	.73	2	73	3.25	.70
3	98	3.62	.61	3	73	3.15	.79

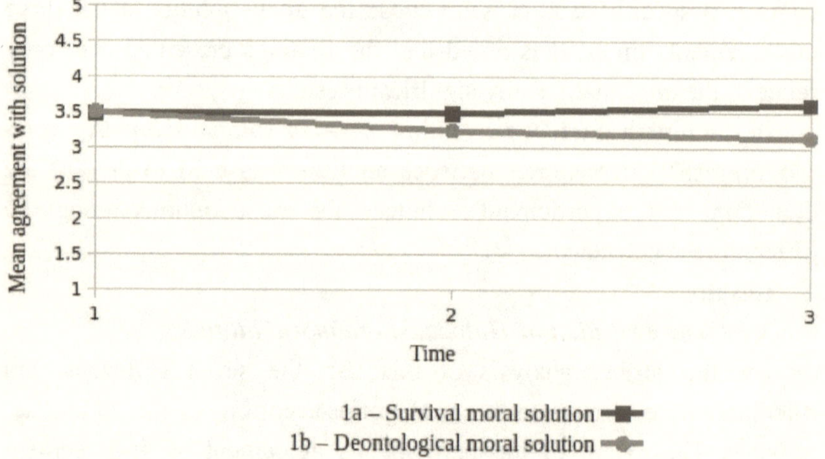

Figure 3.2.1: The evolution of mean results for category 1-"The collaboration dilemmas"

The results indicate that agreement with the survival moral solution (1a) increased over the three different measuring points (T) of the research in a manner that was not significant (F=1.69, p>0.05). On the other hand, agreement with solutions based on deontological morality (1b) decreased over the different measuring points (T) in a significant manner (F=5.32, p<0.01). Post-hoc pairwise comparisons T1-T3 (p<0.05, d'=0.44) were significant while the rest were not: T1-T2 (p>0.05, d'=0.336); T2-T3 (p>0.05, d'=0.13).

Table 3.2.2: The evolution of mean results for category 1- " The collaboration dilemmas ", between Time 1-3

Dilemmas categories	Mean T1	Mean T3	Mean T3-T1
Category 1a- "The collaboration dilemmas", survival moral solution	3.48	3.62	0.14
Category 1b- "The collaboration dilemmas", deontological moral solution	3.51	3.15	-0.36

The results indicate that the evolution of participants' responses between T1 - the beginning of learning and T3 – the end of learning showed an increase of 0.14 (3.62-3.48) in agreement with the survival moral solution (1a) and a decrease of 0.36- (3.15-3.51) in agreement with the deontological moral solution (1b). However, both contradicting solutions were awarded agreement throughout the entire learning process (T1-T2-T3).

Category 2 – *"The acute dilemmas"*: including the 'Crying baby dilemma' and the 'Thief's dilemma'. Moral deliberation exists between deontological morality and survival morality. The main common characteristic of this category is the direct influence of the individual's decision on a specific other individual within a very close social circle - his family or a small group of Jews in hiding in the 'crying baby dilemma' and the group of prisoners in the extermination camp in the 'thief's dilemma'. These dilemmas are defined as ***"acute dilemmas"*** because the individual needs to make a fast decision with no way back.

Table 3.2.3: Mean results for category 2 - "The acute dilemmas"

2a - survival moral solution				2b - deontological moral solution			
Time	N	Mean	SD	Time	N	Mean	SD
1	60	2.75	.95	1	77	3.90	.65
2	60	3.00	.90	2	77	3.68	.77
3	60	3.11	.96	3	77	3.58	.80

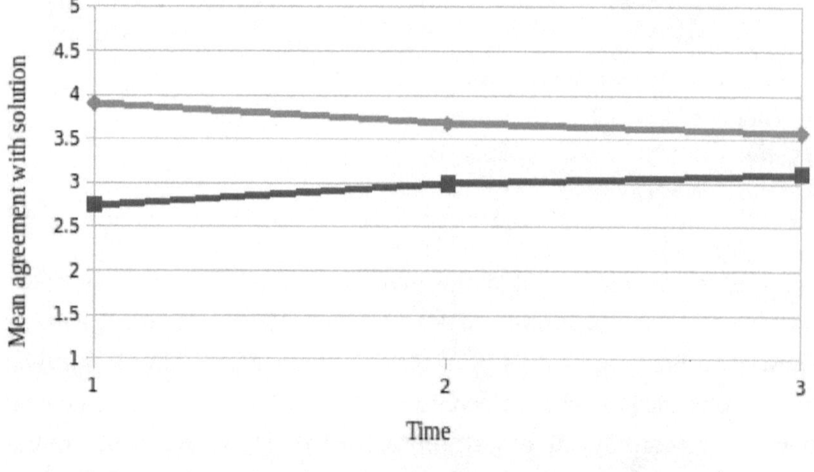

Figure 3.2.2: The evolution of mean results for category 2 - " The acute dilemmas"

The results indicate that the extent of agreement with the survival moral solutions (2a) changed from "disagreement" at T1 (the beginning of the learning) to "uncertain" at T2 (in the middle of the learning) and "agreement" at T3 (the end of the learning). However, the increase in agreement over the different measuring points of the research was not significant (F=0.98, p>0.05). At the same time the level of agreement with solutions based on deontological morality (2b) decreased over the different measuring points of the research in a significant manner (F=4.64, p<0.05) but remained "agreement". The post-hoc pairwise comparison T1-T3 (p<0.05, d'=0.439) is significant while the rest are not: T1-T2 (p>0.05, d'=0.308) T2-T3 (p>0.05, d'=0.127).

Table 3.2.4: Evolution of mean results for category 2- "The acute dilemmas", between T1-T3

Dilemmas categories	Mean T1	Mean T3	Mean T3-T1
Category 2a- " *The acute dilemmas*", survival moral solution	2.75	3.11	0.36
Category 2b- " *The acute dilemmas*", deontological moral solution	3.90	3.58	-0.32

The results indicated that the evolution of participants' responses between T1 (the beginning of the learning) and T3 (the end of the learning) showed a general increase in agreement with the survival moral solution (2a) and decrease in agreement with the deontological moral solution (2b). Specifically, there was an increase of 0.36 (3.11-2.75) in agreement with the survival moral solution between T1 and T2. For this solution, participants' attitudes changed from disagreement at the beginning of the learning (Mean=2.75) to agreement at T3 – the end of learning (Mean=3.11). At the same time, there was a decrease of -0.32 (3.58-3.90) in the level of agreement with the deontological moral solution. However, at the end of the learning agreement with the deontological moral solution is still higher.

Category 3 – *"The parental dilemmas":* including the 'Little Smuggler dilemma' and the 'Giving children away dilemma'. Moral deliberation exists between deontological morality and survival morality. The main common characteristic of this category is the direct influence of the individual – the parent's decision on the fate of his child or children.

Table 3.2.5: Mean results for category 3 – " The parental dilemmas"

3a - survival moral solution				3b - deontological moral solution			
Time	N	Mean	SD	Time	N	Mean	SD
1	99	3.92	.72	1	N=36	3.39	1.01
2	99	4.00	.78	2	N=36	2.74	1.10
3	99	3.96	.63	3	N=36	2.69	0.80

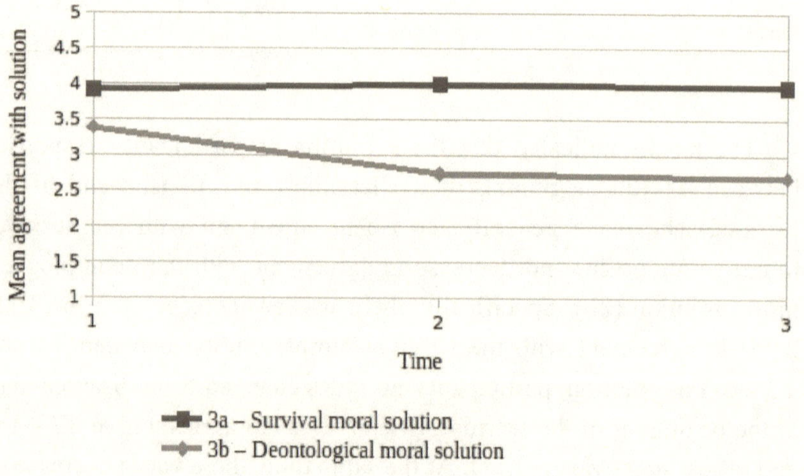

Figure 3.2.3: The evolution of mean results for category 3 - " The parental dilemmas"

The results indicate that the level of agreement with the survival moral solution (3a) increased over the different measuring points of the research in an insignificant manner (F=0.47, p>0.05). However, the level of agreement with the deontological moral solutions (3b) decreased from "agreement" at T1 (the beginning of learning) to "disagreement" at T2 (middle of learning) and T3 (end of learning) in a significant manner (F=8.27, p<0.01). Two of the post-hoc pairwise comparisons were significant: T1-T2 (p<0.05, d'=0.61); T1-T3 (p<0.05, d'=0.768). The post-hoc pairwise comparison T2-T3 (p>0.05, d'=0.05) was not significant.

Table 3.2.6: Evolution of mean results for category 3-" The parental dilemmas", between T1 and T3

Dilemmas categories	Mean T1	Mean T3	Mean T3-T1
Category 3a- " *The parental dilemmas*", survival moral solution	3.92	3.96	0.04
Category 3b- " *The parental dilemmas*", deontological moral solution	3.39	2.69	-0.70

The results indicate that the evolution of participants' responses between −T1 (the beginning of learning) and T3 (the end of learning) showed an increase of 0.04 (3.96-3.92) in the level of agreement with the survival moral solution (3a) and a decrease of -0.70 (2.69-3.39) in the level of agreement with the deontological moral solution (3b). However, both contradicting solutions were awarded agreement over the entire learning process (T1, T2 and T3).

It can be concluded, overall that the learning process regarding Holocaust era dilemmas led to an insignificant increase in the level of participants' agreement with survival moral solutions and a significant decrease in the level of their agreement with deontological moral solutions. The following tables (3.2.7 + 3.2.8) illustrate the amount of difficulty expressed by the participants to agree with the different solutions.

Table 3.2.7: The extent of difficulty to agree with the survival moral solution

Most difficult to agree	Dilemmas Categories 1,2, and 3 The survival moral solution	T1 Mean	T3 Mean	T3-T1 Mean
1	**Category 2a-** "The acute dilemmas"	2.75	3.11	+0.36
2	**Category 1a-** "The collaboration dilemmas"	3.48	3.62	+0.14
3	**Category 3a-** "The parental dilemmas"	3.92	3.96	+0.04

This table underwent analysis of variance – repeated measures (ANOVA). This analysis showed a significant effect for category ($F=67.76$, $p<0.01$), a marginally significant effect for time ($F=3.1$, $p<0.05$) and no significant interaction ($F=0.87$, n.s.).

A linear contrast, conducted according to the order of the categories in Table 3.2.7, reached significance ($F=117.9$, $p<0.01$) and thus supports the order presented in the first column of the table ("Most difficult to agree"). The results indicate that at origin (T1 - beginning of learning) the greatest difficulty to agree with the survival moral solution appeared in category 2a, followed by less difficulty in category 1a and least difficulty in category 3a. The evolution: In general - the level of agreement with the survival solution increased over time. Specifically - insofar as the level of agreement with the survival solution was lowest at origin (T1), then the level of agreement with this solution increases over time until at the end of learning (T3) it is at the highest level.

Table 3.2.8: The extent of ease to agree with the deontological moral solution

Most easy to agree	Dilemmas Categories 1,2 and 3 The deontological moral solution	T1 Mean	T3 Mean	T3-T1 Mean
1	**Category 2b-** "The acute dilemmas",	3.90	3.58	-0.32
2	**Category 1b-** "The collaboration dilemmas"	3.51	3.15	-0.36
3	**Category 3b-** "The parental dilemmas"	3.39	2.69	-0.70

This table underwent analysis of variance – repeated measures (ANOVA). This analysis showed a significant effect of category (F=16.6, p<0.01), a significant effect of time (F=11.4, p<0.01) and no significant interaction (F=0.83, n.s.).

A linear contrast, conducted according to the order of the categories in Table 3.2.8, reached significance (F=28.9, p<0.01) and thus supports the order presented in the first column of the table ("Most easy to agree"). The results indicate that the greatest ease in agreeing with the deontological solution appears at origin (T1- beginning of learning) in category 2b, with less ease in category 1b and the least ease in category 3b. The evolution: In general - the level of agreement with the deontological solution decreased over time. Specifically - insofar as the participants' level of agreement with the deontological solution is highest at origin (T1), then there is a decrease of agreement with this solution over time until the end of learning (T3) when the level of agreement with this solution is lowest.

Significant differences in the evolution of Holocaust-era moral attitudes:

In order to address the question of whether there are significant differences in the evolution of Holocaust-era moral attitudes between the different stages of learning, a comparison was drawn between the changes at the different stages. Table 3.2.9 presents the results of this test/OR comparison.

Table 3.2.9: Summary of significant differences in the evolution of Holocaust-era moral attitudes

Category	Solution	Total evolution
1a-"The collaboration dilemmas"	survival morality	No significant change
1b-"The collaboration dilemmas"	deontological morality	Agreement decreased significantly
2a - "The acute dilemmas"	survival morality	No significant change
2b - "The acute dilemmas"	deontological morality	Agreement decreased significantly
3a – "The parental dilemmas"	survival morality	No significant change
3b – "The parental dilemmas"	deontological morality	Agreement decreased significantly

It can be concluded that the evolution of the participants' moral attitudes towards Holocaust-era dilemmas showed a non-significant increase in level of agreement with survival moral solutions and a significant decrease in level of agreement with deontological moral solutions. There are no prominent results for significant differences between times intervals. Therefore, it seems that there was no particular stage or event during the learning process which had a more systematic effect than other stages.

3.2.2 The evolution of Post-Holocaust era moral attitudes

This part describes the evolution of participants' moral attitudes towards the different Post-Holocaust dilemma categories.

Category 4 – *"The perception of Jewish behavior towards the Nazis":* including the 'Like Lambs to the slaughter dilemma', the 'Kapo dilemma', the 'Kastner dilemma' and the 'Resistance dilemma'. The main common characteristic of this category is the attempt to understand and evaluate the way that Jews behaved towards the Nazis from different perspectives. Moral deliberation for this category exists between "judgmental" versus "acceptance" moral attitudes.

. . .

Table 3.2.10: Mean results for category 4 – *"The perception of Jewish behavior towards the Nazis"*

4a - Judgmental moral solution				4b - Acceptance moral solution			
Time	N	Mean	SD	Time	N	Mean	SD
1	58	2.67	.96	1	99	4.02	.55
2	58	2.51	.95	2	99	3.88	.70
3	58	2.54	.86	3	99	3.91	.67

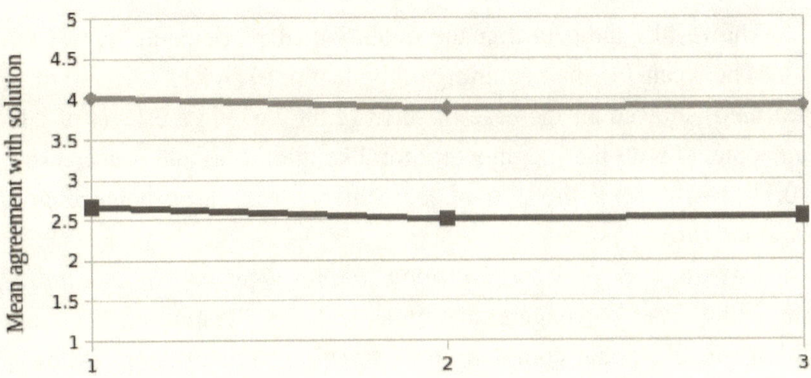

Figure 3.2.4: The evolution of mean results for category 4 – "The perception of Jewish behavior towards the Nazis"

The results indicate that the level of "disagreement" with the judgmental moral solution (4a) increased over the different measurement points in a manner that was not significant (F=0.71, p>0.05, d'=0.14). At the same time the level of "agreement" with the acceptance moral solutions (4b) decreased in a manner that was also not significant (F=1.72, p>0.05).

Table 3.2.11: Evolution of mean results for category 4- "The Perception of Jewish behavior towards the Nazis", between times 1-3

Dilemmas categories	Mean T1	Mean T3	Mean T3-T1
Category 4a- "The perception of Jewish behavior towards the Nazis", the judgmental moral solution	2.67	2.54	-0.13
Category 4b- "The perception of Jewish behavior towards the Nazis", the acceptance moral solution	4.02	3.91	-0.11

The results indicate that the evolution of participants' moral attitudes between T1 (the beginning of the learning) and T3 (the end of the learning) showed an increase of -0.13 (2.54-2.67) in the level of "disagreement" with the judgmental moral solution (4a) and a decrease of -0.11 (3.91-4.02) in the level of "agreement" with the acceptance moral solution (4b).

Category 5 – *"Consideration of revenge and compromise"*: including The 'Revengers dilemma' and the 'Restitution Payments dilemma'. The main common characteristic of this category is Jewish thinking and decisions concerning the way in which to treat the crimes of former Nazis in the post-Holocaust era. Moral deliberation exists between "affective-intuitive" versus "rational-utilitarian" moral solutions.

Table 3.2.12: Mean results for category 5 - "Consideration of revenge and compromise"

5a- Affective-intuitive moral solution				5b- Rational-utilitarian moral solution			
Time	N	Mean	SD	Time	N	Mean	SD
1	47	3.38	1.11	1	96	4.06	.70
2	47	2.84	.99	2	96	3.91	.90
3	47	2.95	1.01	3	96	4.08	.75

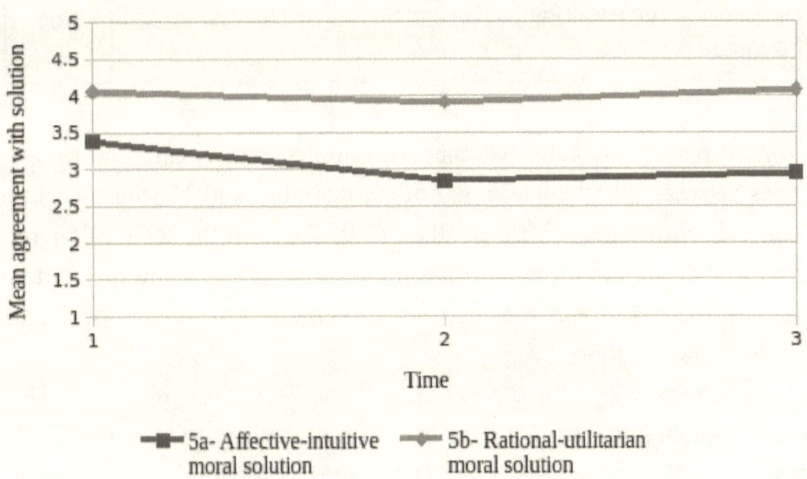

Figure 3.2.5: The evolution of mean results for 5 - "Consideration of revenge and compromise"

The results indicate that the participants' level of "agreement" with the affective-intuitive moral solution (5a) decreased over the different measurement points of the research in a significant manner (F=5.13, p<0.01). One of the post-hoc pairwise comparisons was significant: T1-T2 (p<0.05, d'=0.51) while the others were not significant: T2-T3 (p>0.05, d'=0.10); T1-T3 (p>0.05, d'=0.40). At the same time, the level of "agreement" with the rational-utilitarian moral solution (5b) increased over the different measurement points of the research in a manner that was not significant (F=1.74, p>0.05).

Table 3.2.13: Evolution of mean results for category 5- "Consideration of revenge and compromise", between times 1-3

Dilemmas' categories	Mean T1	Mean T3	Mean T3-T1
Category 5a- "Consideration of revenge and compromise" , the affective-intuitive moral solution	3.38	2.95	-0.43
Category 5b- "Consideration of revenge and compromise", the rational-utilitarian moral solution	4.06	4.08	0.02

The results indicate that the evolution of participants' moral attitudes between T1 (the beginning of the learning) and T3 (the end of the learning) shows a decrease of -0.43 (2.95-3.38) in the level of "agreement" with the affective-intuitive moral solution (5a) and an increase of 0.02 (4.08-4.06) in the level of agreement with the rational-utilitarian moral solution (5b).

Category 6 – *"The Perception of the Holocaust as a historical event"*: including the 'Comparison of the Holocaust dilemma'. The essence of the dilemma is whether or not to compare the Jewish Holocaust to other genocides in history. Moral deliberation exists between "universal" versus "Jewish-particular" moral solutions.

Table 3.2.14: Mean results for category 6 –"The Perception of the Holocaust as a historical event"

6a - Universal moral solution				6b - Jewish-Particular moral solution			
Time	N	Mean	SD	Time	N	Mean	SD
1	45	3.20	1.29	1	46	3.91	1.13
2	45	3.22	1.22	2	46	3.89	1.04
3	45	2.67	1.33	3	46	3.89	1.06

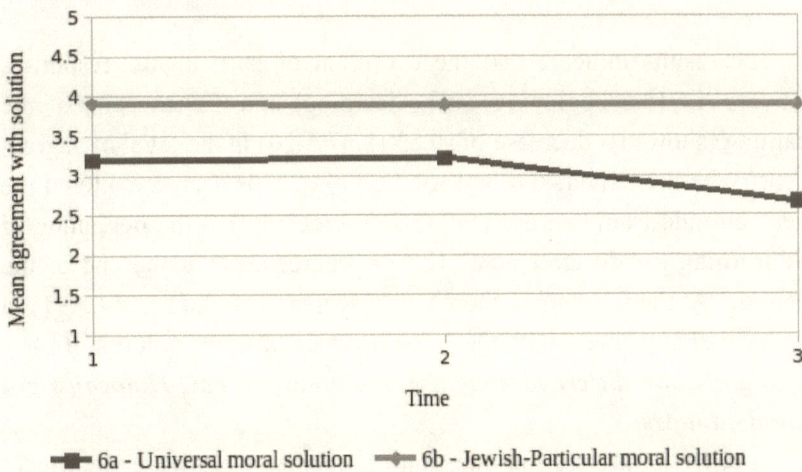

Figure 3.2.6: The evolution of mean results for category 6 – "The Perception of the Holocaust as a historical event"

The results indicate that the level of agreement with the universal moral solution (6a) decreased over the different measurement points of the research in a significant manner (F=6.41, p<0.01). Two of the post-hoc pairwise comparisons were significant: T2-T3 (p<0.05, d'=0.01); T1-T3 (p<0.05, d'=0.40), while the T1-T2 comparison (p>0.05, d'=0.01) was not significant. At the same time the level of "agreement" with the Jewish-Particular moral solution (6b) decreased over the different measurement points of the research in a manner that was not significant (F=0.01, p>0.05).

Table 3.2.15: The evolution of mean results for category 6- "The perception of the Holocaust as a historical event", between T1-T3

Dilemmas categories	Mean T1	Mean T3	Mean T3-T1
Category 6a- "The perception of the Holocaust as a historical event", universal moral solution	3.20	2.67	-0.53
Category 6b- "The perception of the Holocaust as a historical event", Jewish-particular moral solution	3.91	3.89	-0.02

The results indicate that the evolution of participants' responses between T1 (the beginning of the learning) and T3 (the end of the learning) showed a decrease of -0.53 (2.67-3.20) in the level of "agreement" with the universal moral solution (6a). This decrease altered the mean attitude from "agreement" (3.20=agreement) at the beginning of the learning to "disagreement" (2.67=disagreement) at the end of the learning. At the same time, there was a decrease of -0.02 (3.89-3.91) in the level of agreement with the Jewish-particular moral solution (6b).

Significant differences in the evolution of Post-Holocaust-era moral attitudes:

In order to address the question of whether there were significant differences in the evolution of Holocaust-era moral attitudes between the different stages of learning, a comparison was drawn between the changes at the different stages. Table 3.2.16 shows the results of this comparison.

Table 3.2.16: Summary of significant changes in the evolution of Post-Holocaust era moral attitudes

Category	Solution	Total evolution
4a - "The perception of Jewish behavior towards the Nazis"	judgmental moral solution	No significant change
4b - "The perception of Jewish behavior towards the Nazis"	Acceptance moral solution	No significant change
5a - "Consideration of revenge and compromise"	affective-intuitive moral solution	Agreement decreased significantly
5b – "Consideration of revenge and compromise"	rational-utilitarian moral solution	No significant change
6a -"The Perception of the Holocaust as a historical event"	Universal moral solution	Agreement decreased significantly
6b -"The Perception of the Holocaust as a historical event"	Jewish-Particular moral solution	No significant change

It can be concluded that the evolution of the participants' attitudes towards Post-Holocaust era moral dilemmas demonstrates significant change only for certain dilemmas' categories. There are no prominent results for significant differences between the different stages. Therefore, it cannot be concluded that a particular stage or event during the learning process had more effect than others.

3.2.3 Moderators of change in moral attitudes

This part presents three significant results regarding the influence of moderators of change for the evolution of participants' moral attitudes through the three research stages. The potential moderators are: gender, having a family relative who was a Holocaust victim or survivor and participation in the journey to Poland. The results are presented according to the dilemmas' categories.

First, deductive statistic including repeated measures profile analysis is used to describe the mean results that illustrate the evolution of participants' attitudes. A two-way ANOVA model is used for each analysis, in which the first factor is the intervention and the second factor is the moderator. F constitutes the statistical indicator in each analysis regarding the interaction between the intervention and the moderator. A statistically significant F for the interaction means that the two comparison pairs evolved in a significantly different way from one measurement point to another. This kind of result suggested a moderation effect which was then further investigated by targeted comparisons using t-tests and the effect size indicator (d). This is followed by the presentation of the evolution of the results between T1(the beginning of the process), and T3(the end of the process), using descriptive statistical analysis, calculating difference between mean results.

I. A family relative who was a Holocaust victim or survivor as a moderator

Category 4 – *"The perception of Jewish behavior towards the Nazis"*, including the 'Like Lambs to the Slaughter dilemma', the 'Kapo dilemma', The 'Kastner dilemma' and the 'Resistance dilemma'. Moral tension exists between "Judgmental" versus "Acceptance" moral solutions. The main common characteristic of this category is the attempt to understand and evaluate the way that Jews behaved towards the Nazis from different perspectives.

Table 3.2.17: The evolution of Mean results for category 4b – *"The perception of Jewish behavior towards the Nazis"*, for the acceptance moral solution, comparison between having and not having of a Holocaust survivor or victim as a relative {Yes/No}

Time	The Moderator: Having a relative who was a Holocaust survivor or victim	N	Mean	SD
1	Yes	60	4.12	0.48
	No	38	3.87	0.62
2	Yes	60	3.83	0.76
	No	38	3.95	0.60
3	Yes	60	3.87	0.70
	No	38	3.96	0.65

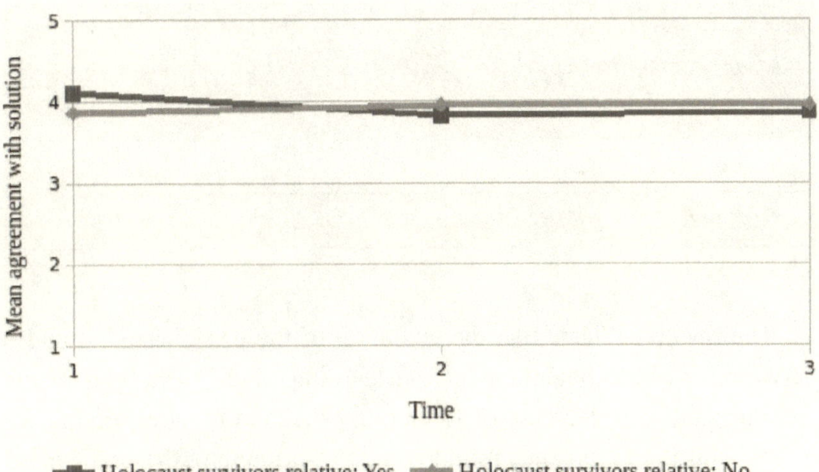

Figure 3.2.7: The evolution of Mean results for category 4b – *"The perception of Jewish behavior towards the Nazis"*, for the acceptance moral solution, comparison between having and not having Holocaust survivors as relatives

A significant interaction effect (F=3.156, p<0.05) was found between the Holocaust Learning Program and the moderator 'having or not having a relative who was a holocaust victim or survivor' in the evolution of "agreement" with the acceptance moral solution (4b). Two of the post-hoc pairwise comparisons for relatives of holocaust victims or survivors were significant: YT1-YT2 (p=0.05, Cohens` d=0.456); YT1-YT3 (p=0.054, Cohens` d=0.416). The other post-hoc pairwise comparisons were not significant. This means that agreement with the acceptance moral solution among participants who have relatives who were Holocaust survivors or victims decreased significantly over time.

Table 3.2.18: The evolution of mean results in category 4-"*Perception of Jewish behavior towards the Nazis*", the acceptance moral solution, between T1 and T3 for the moderator "Family relationship with Holocaust victims or survivors"

The Moderator: *Family relationship with Holocaust victim or survivor*	Mean T1	Mean T3	Mean T3-T1
Yes	4.12	3.87	-0.25
No	3.87	3.96	0.09

The results indicate that the evolution of the participants' attitudes between −T1 (the beginning of the learning) andT3 (the end of the learning) shows a decrease of -0.25 (3.87-4.12) in the level of "agreement" with the acceptance moral solution (4a) among the participants who had a family relative who was a Holocaust victim or survivor. For the participants who did not have such a family relative there was an increase of 0.09 (3.96-3.87) in the level of agreement with the acceptance moral solution over the same period.

II. Gender as a moderator

Category 5 - *"Consideration of revenge and compromise"*: including The 'Revengers dilemma' and the 'Restitution Payments dilemma'. Moral tension exists between "affective-intuitive" versus "rational-utilitarian" moral solutions. The main common characteristic of this category is Jewish thinking and decisions concerning the way to treat the crimes of former Nazis in the post-Holocaust era. Moral tension exists between "affective-intuitive" versus "rational-utilitarian" moral solutions.

Table 3.2.19: Mean results for category 5a - *"Consideration of revenge and compromise"*; for the affective-intuitive moral solution, comparison between male and female participants

Time	The Moderator: Gender	N	Mean	SD
1	Male	22	3.07	1.16
	Female	25	3.66	1.01
2	Male	22	2.98	1.05
	Female	25	2.72	0.94
3	Male	22	3.20	0.85
	Female	25	2.72	1.09

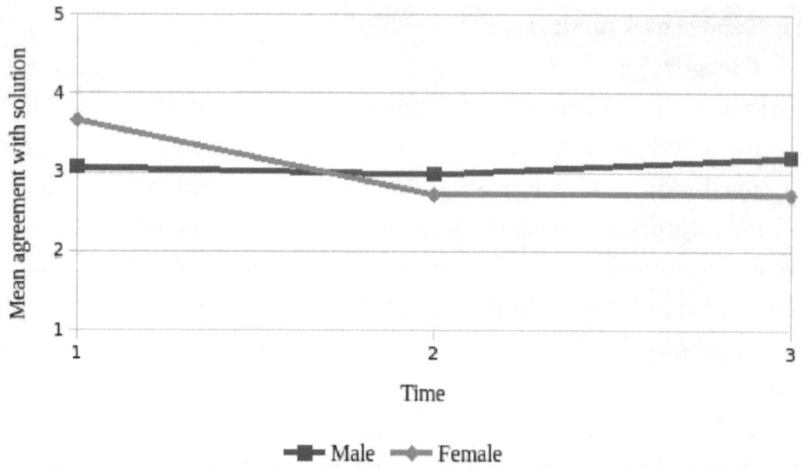

Figure 3.2.8: The evolution of mean results for category 5a- *"Consideration of revenge and compromise"*, for the affective-intuitive moral solution, comparison between male and female participants

A significant interaction effect (F=5.45, p<0.01) was found between the Holocaust Learning Program and gender in the evolution of agreement with the affective-intuitive moral solution (5a). Post-hoc pairwise comparisons yielded two significant differences in the female group: FT1-FT2 (p<0.01, Cohens` d=0.963); FT1-FT3 (p=0.01, Cohens` d=0.894). No other significant differences were found. This means that the level of agreement with the affective-intuitive moral solution among the female group decreased significantly over time and changed from "agreement" to "disagreement".

Table 3.2.20: The evolution of mean results in category *5a*-"Consideration of revenge and compromise"*, the affective-intuitive moral solution between T1 and T3 for the moderator Gender, {Male / Female}

The Moderator: Gender	Mean T1	Mean T3	Mean T3-T1
Male	3.07	3.20	0.13
Female	3.66	2.72	-0.94

The results indicate that the evolution of participants' moral attitudes between –T1 (the beginning of learning) and T3 (the end of learning) shows a decrease of -0.94 (2.72-3.66) in the females' level of agreement with the affective-intuitive moral solution (5a). For the boys there was an increase of 0.13 (3.20-3.07) in the level of agreement with the affective-intuitive moral solution over the same period. This means that the extent of agreement with the affective-intuitive moral solution among the girls decreased significantly over time and changed from "agreement" to "disagreement" while for the boys the level of agreement with the affective-intuitive moral solution increased insignificantly over the same period.

Category 6 – *"The perception of the Holocaust as a historical event":* only including the 'Comparison dilemma'. The essence of the dilemma is whether or not to compare the Jewish Holocaust to other genocides in history. Moral tension exists between "universal" versus "Jewish-particular" moral solutions.

Table 3.2.21 - Mean results for category 6a – *"The perception of the Holocaust as a historical event"*, for the Jewish particular moral solution, comparison between participant's genders

Time	The Moderator: Gender	N	Mean	SD
1	Male	12	3.08	1.08
	Female	34	4.21	1.01
2	Male	12	3.83	1.03
	Female	34	3.91	1.06
3	Male	12	3.83	0.72
	Female	34	3.91	1.16

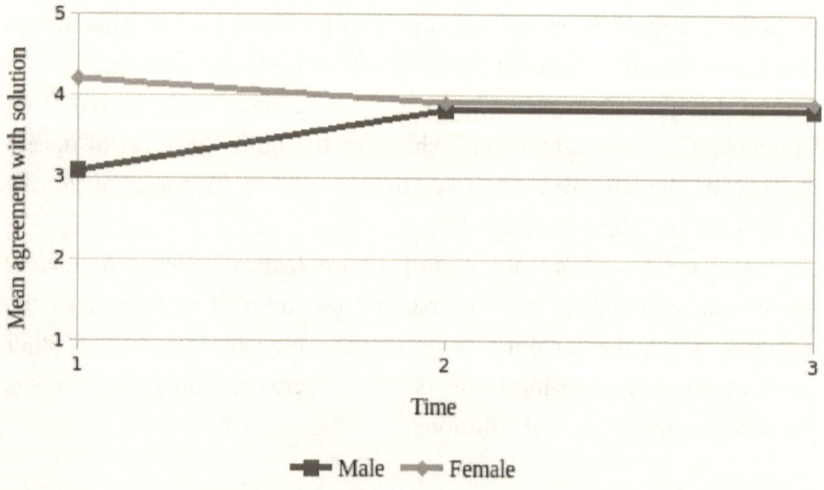

Figure 3.2.9: The evolution of mean results for category 6a- *"The perception of the Holocaust as a historical event"*; for the Jewish-particular moral solution, comparison between males and females

A significant interaction effect (F=3.223, p-0.01) was found between the Holocaust Learning Program and gender in the evolution of agreement with the Jewish-particular moral solution. However Post-hoc pairwise comparisons did not yield any significant difference: MT1-MT2 (p>0.05, Cohens`d=0.71); MT2-MT3 (p>0.05, Cohens`d=0.000); MT1-MT3 (p>0.05, Cohens`d=0.894); FT1-FT2 (p>0.05, Cohens`d=0.289); FT2-FT3 (p>0.05, Cohens`d=0.000); FT1-FT3 (p>0.05, Cohens`d=0.275). Nevertheless, Post-hoc pairwise comparisons did yield a marginally significant difference between males and females at T1: T1M-T1F (p=0.08, Cohens`d=1.08). No other pairwise comparison was significant. This means that the gap in the extent of agreement with the Jewish-particular moral solution between boys and girls became significantly smaller over time.

Table 3.2.22: The evolution of mean results in category 6*a*-" The perception of Holocaust as a historical event", the Jewish-Particular attitude, between T1 to T3 for the moderator Gender, (Male / Female)

The Moderator: Gender	Mean T1	Mean T3	Mean T3-T1
Male	3.08	3.83	0.75
Female	4.21	3.91	-0.30

The results indicate that the evolution of participants' moral attitudes between T1 (the beginning of the learning) and T3 (the end of the learning) is an increase of 0.75 (3.83-3.08) in the level of agreement with the Jewish-Particular moral solution (6a) among the boys. For the girls, there was a decrease of -0.30 (3.91-4.21) in the level of agreement with the Jewish-Particular moral solution over the same period. This means that the difference between the extent of agreement with the Jewish-particular moral solution between boys and girls became significantly smaller over time but remains "agreement".

3.2.4 The evolution of "No opinion" and "Other solutions" options

This part presents the result for the "Other solutions" and "No opinion" options.

The moral attitudes questionnaire gave respondents the possibility of writing an **"Other solution"** (alternative solution) to the extent that they did not choose one of the two predetermined given solutions (A or B). Three main types of such "other solutions" were identified during the data analysis:

- **Type 1** - Unrealistic or imaginary solutions.
- **Type 2** - Solutions that were actually explanations that the respondent gave for their choice of a predetermined given solution, A or B
- **Type 3** - Solutions that are genuinely different from solutions A or B.

"Other solutions" were written by participants at each of the research stages, but they became fewer in stage T2 relative to stage 1 (T1) and then fewer in stage 3 (T3) relative to stage 2 (T2). These solutions mainly stemmed from the participants' lack of knowledge, emotional difficulty or a desire to express a personal opinion. Most of these solutions were, in fact explanations for the choice of solution A or solution B given in the questionnaire, and so they actually reinforced the choices of these options from the participant's point of view. Because "Other solutions" were not calculated by the SPSS software, they didn't actually affect the results directly, but the decrease in the use of this option increased the choices of given solutions throughout the research.

The attitudes questionnaire also gave participants the possibility of writing an **"I have no opinion"** as an option. The "I have no opinion" option was used by participants at each of the research stages, but it was used less frequently at T2 than at to T1 and even less frequently at T3 than at T2. The following tables and figures summarize these results:

Table 3.2.23: Summary of "no opinion and "other solution" for Holocaust era dilemmas (Dilemmas 1-7)

Time	No opinion	Cumulative %	Alternative solution	Cumulative %
1	49	-	71	
2	29	-40%	52	-27%
3	17	-40%	28	-46%
T3-T1		-65%		-60%

Figure 3.2.10: The decrease in use of "no opinion and "other solutions" for Holocaust era dilemmas (Dilemmas 1-7)

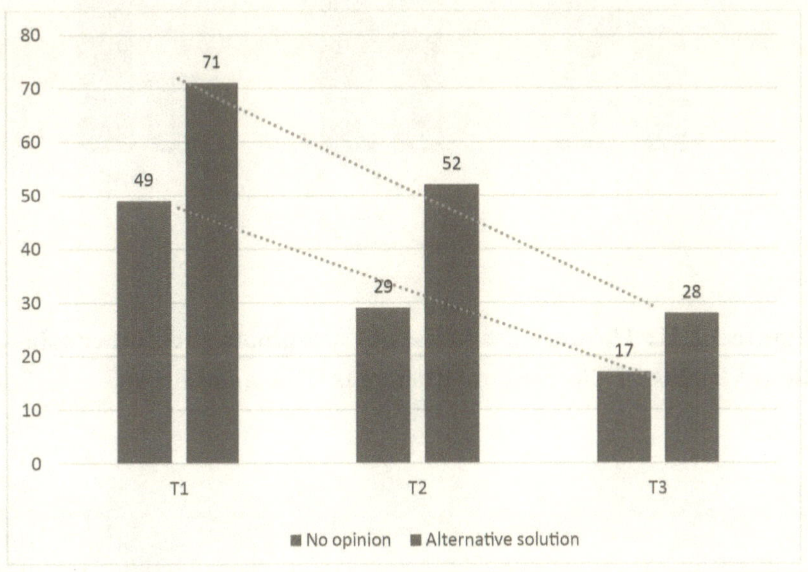

Table 3.2.24: Summary of "no opinion and "other solution" for Post-Holocaust era dilemmas (Dilemmas 8-14)

Time	No opinion	Cumulative %	Alternative solution	Cumulative %
1	40		118	
2	50	25%	70	-40%
3	26	-48%	69	-1%
T3-T1		-35%		-42%

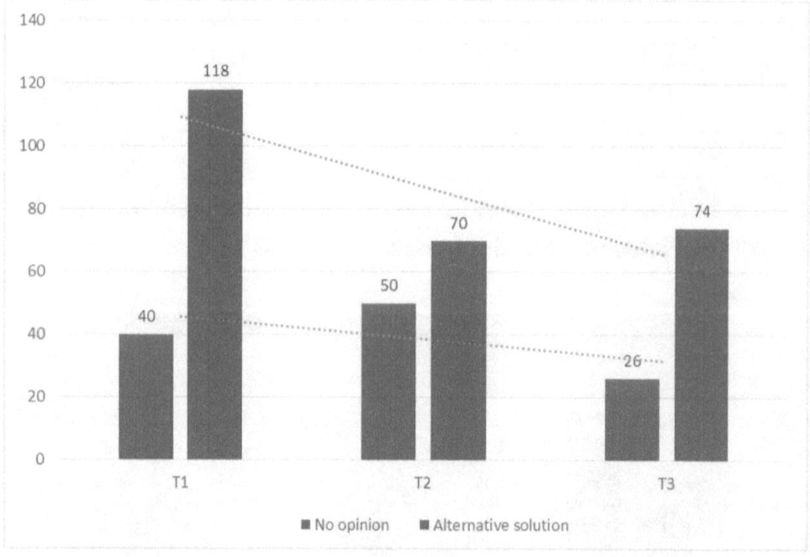

Figure 3.2.11: The decrease in use of "no opinion and "other solutions" for Post-Holocaust era dilemmas (Dilemmas 8-14)

3.2.5 Discussion and conclusions

Discussion on the evolution of Holocaust-era moral attitudes

The first research aim of this study was to test whether the Holocaust Learning Program generated changes in the participant's moral attitudes. General observation of the results indicates that the evolution of Holocaust-era moral attitudes demonstrates a non-significant increase in the level of participants' agreement with survival moral solutions and a significant decrease in the level of their agreement with deontological moral solutions in all three categories. This result leads to the two initial conclusions: **the first conclusion** is that the learning process is the main cause for this evolution.

The second conclusion is that it is easier to decrease the level of agreement with deontological moral solutions than to increase the level of agreement with survival moral solutions. However, when we look closely at the different dilemmas' categories we find differences. The described trend of increasing agreement with survival moral solutions and decreasing agreement with deontological solutions forms a hierarchy which is maintained throughout the whole learning process: it was most difficult to agree with the survival moral solution and easiest to agree with the deontological moral solutions primarily in **category 2** - the 'acute dilemmas' in which an individual decides to take personal direct action, killing another person in order to save his own life. This was less true in **category 1** –the 'collaboration dilemmas' where an individual's moral decision influences the fate of many people but less directly, and least true in **category 3** –the 'parental dilemmas' where the individual's moral decision involves the consideration of a chance to rescue his children although high risk of harm to the child is involved. The difference between the three categories can be explained by the nature of the dilemmas. As mentioned before all Holocaust era dilemmas are "harm to save" (H2S) dilemmas, where one must decide whether to hurt another person in order to save more or other lives (Koenigs et al., 2007). In this context, the dilemmas of category 2 and especially the 'Crying baby' dilemma are the most extreme and hard to cope with. The reasons are mainly the direct and immediate connection between the action and the outcome and the personal connection

between the killer and the victim. This interpretation is supported by
the findings of Gillath, McCall, Shaver and Blascovich (2008), which
indicated that dilemmas relating to physical injury and especially
killing of humans are more meaningful and arouse stronger emotional
reactions. Furthermore, an interesting process was also observed with
regard to the gap or the difference between the contradicting moral
solutions in the three categories: insofar as the level of agreement with
the survival solution is at its lowest at the beginning of the learning,
then the increase in level of agreement with this solution is highest
over time. Simultaneously insofar as the agreement with the deontological solution is highest at the beginning of the learning, then the
decrease in the level of agreement with this solution is lowest over
time.

The third conclusion is that we can arrange the three Holocaust
dilemmas' categories (1, 2 and 3) which have the same kind of moral
decision mechanism (deontological versus survival) according to the
level of difficulty and the extent of the change in the level of
agreement.

The fourth conclusion is that the acquisition of knowledge
through learning gradually changes the participant's moral attitudes. It
increases the level of agreement with survival moral solutions and
decreases the level of agreement with deontological solutions. The
reason for this evolution is that participants acquire greater cognitive
understanding and emotional acceptance of the unique reality of the
Holocaust moral dilemmas through the learning process.

At the end of this discussion we can compare the findings
regarding attitudes towards the dilemmas from the Holocaust era to
previous research of the moral dilemmas domain. As observed, traditional theories of moral development emphasize the role of controlled
cognition in mature moral judgment, while a more recent trend emphasizes intuitive and emotional processes. In the course of time a dual-
process theory synthesizing these perspectives was also developed.
This theory associates utilitarian moral judgment (approving harmful
actions that maximize good consequences) with controlled cognitive
processes and associated non-utilitarian moral judgment. The theory

suggests that cognitive load manipulation selectively interferes with utilitarian judgment. This interference provides direct evidence for the influence of controlled cognitive processes in moral judgment and more specifically in utilitarian moral judgment (Greene et al. 2007). As has been observed in reliance on this theory, in this research the initial attitudes of the participants towards Holocaust era dilemmas tended toward deontological moral solutions, which have much emotional impact (but with much deliberation). Then, over the learning process, their attitudes tended to move more towards the survival (utilitarian), more cognitive affected solutions.

The fifth conclusion therefore is that the process of learning about Holocaust moral dilemmas reinforced and strengthened the cognitive adoption of moral attitudes which justify harmful actions that maximize good in an extreme situation involving a threat to life. Based on the understanding that a moral attitude involves both emotional and cognitive components we can draw another conclusion from a wider perspective.

The sixth conclusion is that the participants' initial intuitive reaction to moral dilemmas (especially Holocaust like moral dilemmas) is mostly emotional and this reaction leads to more agreement with deontological moral solutions. However, later during the learning process, a combination of acquired knowledge on the Holocaust dilemmas, understanding of the moral conflicts involved and development of moral thinking about different solutions over a significant period of time, moderated the participants' initial emotional reactions. It`s also balancing and dipping moral thinking and eventually leading to more agreement with survival (utilitarian) moral attitudes.

Discussion on the evolution of Post-Holocaust era moral attitudes

In category 4- "the perception of Jewish behavior towards the Nazis", the results revealed an increase in the level of agreement with the 'acceptance moral solution' regarding the way that Jews behaved towards the Nazis' oppression and murderous actions during the Holocaust. Yet this trend was reduced by the great deliberation that existed in this category. One explanation for this result is the complicated structure and components of the dilemmas in this category. This interpretation is supported by Moll & de Oliveira-Sousa (2007) who claimed that insofar as the dilemma is more realistic and clearer, the examinee's ability to make a decision will increase and vice versa. In relation to this research it seems that learning process helped the participants to clarify the issues involved and make up their minds regarding the dilemmas. Another explanation relates to the emotional aspect. Guglielmo, Monroe & Molle (2009) explained that emotions have a significant if not decisive influence on thinking and especially on moral decisions concerning moral dilemmas. This explanation fits our results since the participants demonstrated serious deliberation concerning the heavily emotional nature of the dilemmas to which they were asked to react. Nevertheless, the participants demonstrated that their learning helped them to define their attitudes more clearly and this is in line with the findings of Greene (2011), who claimed that when the examinees are more emotionally involved in the dilemma their ability to make clearer moral decisions will increase, although they are more influenced by the emotional aspect. **The conclusion** is that continuous learning and deeper understanding of the dilemmas led participants to become more emotionally involved but they also acquired more understanding of the complexity and difficulty involved in making moral decisions and especially regarding moral behavior in the reality of the Holocaust. This combination of factors led the participants to greater understanding and acceptance of the way that Jewish people coped with the horror and moral challenges of the Holocaust.

In category 5- "consideration of revenge and compromise", the results indicate that there was an increase in the level of agreement with the 'rational-utilitarian moral solution' concerning the way to treat Nazi crimes after the Holocaust. This means that there was support for the normalization of relationships between the Jewish people, the State of Israel, Germany and the German people after the Holocaust, and this was accepted by the participants as the more correct moral attitude despite strong bitter feelings that still seem to exist. This attitude is of course affected by the financial and other benefits of normalization. Our results are supported by Greene & Haidt (2002), who noted that there might be a substantial difference between moral consideration and a moral decision. There are cases in which examinees will think in one direction, but make a decision in another direction. This is primarily influenced by the balance between personal utilitarian factors versus the principled moral factor. More reinforcement for this interpretation is given by the findings of Haidt & Joseph (2007). They claimed that intuition is an important factor in moral decision-making although it is possible that later, when explaining their cognitive considerations for the making of the decision, actors will not provide sufficient consideration for this element. **The conclusion is** that continuous learning and deeper understanding of the dilemmas will weaken or at least moderate the initial emotional response and then the individual will adopt more rational-utilitarian moral attitudes.

In category 6- "the perception of the Holocaust as a historical event", the results revealed an increase in the level of agreement with the 'Jewish-particular moral solution' which apprehend the Holocaust as a unique "Jewish only" event which cannot be compared to other genocides. It seems that at the beginning of the learning, the first or perhaps the intuitive attitude of the participants was to also support the 'universal moral solution' which grasps the Holocaust as one of many worldwide terrible phenomena – genocides. However later on, this approach was weakened by the effect of learning and educational emphases. This is no surprise in light of the strong tendency in Israeli society and education to think of the Holocaust as a unique "Jewish only" event that cannot be compared to anything else (Oron, 2006). This interpretation is strengthened by the claim of Haidt & Joseph (2007) that intuition is an important factor in moral decision-making, although it is possible that later, when explaining the cognitive considerations for the making of the decision, people will not provide sufficient consideration for this element. Reinforcement for this claim was presented by Aquino & Reed, (2002), who found that personal states and specific circumstances will have significant influence both on an individual's moral judgment and also on their moral decision-making. **The conclusion** is that the participants in our research changed or at least moderated their earlier support for the 'universal moral solution' and subsequently gave more support for the 'Jewish-particular moral solution', as a result of educational direction and guidance during the learning process which emphasizes this line of thinking.

Discussion on the effect of different moderators on the participants' moral attitudes

The research aim was to test whether changes in the participant's moral attitudes during their Holocaust Learning Program are moderated by different potential moderators - gender, having a relative who was a Holocaust victim or survivor and the participation in the journey to Holocaust memorial sites in Poland. It should be noted that no significant differences were found for the moderator 'participating in the journey to Poland'.

Discussion on differences regarding the moderator 'having or not having a relative who was a Holocaust victim or survivor':

The results indicate that a significant difference was only found in dilemmas' category **4** - "The Perception of Jewish behavior towards the Nazis", between the group of students who had relatives who died in or survived the Holocaust survivors relatives and those who did not have such relatives, in the evolution of their agreement with the 'acceptance moral solution'. Among the participants who had a family connection to Holocaust victims or survivors there was a significant decrease in the level of agreement with the 'acceptance moral solution', while for the participants who did not have such a family connection there was an opposite process of insignificant increase in the level of their agreement with the 'acceptance moral solution'. How can we explain this difference? Former research has emphasized the great emotional sensitivity of Holocaust victim's and survivor's relatives to anything relating to the Holocaust (Fuchs, 2009). Nevertheless, from a psycho-social and historical aspect it is now more possible for the third and fourth generations to develop new perceptions of the Holocaust and new directions of thinking (Litvak-Hirsch & Brown, 2008). A possible explanation is that although family members of Holocaust victims and survivors did embrace the 'acceptance moral attitude' at the beginning of learning and continued to hold this attitude when learning continued, they also had emotional difficulty to really except the Jews' helplessness in the face of Nazi aggression with so much understanding. This interpretation is supported by the claim of Guglielmo, Monroe & Molle (2009) that emotions have a significant, if not decisive influence on thinking and especially on moral decisions concerning moral dilemmas. Reinforcement for this view is giving by Aquino & Reed, (2002) who found that personal states and specific circumstances will have significant influence both on moral judgment and also on moral decision-making. **The conclusion** is that the initial emotional instinctive tendency among relatives of Holocaust survivors or victims, to accept the "passive" way that Jews behaved towards the Nazis, was reduced by the learning process although it still remained supportive.

Discussion on gender differences

The results revealed two cases of gender differences which will be discussed here:

1. In category 5 - *"Consideration of revenge and compromise"* a significant difference was found between boys and girls in the evolution of their level of agreement with the 'affective-intuitive moral solution'. Both boys and girls decreased the level of their agreement with the 'affective-intuitive moral solution', but while for the girls it was a significant decrease to the level of disagreement, the decrease in the boys' level of agreement was not significant. These results are in line with those of Greene et al. (2007), which indicated that women may experience stronger affective responses to harm than men, leading to systematic gender differences in deontological judgments. **The conclusion** is that girls were more affected by the cognitive aspect of learning process, were more realistic, less emotional and had less desire to support killing of Nazis as an act of revenge. At the same time boys were more affected by emotional reasoning and had more desire to support acts of revenge against Nazis.

2. In category 6 - "The perception of the Holocaust as a historic event", a significant difference was found between boys and girls in the evolution of the level of their agreement with the 'Jewish-particular moral solution'. The results indicate that there was an increase in the level of agreement with the 'Jewish-Particular moral solution' among the boys and a decrease in the level of agreement among the girls. Previous research regarding gender differences can give us some insight into these results. Researchers found that women tend to experience stronger emotional responses than men (Brody & Hall, 2000; Cross & Madson, 1997; Fischer & Manstead, 2000; Gross & John, 1998). In addition they are more easily persuaded by messages appealing to emotion (Meyer & Tormala, 2010) and score higher on measures of empathic concern (Eisenberg & Lennon, 1983). In contrast, men were found to be significantly more willing to give utilitarian answers to personal moral dilemmas than women (Fumagalli et al., 2010). These findings from previous research can give a partial explanation for our results because agreement with the 'Jewish-Particular moral solution', which highlights the horror of Holocaust and the particularly immense suffering of the Jewish people, is more emotional than rational. However, in this research there was an opposite change in attitudes which can only be explained by the learning process itself. **The conclusion** is that during the learning process boys were affected more than girls by educational messages which emphasized the 'Jewish-particular solution' and presented the Holocaust as a unique "Jewish only" historical event while girls gradually rejected some of these messages.

Discussion on the evolution of the choice of "Other solutions" and "No opinion" options

The results indicate that as the research progressed through the different stages there was a clear decrease both in the number of "Other solution" and "I have no opinion" options. The reduction of "I have no opinion" answers can be attributed to an authentic effort by the participants to cope with the dilemmas and the contribution of the learning process and maturation over time. In the dilemmas from the Holocaust era there were more participants who chose the option "I have no opinion" than in the post-Holocaust era dilemmas. This testifies to the greater strength of the dilemmas from Holocaust era and the serious difficulty that participants had to cope with them. It seems that the main reasons to write an "Other solution" were a lack of knowledge (mainly at the beginning of the learning), emotional difficulty and cognitive confusion about the justification for the different given solutions as well as a will to explain in words the moral choices they had marked in the questionnaire. **The conclusion** is that the learning process which provided more knowledge and clarified the issue of Holocaust moral dilemmas, along with maturation processes over time and participants' motivation reduced the use of both "no opinion" responses and the writing of "other solutions".

3.3 Study 3 - Perceived influences and lessons learned

Introduction

The first aim of this study was to identify whether and how social and educational factors were perceived by participants as influencing their moral attitudes. In Israel the issue of the Holocaust is an important unifying element, held in consensus by all parts of the Jewish society as part of the national ethos (Gottwein, 1998). Israelis experience the subject of the Holocaust in many ways from early childhood, especially in school (Machman, 1998). Therefore, it was natural to assume that all kinds of social and educational factors would be perceived as having an influence on participants' moral attitudes towards the Holocaust. This study questioned not only the nature of those perceived influential factors but also the hierarchy of importance between them.

The second aim of this study was to identify the moral lessons that participants perceived they had learned from the Holocaust Learning Program. This program has different goals including the "traditional" goals of helping the participants to identify with the tragedy of Holocaust and its victims (Cohen, 2010) along with newer goals relating to the learning of Jewish values and international humanistic values (Ministry of Education, General Manager's Directive, 2014). It was important to understand not only the nature of participants' moral attitudes but also what could be possible moral lessons that the Holocaust learning program would be perceived as producing. The question that arose was therefore how did participants react to such lessons and what would be the hierarchy of importance between the different lessons learned.

Method

This study presents results and discussion concerning the responses of the participants to the Perceived Influence Factors and Lessons Learned Questionnaire. The questionnaire was filled in by 102 participants in January 2016, when the participants were in the middle of Grade 12, at the end of the Holocaust Learning Program. The Perceived Influence Factors and Lessons Learned Questionnaire that they completed consisted of two parts: Part A related to different influence factors perceived by participants as having an influence on their moral attitudes towards the Jews' ways of coping with Holocaust and post-Holocaust dilemmas. Part B is related to moral lessons that they perceived they had learned during the Holocaust Learning Program. The different influences and lessons were first analyzed separately for each item and then sorted into categories according to similar characteristics, in order to create a higher level of analysis.

The perceived influences were derived from major domains in the participant's life. The perceived lessons were partly drawn from Jewish-Israeli discourse over the Holocaust and can be found in literature, newspapers, television, movies and mainly in school learning

Data analysis first used descriptive statistics to describe the distribution (in percentages) of the factors perceived by the participants as influencing their moral attitudes and also the extent of their agreement with the different lessons, by individual items. Additionally, the central tendency index (mean) and deviant tendency index (SD) are given for the responses to each of the items in this questionnaire. Secondly, comparative deductive statistics were deduced using t-tests. This was done to find significant differences between possible moderators (participant's gender, having Holocaust relatives and participation in the journey to Poland) and the way they moderated the categories of perceived influence factors that were assembled from the individual items. The same action was performed for the categories of lessons. Cohens'd size effect was calculated to measure the size effect of the significant differences.

Results

3.3.1 Perceived influences over the moral attitudes

This part presents the different influences perceived to have an effect on the participants' moral attitudes towards the Jews' way of coping with Holocaust and post-Holocaust dilemmas.

1. Analysis of particular perceived influences items:

The first step of data analysis related to particular perceived influences items, shown in Table 3.3.1:

Table 3.3.1: Influences perceived to have an effect on participants' moral attitudes, by particular items

The Factor	No influence 1	Slight influence 2	Medium influence 3	Strong influence 4	strongest influence 5	%	N	Mean	SD
1. Learning for Matriculation in Holocaust Studies	10.78%	6.86%	29.41%	39.22%	13.73%	100	102	3.38	1.14
2. Prior knowledge and experiences until Grade 11	3.92%	16.67%	37.25%	30.39%	11.76%	100	102	3.29	1.01
3. Nuclear Family	11.76%	16.67%	27.45%	28.43%	15.69%	100	102	3.20	1.24
4. Participation in this research	21.57%	24.51%	31.37%	13.73%	8.82%	100	102	2.64	1.22
5. Close friends	24.51%	23.53%	34.31%	11.76%	5.88%	100	102	2.51	1.16

The results indicated that the first influence factor, most perceived by the participants to have an effect on their moral attitudes was learning for the matriculation in Holocaust studies, the second was prior knowledge and experiences until Grade 11, third was the nuclear family, fourth was participation in the research while fifth and last was the participants' close friends.

2. Analysis of perceived influences categories

The second step of data analysis was to sort the different perceived influences into the following two categories:

A. Perceived educational-learning influences, including - learning for Matriculation in Holocaust Studies and participation in this research.

B. Perceived socio-cultural influences, including - prior knowledge and experiences until Grade 11, the nuclear family and the participants' close friends.

Table 3.3.2: Results of perceived influences categories (2 = slight influence, 3 = medium influence, 4 = strong influence)

Categories of perceived influences	N	Mean	SD	Paired Samples t-test (df)
A. Educational-learning influences	102	**3.01**	.07	0.09 (101) n.s.
B. Socio-cultural influences	102	**3.00**	.08	

n.s. - non-significant p>0.005

*There were no significant differences between the two categories.

3. Gender, the journey to Poland and family relation to Holocaust victims or survivors as moderators of perceived influences categories

The third step of data analysis was to look for significant differences between gender, participation in the journey to Poland and having or not having family relatives who were Holocaust victims or survivors, as moderators of perceived influences categories. First Table 3.3.3 presents the perceived socio-cultural influences and then the perceived educational-learning influences.

Table 3.3.3: Results for measurement of perceived socio-cultural influences as a function of the moderators

Moderators	Section	N	Mean	SD	t-test value (df)
1. Participant gender	Male	36	3.05	.75	t=0.45
	Female	66	2.97	.78	(100)
2. Whether the participant has Holocaust family relatives	Yes	61	3.14	.71	t=2.18*
	No	40	2.81	.82	(99)
3. Whether the participant took part in the journey to Poland	Yes	71	2.93	.77	t=-1.31
	No	31	3.15	.76	(100)

*significant differences were found in these parameters p<0.05

The results indicate that there were significant differences in the perceptions of socio-cultural factors that influenced their moral attitudes between participants who had relatives who were Holocaust victims or survivors and participants who did not have such relatives: mean = 3.14 for those who had such relatives in comparison to 2.81 for those who did not have such relatives (t=2.18, p<0.05). Cohens'd size effect between the mean results is 0.430 (medium effect). The meaning of these results is that if you have a relative, who was a Holocaust victim or survivor your moral attitudes will be more influenced by socio-cultural factors.

Table 3.3.4: Results for measurement of perceived educational-learning influences as a function of the moderators

Moderators	Section	N	Mean	SD	t-test value (df)
1. Participant gender	Male	36	3.28	.69	t=-1.28
	Female	66	3.47	.73	(100)
2. Whether the participant has Holocaust family relatives	Yes	61	3.29	.69	t=-2.07*
	No	40	2.58	.73	(99)
3. Whether participant took part in the journey to Poland	Yes	71	3.42	.67	t=0.37
	No	31	3.36	.82	(100)

*significant differences were found in these parameters p<0.05

In relation to the participants' perceptions of the educational-learning influence factors that affected their moral attitudes, the results indicate that there were significant differences between participants who had a relative who was a Holocaust victim or survivor and those who did not have such a relative: mean = 3.29 for those who had such a relative in comparison to 2.58 for those who did not have such a relative (t=-2.07, p<0.05). Cohens'd size effect between the mean results is 0.999 (large effect). The meaning of these results is that if you have Holocaust family relatives your moral attitudes will be more influenced by educational-learning factors.

3.3.2 Perceived moral lessons derived from Holocaust learning

This part presents different perceived moral lessons deriving from Holocaust learning.

1. Analysis of moral lessons items

The first step of data analysis related to participants' perceptions of particular moral lessons learned from the program, shown in Table 3.3.5:

Table 3.3.5- Extent of agreement with the different perceived lessons

The Lesson	No agreement 1	Slight agreement 2	Medium agreement 3	Strong agreement 4	Strongest agreement 5	%	N	Mean	SD
1. It`s important to learn about Holocaust moral dilemmas		1.96%	4.90%	31.37%	61.76%	100	102	**4.53**	.69
2. The strong must avoid harming the weak	1.96%	3.92%	11.76%	47.06%	35.29%	100	102	**4.10**	.90
3. If we lose our morals we may become like the Nazis	9.80%	19.61%	17.65%	28.43%	24.51%	100	102	**3.38**	1.31
4. Moral dilemmas are not relevant in war situations	20.59%	30.39%	34.31%	13.73%	.98%	100	102	**2.44**	1.00
5. Since the Nazis harmed us, we can harm others	59.80%	30.39%	7.84%	1.96%		100	102	**1.52**	.73

The results indicate that the highest level of agreement was with the lesson "it is important to learn about the moral dilemmas of the Holocaust", the second was "the strong must avoid harming the weak" and the third was "if we lose our morals we may become like the Nazis". The lowest level of agreement ("slight agreement") was with the lesson "moral dilemmas are not relevant in war situations". The lesson "since the Nazis harmed us, we can harm others" was not awarded any agreement.

2. Analysis of lessons categories

The second step of data analysis was to sort the different lessons into the two following categories:

A. Perceived Humanist-liberal moral lessons, including – "it is important to learn about Holocaust moral dilemmas", "the strong must avoid harming the weak" and "if we lose our morals we may become like the Nazis".

B. Perceived Nationalist-utilitarian moral Lessons, including – "moral dilemmas are not relevant in war situations" and "since the Nazis harmed us, we can harm others".

Table 3.3.6- Results for lessons categories (2 = slight agreement, 3 = medium agreement, 4 = strong agreement)

Categories of Lessons	N	Mean	SD	Paired Samples t-test (df)
A. Humanist-Liberal moral lessons	102	**4.00**	.06	
B. Nationalist-Utilitarian moral lessons	102	**1.98**	.07	-18.36** (101)

**significant differences p<0.01

The results indicate that the extent of agreement with the Humanist-Liberal moral lessons (Mean = 4.00), was significantly higher in comparison with the extent of agreement with the Nationalist-Utilitarian moral Lessons (Mean=1.98); (t=-18.36, p<0.01). Cohens'd size effect between mean results for **A-** Humanist-Liberal moral Lessons category and **B-** Nationalist- Utilitarian moral Lessons category is 30.985 (very large size effect).

3. Gender, the journey to Poland and having a family relative, who was a Holocaust victim or survivor as moderators of the perceived lessons categories

The third step of data analysis was to look for significant differences between gender, participation in the journey to Poland and having relatives who were Holocaust victims or survivors as moderators of perceived lessons categories. We shall now present the results of this investigation first for the nationalist-utilitarian moral lessons category and then for the humanist-liberal moral lessons category.

Table 3.3.7; Measurement of the difference between perceived nationalist-utilitarian moral lessons as a function of the moderators

Moderators	Section	N	Mean	SD	t-test value (df)
1. Participant gender	Male	36	2.25	.78	t=2.91**
	Female	66	1.83	.64	(100)
2. Whether the participant has relatives who were Holocaust victims or survivors	Yes	61	1.91	.69	t=-0.98
	No	40	2.05	.72	(99)
3. Whether the participant took part in the journey to Poland	Yes	71	1.89	.67	t=-1.86
	No	31	2.18	.80	(100)

****significant differences were found in these parameters p<0.01**

Significant differences were found between males and females in relation to the extent of agreement with nationalist-utilitarian lessons categories. Males expressed a significantly higher extent of agreement than the females: mean=2.25 among the males in comparison to 1.83 among the females (t=2.91, p<0.01). Cohens'd size effect between mean results of the moderator "participant's gender" for nationalist-utilitarian moral lessons category is 0.588 (medium size effect). The meaning of these results is that if you are a male than you will be more likely to support nationalist- utilitarian lessons.

No significant differences were found in the extent of the agreement by the participants with humanist-liberal moral lessons.

.   .   .

3.3.3 Discussion and conclusions

Discussion on the results regarding the perceived influences:

The research aim was to identify whether and how social and educational factors are perceived by participants as influencing their moral attitudes. The first results indicated that educational-learning and socio-cultural influences were perceived as having almost the same influence on the participants' moral attitudes. This demonstrates the influence of education and learning together with the influence of culture and society on the formation of moral attitudes regarding Holocaust moral dilemmas. The second result was that participants who had relatives, who were Holocaust victims or survivors were found to be more influenced by both socio-cultural and educational-learning influences on their moral attitudes in comparison with the participants who did not have such relatives. It seems that family proximity to the Holocaust creates both intellectual curiosity and emotional involvement. This explanation is supported by Litvak-Hirsch & Brown (2008) who found that there is a strong inter-generation sensitivity towards the Holocaust among the descendants of those who endured the Holocaust. **The conclusion** is that we were able to identify the continued inter-generational transfer among our participants, who were third and fourth generation after the Holocaust, and this transfer was most meaningful in shaping their moral attitudes regarding Jewish moral dilemmas during and after the Holocaust.

Discussion on the results of the perceived lessons

The research aim was to identify the perceived moral lessons that emerged from the Holocaust Learning Program. The results reveal that the extent of agreement with humanist-liberal moral lessons was much higher in comparison with the extent of agreement with national-utilitarian moral lessons. These results can be explained in three ways: The first explanation is that the latest criticism of the journeys to Poland, which claims that they emphasize national values and ignore universal values (Maltz 2016; Starkman & Dattel, 2016) is not so accurate or not so meaningful. The second explanation is that universal and humanistic values are adopted by Jewish-Israeli high-school students or at least those who participated in this research. This explanation is supported by Gutman, (1990a) and Machman (1998) who emphasized the socio-cultural-educational adherence of Jewish people to a tradition of universal moral values and a lifestyle of cohesion, mutual assistance and backing in times of prosperity and of distress. The third explanation is that participation in the research has a significant impact. This interpretation relies on the fact that the lesson "it`s important to learn about holocaust moral dilemmas" was awarded the highest amount of agreement in the part of the questionnaire relating to the lessons learned.

The conclusion is that the prefer adoption among the participants of humanist-liberal lessons stemmed from Holocaust learning; is an evidence for the effect of moral education on moral judgment. Another interesting result is that significant differences were found between boys and girls in relation to the extent of agreement with nationalist-utilitarian lessons. Boys expressed a significantly higher extent of agreement than the girls with these lessons. These results are supported first by Aleman & Swart (2008) who found gender specificities in moral development and behavior. More specific support is provided by the findings of Friesdorf, Gawronski & Conway (2014), who suggested that men showed a stronger preference for utilitarian over deontological judgments than women in deciding between conflicting moral decisions. This conclusion was also based on previous research performed by Conway & Gawronski (2013) who found that the use of a deontological moral approach as the cause of an action depends on its consistency with moral norms while the utilitarian moral approach implies that the morality of an action depends on its consequences. Boys and girls who participated in this research learned the same things and had the same experiences but nevertheless, they differ in their level of agreement with nationalist-utilitarian lessons.

The second conclusion is that because of psychological gender differences it is more likely that boys will demonstrate more support for nationalist-utilitarian lessons. This natural tendency seems to be supported by perceived implications of present consideration in the reality of living in Israel which is involved in continuous military conflict with some of her neighboring countries.

Until now this sub-chapter presented and discussed the perceived influences and lessons learned by participants. In study 4 we shall attempt to discover possible correlations between the participant's moral attitudes at the end of their Holocaust Learning Program and the moral lessons that they perceived that they learned during this time.

3.4 Study 4 –Associations between moral attitudes and moral lessons

Introduction In study 1- the initial moral attitudes of the participants were identified and in study 2 we examined the evolution of these attitudes over the Holocaust Learning Program. Then in study 3, moral lessons that were perceived as emerging from this learning were identified. Now a further question is posed: are there correlations between moral attitudes and perceived moral lessons? In this study, we try to answer this question. Therefore, the research aim of this study is to examine whether specific moral attitudes associated with specific lessons perceived to have been acquired from the Holocaust Learning Program. This aim is an innovating attempt to look for these kinds of correlations. The study is divided into two parts: the first part presents the correlations found between Holocaust era dilemmas categories and the lessons categories. The second part presents the correlations found between the Post-Holocaust era dilemmas categories and the lessons categories.

Method

The study was conducted at the end of the research after all the data were collected from the three Moral Attitudes Questionnaires and the Lessons Questionnaire completed by the 102 research participants. The statistical data analysis was performed with a correlation matrix using "Pearson" coefficients in order to examine possible linear connections (correlations) between the mean results for Holocaust and Post-Holocaust dilemmas categories and lessons categories. The two different moral solutions for each moral attitude category were correlated with the Humanist-liberal moral lessons category and with the Nationalist-utilitarian moral lessons category.

Results

3.4.1 Correlations between Holocaust moral attitudes and moral lessons

Table 3.4.1: Correlations between Holocaust moral attitudes and moral lessons

	Dilemmas and Lessons	1	2	3	4	5	6	7	8
1	**Category 1a-** "The collaboration dilemmas", survival moral solution								
2	**Category 1b-** " The collaboration dilemmas", deontological moral solution	-.14							
3	**Category 2a-** "The acute dilemmas", survival moral solution	.41**	.14						
4	**Category 2b-** "The acute dilemmas", deontological moral solution	-.08	.16	-.50**					
5	**Category 3a-** "The parental dilemmas", survival moral solution	.45**	-.27*	.26*	-.23*				
6	**Category 3b-** "The parental dilemmas", deontological moral solution	-.14	.51**	-.12	.44**	-.36**			
7	**Nationalist- Utilitarian** Lessons	-.03	-.12	-.09	-.02	.002	-.08		
8	**Humanist-Liberal** Lessons	.33**	-.05	.35**	-.03	.28**	-.04	-.34**	

**p<0.01 *p<0.05

The results indicate that:

In category 1a: "The collaboration dilemmas": a medium positive significant linear correlation was found between the results for the survival moral solution and the results for the Humanist-Liberal moral lessons (r=0.33, p<0.01). This means that if the extent of agreement with the survival moral solution is higher, then the extent of agreement with Humanist-Liberal moral lessons will also be higher.

In Category 2a: "The acute dilemmas": a medium positive significant linear correlation was found between the results for the survival moral solution and results for the Humanist-Liberal moral lessons (R=0.35, p<0.01). This means that if the extent of agreement with the survival moral solution is higher, then the extent of agreement with Humanist-Liberal moral lessons will also be higher.

In Category 3a: "The parental dilemmas": a medium positive significant linear correlation was found between the results for the survival moral solution and the results for the Humanist-Liberal moral lessons (R=0.28, p<0.01). This means that if the extent of agreement with the survival moral solution is higher, the extent of agreement with Humanist-Liberal moral lessons will also be higher.

No significant linear correlations were found between Holocaust moral dilemmas categories and Nationalist-utilitarian lessons, for either one of the moral solutions.

3.4.2 Correlations between Post-Holocaust moral attitudes and moral lessons

Table 3.4.2: Correlations between Post- Holocaust moral attitudes and moral lessons

	Dilemmas and Lessons	1	2	3	4	5	6	7
1	**Category 4a:** The perception of Jewish behavior towards the Nazis, judgmental moral solution							
2	**Category 4b:** The perception of Jewish behavior towards the Nazis, acceptance moral solution	-.03						
3	**Category 5a:** Consideration of revenge and compromise, affective-intuitive moral solution	.14	-.13					
4	**Category 5b:** Consideration of revenge and compromise, rational-utilitarian moral solution	.01	.33**	-.31*				
5	**Category 6a:** The perception of the Holocaust as a historical event, universal moral solution	.03	.05	-.03	.34**			
6	**Category 6b:** The perception of the Holocaust as a historical event, Jewish-particular moral solution	.162	1.00	.37**	-.06	-.80**		
7	**Humanist-Liberal** Lessons	-.16	.35**	-.16	.21*	.26*	-.02	
8	**Nationalist- Utilitarian** Lessons	.22*	-.16	.32**	-.06	-.07	-.08	-.34**

**p<0.01 *p<0.05

The results indicate that:

In Category 4a: "The perception of Jewish behavior towards the Nazis": a medium positive significant linear connection (correlation) was found between the results for the judgmental moral solution and the results for the nationalist-utilitarian moral lessons ($r=0.22$, $p<0.05$). This means that if the extent of agreement with the judgmental moral solution is higher, then the extent of agreement with nationalist-utilitarian moral lessons will also be higher.

In Category 4b: "The perception of Jewish behavior towards the Nazis": a medium positive significant linear correlation was found between the results for the moral acceptance solution, and the results for the humanist-liberal moral lessons ($R=0.35$, $p<0.01$). This means that if the extent of agreement with the acceptance moral solution is higher, then the extent of agreement with humanist-liberal moral lessons will also be higher.

In category 5a: "Consideration of revenge and compromise": a medium positive significant linear correlation was found between the results for the affective-intuitive moral solution and the results for the nationalist-utilitarian moral lessons ($R=0.32$, $p<0.01$). This means that if the extent of agreement with the affective-intuitive moral is higher, then the extent of agreement with nationalist-utilitarian moral lessons will also be higher.

In category 5b: "Consideration of revenge and compromise": a positive medium significant linear correlation was found between the results for the rational-utilitarian moral solution and the results for the humanist-liberal moral lessons ($R=0.21$, $p<0.05$). This means that if the extent of agreement with the rational-utilitarian moral solution is higher, then the extent of agreement with humanist-liberal moral lessons will also be higher.

In category 6a: "The Perception of the Holocaust as a historical event": a positive medium significant linear correlation was found between the results for the universal moral solution and the results for the humanist-liberal moral lessons ($R=0.26$, $p<0.05$). This means that if the extent of agreement with the universal moral attitude is higher, then the extent of agreement with humanist-liberal moral lessons will also be higher.

3.4.3 Discussion and conclusions

This discussion relates to research aim 6 - to examine whether moral attitudes are associated with perceived moral lessons from Holocaust Learning Program. The results revealed that a significant linear connection (correlation) was found between participants' moral attitudes regarding all six Holocaust and post-Holocaust dilemma categories and at least one of the two lessons categories as will be discussed below.

Previous research has already recognized possible connections between Holocaust learning and different messages, which may have an impact on learners' deduction of conclusions and the lessons that they learn. Gurani (2015) noted that Holocaust learning and especially the journeys to Poland deliver different messages, mainly from two different angles: 1. the universal message of the Holocaust, which sees the Holocaust as parallel to other cases of genocide. 2. The Jewish-national message of the Holocaust that sees the Holocaust as a unique event for the Jewish people and refuses to assign the term "holocaust" to other cases of genocide. If we replace the term "message" with the term "conclusion" or "lesson" we can surmise two possible different outcomes of Holocaust learning: one negative and the other positive. An example of a negative outcome can be found in the findings presented by Davidovich & Hazan (2011), which indicated that the journey to Poland increased negative consideration of the Poles among most of the students who saw Poles as anti-Semites and collaborators with the Nazis during the persecution of the Jews in the Holocaust. Another example of a negative outcome is from the research conducted by Kimchi (2011), who found that the journey to Poland led participants to strengthen their Israeli identity and have greater identification with Zionist values but also radicalized their feelings towards Arabs as a group endangering the security of Israel. On the other hand, a more positive outcome was found by Ganor, (2006) who investigated the Israeli Defense Forces (IDF) journeys to Poland and found that they influenced the soldier's code of ethics by reinforcing humanist values.

Thus too, Davidovich, Amir and Heskel (2011) who also investigated the IDF journeys to Poland found that universal values were strengthened among the soldiers who participated in the journeys.

It appears that drawing conclusions or lessons from Holocaust learning depends to a large extent on the different emphases of the learning program. In this research, participants were exposed to different messages and emphases according to the goals of Holocaust learning program and according to specific emphases given by teachers and the professional tour guides during the journey. In addition, they were exposed to Holocaust moral dilemmas and acquired different moral lessons from the Holocaust as a result of their participation in this research. When we look at the research results regarding the correlations between Holocaust era moral attitudes and the perceived moral lessons we find that agreement with the survival moral solution led in all the three categories to agreement with Humanist-Liberal moral lessons.

The conclusion is that Holocaust learning including exposure to Holocaust moral dilemmas reinforced moral thinking and understanding of human difficulties and needs. When we look at the correlations between Post-Holocaust era moral attitudes and the perceived moral lessons **the conclusion** is that: Insofar as the moral attitude is more critical than the lessons learned will be more extreme. Insofar as the moral attitude is more merciful then the lessons learned will be less radical. Insofar as the moral attitude is more open-minded and flexible, than the lessons learned give more consideration to other people's needs and universal values.

Following those conclusions, we can surmise that learning, understanding and evaluation of Holocaust moral dilemmas increases the probability that students will learn universal lessons such as the need for understanding, closeness and friendship with other people. This insight can strengthen support for the approach that universal lessons can be learned from the Holocaust.

3.5 Study 5 –The experiences of Holocaust learning

Introduction The main aim of this study was to understand the meanings constructed through the participants' narratives regarding their personal experiences of Holocaust Learning Program. Beyond numbers and facts, it is very important to understand the participant's world, the way they felt and their thinking during this learning process. These narratives can offer new insights to the discussion on the educational relevance and power of the Holocaust Learning Program and also the journey to Poland in relation to the development of Holocaust moral attitudes, and moral lessons that can be derived from the program. Examination of the participants' narratives will hopefully give us a deeper understanding of the cognitive and emotional meanings attributed by the participants to different parts of their learning. Specific aims are to answer further questions: What are the participant's experiences from their participation in Holocaust learning program? What did participants learn from these experiences? What are the moral meanings that participants derived from their Holocaust learning?

Method

An individual interview is a very good tool for the study of people's emotions and the meanings they attribute to their experiences (Sabar Ben Yehoshua, 2002; Morgan, 1988; Braun & Clarke 2006). This was the reason why individual in-depth interviews were used in order to gather evidence for this part of the research. Thirteen participants (out of a total of 102 participants in the research) volunteered to take part in individual in-depth interviews conducted during the last phase of the study in January 2016. Four of the interviewees were boys: Boaz, Elad, Asaf and Ronen (all names given are fictive to protect interviewees' confidentiality). Nine of the interviewees were girls - Yonat, Pazit, Noa, Lily, Rachel, Miriam, Sarah, Aia and Dina. Elad, Asaf and Sarah did not participate in the journey to Poland. Ronen, Boaz, Aia, Miriam and Lily do not have family relatives, who are Holocaust victims or survivors. The other interviewees did have such connection, usually a grandmother or grandfather, who was still alive, and they heard about their experiences in the Holocaust at different levels of scope and detail. They are actually members of the third or fourth generation in Holocaust survivors' families. Interviewees were asked questions that touched upon their family connection to the Holocaust, the decision to participate or not to participate in the journey to Poland, their learning experiences regarding the journey, their views towards the moral dilemmas faced by Jews during and after the Holocaust, the moral lessons they learned and they were asked to describe their experience of participation in the study itself.

The interviewee's main characteristics are presented in Appendix 4. The individual in-depth interviews were recorded, transcribed, coded and organized according to themes and sub-themes using thematic analysis (Braun & Clarke 2006). Thematic analysis was chosen in order to reinforce the validity of the data and provide rich and deep information. Additional reasons for choosing thematic analysis as an analytic tool in the qualitative part of this research are that it offers an accessible, efficient and theoretically flexible tool for analyzing qualitative data. It is actually a qualitative analytic method that identifies themes or mutual patterns in qualitative research data (Kassan & Kromer-Nevo, 2010; Shkedi, 2003; Gibton, 2002; Braun & Clarke 2006). Thematic analysis of the results revealed 4 main themes:

- The personal connection with Holocaust.
- The deliberation regarding the decision to join the journey to Poland.
- The experiences gained from the journey to Poland.
- Coping with Holocaust moral dilemmas through learning.

These themes are presented and discussed below.

3.5.1 Exploring the different experiences

The personal connection with Holocaust

Jewish people all around the world and mainly in Israel have memories of experiences from early childhood regarding the Holocaust through stories they heard, ceremonies in which they participated, films they watched etc.. These experiences are stronger when they have family relatives, who were Holocaust victims or survivors. This direct encounter (or indirect through photographs etc) with family members who witnessed the Holocaust creates strong emotions together with the arousal of a need for more information in order to satisfy curiosity.

"I have Holocaust survivors in my family and I think that the encounter with them helped me to understand what they went through and all sorts of things that I would otherwise have been unable to grasp. I am very interested in the Holocaust, I have been thinking about this all year. On Holocaust Memorial Day' my feelings are very strong so I even sometimes need to close myself in my room and try to repress it" (Yonat).

Elad spoke about the way that he tried to find information about the Holocaust in his family:

"In our family we talk a lot about the Holocaust and also about moral dilemmas. We especially talk about "Kastner" because my grandfather was on "Kastner's train" [a train that rescued Jews from Budapest organized by Israel Kastner in July 1944] *"My grandfather is a Holocaust survivor, what he told me about the Holocaust moved me and influenced me a lot"* (Elad).

Pazit gathered information from her father (second generation son of Holocaust survivors):

"My father told me about my grandparents who fought against the Nazis. One of them was awarded medals. Another grandfather was a forced laborer in Warsaw and evacuated the ruins of the "ghetto". All these stories influenced and makes the Holocaust a major field of interest for me" (Pazit).

However, a strong interest in the Holocaust was not exclusive to those who had a relative who was a Holocaust survivor and curiosity about the Holocaust can also be satisfied by auto-didactic learning. An example of such interest was expressed by *Lily* who does not have relatives who went through the Holocaust:

"The Holocaust always fascinated me and I've spent much time thinking about it; I even wrote a story but it is very personal so I don't want to talk about it" (Lily).

Boaz who also does not have Holocaust survivors in his family gave another explanation:

"I read so much about the Holocaust and watched many films…The actions of 'Mengele' [the SS doctor in Auschwitz-Birkenau camp who conducted medical experiments especially on Jewish children] *really shocked me and stressed me at a very difficult level; I also had dreams about the Holocaust, as if I was in the Holocaust and the Nazis were coming to our home"* (Boaz).

Although the mixed emotional - cognitive wish to know what happened in the Holocaust, especially to people that you know is very strong, talking with Holocaust family survivors can be very difficult, as expressed by some interviewees:

"My grandfather is a Holocaust survivor, he is still alive; I know bits of his story, it was difficult to see, hear, understand; I want to talk more with him; he is 92; to my regret and sorrow time marches on; I have to take myself in hand before it is too late" (Aia).

"My grandfather hid in a barn and then in a cave; he was a child aged ten; I read the whole story for my schoolwork on my roots but I don't really remember it in details" (Noa).

"My grandfather is a survivor; there was a meeting of the survivors from his home town; I spoke about it with my father; grandpa doesn't talk much about it; I presume that if I am determined I could talk to him; I really need to know more; I spoke with my father and there are family members who apparently did not survive; they were not together; I had better ask and then it will be clearer to me" (Asaf).

"My grandfather and grandmother are Holocaust survivors…I always wanted to ask them more but I couldn't because I felt their difficulty to talk about it" (Yonat).

It can be concluded that the words of the interviewees reflect a strong interest in the Holocaust followed by a continuous search for more information held by grandparents and parents. This search is emotionally restrained by the mutual difficulty that survivors and their descendants seem to have to touch upon the sensitive issue of the Holocaust.

The deliberation regarding the decision to join the journey to Poland

Israeli high school students undergo serious deliberation regarding their decision whether or not to take part in the journey to Poland (Bondi, 2014). Interviewees referred to their reasons in favor and against this decision. First, they described the different reasons for the decision not to go for the journey. *Elad* spoke about his family's opposition to his participation in the journey, arguing that he was not yet mature enough:

"My father thinks that at my age and in this framework, it is not suitable; I don't know if on a school trip it's possible to achieve the significant experience that is anticipated on a journey to Poland; a school trip includes friends, fun, silliness ... I don't know if this combination is appropriate; my parents are afraid because of our young age and inappropriate behavior that can happen in Poland" (Elad).

Asaf raised another issue - The financial difficulty involved for parents who need to fund the journey:

"It simply costs a lot of money for my parents; it's not worth the cost; you can learn about the Holocaust in Israel too" (Asaf).

While the above consideration can be described as "parental" considerations, other reasons relate to more personal considerations.

Lily: "Some of my friends didn't want to join the journey simply because it is not important enough to them, they do not care so much about the Holocaust or because they didn't wants to make the necessary effort for the journey...they preferred to do other things" (Lily).

Sara pointed up another reason:

"There are students who fear the journey... they are afraid it will arouse emotional difficulties and therefore they didn't go although they are too embarrassed to admit it" (Sara).

As described above, the participants voiced a combination of parental but also personal reasons for their decisions not to participate in the journey to Poland. The following are the reasons that they gave in favor of their participation in the journey. *Boaz* emphasized his family's support for the journey:

"My parents really supported my decision to go for the journey, especially my mother, they said: 'the rewards are justifying the

expense; it's worth the money investment, it's important" (Boaz). *Aia* added:

"It is our family tradition; it's the wish of family members who are survivors; all the grandchildren and all my brothers and sisters have flown there. It's also very important for me to go there; I know it's so important for my grandmother; it's something that I want to experience myself; Grandfather explained it accurately – in which camp, in which block and in which bunk" (Aia).

Rachel emphasized her combined intellectual-emotional deep curiosity – the desire to see everything directly:

"I want so much to see everything with my own eyes, I think it's actually impossible to really understand without seeing; I truly need to touch things" (Rachel).

School tradition and peer pressure played an important role in the decision to travel to Poland, as *Ronen* mentioned:

"Most of the students in our school are going and all my friends for sure; those who didn't go were sorry and had a feeling that they missed something; I believe that it's an experience that one must have and it makes one more mature; it's also benefit for our class team building" (Ronen).

Miriam expressed another thought:

"I don't sure if I'll manage to do such a journey in the future; I assume it will be much more difficult" (Miriam).

Another reason in favor of the journey was the recognition of its historical-national contribution as *Lily* stated:

"It's the history of the Jewish people; these are events that must be remembered so that something like that won't ever happen again; it's something that has to be done by every Jew; I feel it's my moral obligation" (Lily).

For other students, it was difficult to explain inner sense of need to go on the journey, as *Yonat* said:

"At the beginning, I could not decide but then at some stage I suddenly felt that I simply should; I didn`t really knew what we would do there, but I have a strong feeling that it is important" (Yonat).

Sara said:

"I still don't completely understand why it was so important but it really is! Something in my soul told me that I must go... Unfortunately at the end I didn`t go because my father died only a few weeks before the journey" [crying] *I wanted but I just felt that I couldn't handle both things" (Sara).*

As noted the deliberation regarding whether or not to participate in the journey to Poland occupies both parents and students minds.

The experiences of the journey to Poland

Analysis of the results identified two main experiences - Cognitive experience and Emotional experience. In the interviews, participants reported both these types of experiences as they emerged during the journey to Poland.

Miriam explained her experience as a significant learning:

"It was a challenging, difficult and so very busy week [the journey]; *the guides were really good and made it less emotional so that we would really learn and understand what happened there. I did not cry during the journey, it did not affect my emotions; it did make me think and understand"; during the journey everything came together for me and I really saw what had happened and that seriously changed my thinking when I saw everything with my own eyes* (Miriam).

Aia agreed:

"In Poland I learnt a lot more than I learnt in Israel, I saw things visually and what had happened there; I think that there was something important in seeing it all; when you are there you can more clearly imagine how it all was then" (Aia).

On the other hand, some the interviewees had a different experience of not so significant learning. An example of this feeling was expressed by *Noa*:

"I did not really connect with the journey; it did not feel as though it was actually true and it was not possible to absorb things ...it was important but there was nothing very influential that would alter my moral attitudes for example".

Ronen felt much the same:

"In Poland you don`t see so much because so little actually

remains…I expected a lot more, so in a way I was disappointed…it was interesting but not so different from things I already knew" (Ronen).

It can be concluded that the cognitive experiences were a mixture of both significant and less significant learning as was expressed above.

After discussing the cognitive experiences we move to the emotional experiences which emerged from the interviewees' stories. Some of the interviewees reported sadness aroused by the sights and experiences in Poland relating to both concrete and symbolic actions:

"In the Lupochova forest Near the execution ditches it was very cold … when we marched into the forest there was no chirping of birds … there was a ceremony near the ditches … everyone hugged each other and some cried …we lit candles … suddenly we all understood … there was a group of young religious girls that went ahead of us, they sang 'The people of Israel lives' and in that moment I understood the meaning of that phrase, it was really a very strong experience" (Aia).

"I haven't yet internalized completely what I had experience … especially I remember 'Maidenek' and 'Auschwitz' death camps motley because there everything is so concrete; at the ceremony when we read out the names of our families in 'Auschwitz' it was very emotional; on the mound of ashes in 'Maidenek' there was another group of young girls from another journey, they sang very loudly and it was very impressive because it really "shook" the place and moved all of us a lot" (Rachel).

"During the journey my feelings of anger and horror grew stronger. All my emotions were empowered. After visiting different places I thought more about dreadful things and I pitied all those poor people more" (Miriam).

However, other interviewees expressed different emotional reaction, like the pleasure of the social experience:

"I really enjoyed the journey … we had free time in the evenings and I really enjoyed being with my friends" (Ronen).

"The best thing about Poland is having good time with your friends…in this sense it was like another trip abroad" (Boaz)

Some of the interviewees reported emotional satisfaction, and were pleased that they had gone on the journey:

"I remember that when I returned home I firstly went to my grandfather and told him many things about the journey. I showed him my pictures; he was extremely glad and even shed a tear. He told me: "you are a really good girl"; these are things I usually don't hear from my grandfather, so it moved me and pleased me so much" {smiling} (Yonat).

"I am very glad that I made this journey, it was important to do something about the Holocaust' to witness it directly and to know that you have actually been there in that horrible place; I feel proud that I did it as a Jew" (Lily).

Other interviewees reported that they felt bad because they did not feel sad or they did not have emotional difficulty in Poland in contrast to the earlier expectations that they had culled from their surroundings. They felt disappointed in themselves and dissatisfied with their personal emotional reaction to the sights in Poland. They thought that they should have felt a lot more sadness and emotional difficulty, that they should have cried, but they didn't feel the urge to do so. They also felt that they were abnormal and had the impression that their friends had the "correct" feelings.

"I really expected that I will feel more powerful emotions and when it didn't happen I was disappointed that I wasn't moved so much; it was really very interesting but it was not actually difficult; I saw some of my friends crying but I was emotionless so I was disappointed, I felt that When I was interested they felt pain. This feeling made me think all the time 'what kind of person are you'?" (Pazit).

"I felt rather disappointed in myself because in the preparation course we were told all the time that the journey would be difficult and that we shall cry, but in reality it was different" (Noa).

Lily shared the following thoughts:

"I must be honest... [She moved uncomfortably while talking], *when we visited 'Aushwitz-Birkenau' death camp our guide told us about the 'schlyse-commando' - the Jewish prisoners who worked in the latrines. Suddenly me and my friend looked at one another and we*

just burst into so much laughter... everybody stared at us like we were crazy and I felt so bad, not because of they, but because I felt relief while I should have felt bad" (Lily).

It seems that the main experiences noted by the interviewees were emotional experiences, usually connected to things they saw and did in Poland. It can be concluded that there is an emotional gap between prior expectations and the reality that causes a sort of disappointment among the participants. They enjoyed the social experience and the guidance and usually (but not always) derived much from their participation in the journey in terms of learning and experiences.

In themes two and three we focused on the journey to Poland. In the next pages, we observe the moral meaning of the Holocaust for the interviewees by presenting some of the insights and lessons that they perceived that they had learned from the Holocaust Learning Program.

Coping with Holocaust moral dilemmas through learning

Coping with Holocaust moral dilemmas through learning was a new experience for the participants in the research. The reason is that this issue is not included in Holocaust learning programs, nor he has much place in Jewish-Israeli public discourse over the Holocaust. Therefore, it is important and relevant to study the different experiences and reactions of the participants to this new subject. The participants' different experiences when coping with the moral dilemmas were divided into four sub-themes:

- ***Learning about Holocaust moral dilemmas as a new experience:***

During the research and particularly during the interviews it became increasingly clear that the interviewees lacked much knowledge concerning the dilemmas presented to them in the moral attitude questionnaire. This picture altered from dilemma to dilemma and between the different stages of the research but was overall alike. The reason for this is pinned mainly in the fact that this issue of moral dilemmas is not included in Holocaust learning at school. Furthermore, it transpired that even during the preparation for the journey to Poland

and the journey itself, little attention was given to this issue. Because
of these reasons most of the students` knowledge and their exposure to
the moral dilemmas stemmed from their participation in the research.
Examples of the above results can be found in the following explanations given by the interviewees:

*"I don't really understand the dilemma about the comparison of the
Holocaust, I know very little about other genocides; I know a little
about the "Jewish expulsion from Spain" [not actually genocide]: I
heard about the 'Armenian Holocaust' but I really don't know anything
much about it"* (Dina).

*"During the preparations for the journey to Poland and in the
journey itself they [the guides] only touched upon some of the
dilemmas and we heard a few stories about them; In history studies in
our class we deal more with historical details - dates, main events etc.,
less about dilemmas; For example I knew the 'Judenratt dilemma' only
from your research"* (Lily).

*"Most of my knowledge about the dilemmas comes as a result of my
participation in the research. We learnt some of the concepts connected
with some of the dilemmas in the journey to Poland, but in general and
superficially; I never understood a hundred percent what 'selling your
soul to the devil' [in the 'Kastner dilemma'] means and so it's difficult
for me to answer that dilemma"* (Rachel).

*"We learnt a bit about those subjects [the dilemmas] and that influ-
enced my attitudes, although we didn't go deeply into them. I didn't
understand when exactly the 'revengers dilemma' occurred ... now
after you explained it [in the interview], my attitude towards it is
clearer. If we hadn't participated in the research, we would not know so
much about the moral dilemmas"* (Sara).

After hearing these narratives, it can be assumed that deeper
learning and a broader understanding of the dilemmas would have
probably altered the attitudes of at least some of the students for at
least some of the dilemmas.

• *The creation of moral attitudes through learning:*

Participation in the research gave the interviewees the opportunity to meet for the first time with the complex issue of Holocaust moral dilemmas. This encounter enabled them to define their moral attitudes towards the dilemmas as a new experience. We shall now present examples: *Ronen* and *Sara* explained how their moral attitudes had developed through learning:

"The research influenced me since it made me think about the dilemmas posed in the questionnaire although we had not learned about a large proportion of them; as a result of the questionnaires I thought about my attitudes" (Ronen).

"My participation in the research really helped because suddenly I paid attention to the dilemmas themselves and really examined myself; before I had not thought about these things at all so actually my participation in the research formed my attitudes; The research renewed my knowledge on many things that I had not known previously and which I had not learnt in other places" (Sara).

Elad and *Pazit* talked about the connection they found between Holocaust moral dilemmas and actual morality:

"Many students in our school [those who participated in the research] *are now aware of a lot of important things that they had not been aware of; before the research I hadn't thought about moral questions at all... When I began to think about the moral dilemmas it really influenced me and made me think about those situations; the research opened up all sorts of new facets of knowledge and thinking so it had a strong influence on me and probably on many of my friends too; Moral thinking can help us in everyday situations and maybe later when we become soldiers"* (Elad).

"It's good that you did the research in stages, because that can demonstrate our development and I think that my attitudes and opinions developed. The research helped us to think about it more and in greater depth and then to connect it to the present because today there are also horrors that are happening now such as the horrors perpetrated by 'ISIS' [the 'Islamic State'] *... the research really touched me*

personally and helped me to think what I would do in those situations ... I am very happy that there was this research ... perhaps it will also influence me in my life because I will think more about morality and the decisions that I make" (Pazit).

Aia provided another viewpoint. She emphasized the deeper understanding of human feelings and the complexity of the connection between emotions and moral decisions:

"The dilemmas provide another facet of the Holocaust. We always learn about technical matters, what is a 'ghetto', what is the 'Judenratt' etc. The dilemmas speak about people, how they felt and how they acted. It's more personal and emotional; it puts you into the situation so that you need to think how you would have acted. The dilemmas touch upon emotions and it is very important to learn about them" (Aia).

It can be concluded that the new exposure to the issue of moral dilemmas, created awareness, motivated moral thinking and helped to create and shape moral attitudes.

• *The evolution of moral attitudes through learning:*

Interviewees expressed three main factors that caused them to change their attitudes through learning: maturation processes, learning processes and the repetition of filling out the questionnaires three times.

The first factor was the maturation process they underwent during the year in which the research was conducted. This process led them to be more aware of the complexity of the dilemmas and to be less naive. *Miriam* and *Noa* explained:

"Now it is more difficult for me to decide ... in all the dilemmas I wanted to write 'uncertain' ... it is not because of the journey to Poland ... I have matured and I value my life more and that of other people and this makes it more difficult for me to determine my attitudes" (Miriam).

"When I completed the questionnaire for the first time, I thought that I needed to be terribly moral ... I would do nice things and write

that I was against anything that would harm others ... now I understand that I simply have to live... I think that at first I looked at things from our period in time and I understood less what the Jews really underwent, and now I understand things better" (Noa).

The second factor was the different learning processes that the students underwent as expressed by the interviewees:

"After we spoke more about the "thief's dilemma" I understood that everyone stole from everyone else in order to survive... it's a momentary decision, it's not a moral consideration, you don't think about someone - who he is and what he is - you just want to live" (Asaf).

"Because of this extensive knowledge [at the end of the research] I changed my opinion to kill the baby (in the 'crying baby' dilemma) ... the situation now is clearer. I understand now that there is nowhere to escape ... to save the life of the majority if there is no alternative then we have to kill him in order to survive" (Yonat).

The third factor was the fact that they filled in the questionnaire three times. Repeating the same process three times engendered changes in attitudes as *Ronen* explained:

"The fact that the research was in stages had an influence, because that gave us time to think; Time gave me deeper and greater understanding... because I had more time to think, I also deliberated more before making a decision".

Rachel gave her own interpretation and mentioned how difficult it was to determine a moral decision:

"I really felt that I could not answer this question about the baby [in the 'crying baby' dilemma]... it was just too hard... in the 'thief's dilemma' I truly tried to cope with it but I simply couldn't because both solutions are right... The more I learned the more I deliberate... for the 'Judenratt dilemma' I marked 'I have no opinion'... I felt that I didn't have enough knowledge to answer some of the dilemmas, so at different times I chose to mark 'I have no opinion'; at the end of day I think that time gave me better perspective" (Rachel).

Lily emphasized the cognitive aspect:

"The fact that we did the questionnaire several times had an influence and I am sure that there was a change ... I continually tried to

understand the scenarios; the time that passed between the question-naires gave us time to think about things and attitudes changed over that time, each time a little. There is a process in which you have time and opportunities to choose a different choice each time and that helps you to learn. You undergo a process like people who were actually there and think about yourself as if you were there. You choose some-thing and examine it along the axis of time from time to time, until you feel that you are learning to choose the most correct thing to do and that is a process" (Lily).

It can be concluded that changes in attitudes stemmed from the acquisition of knowledge during learning, maturation processes and due to the time that passed between the three points at which the students filled out the questionnaires.

- ***The importance of learning about Holocaust moral dilemmas:***

The interviewees noted five main contributions that they derived from learning about Holocaust moral dilemmas. ***The first*** was that they felt it deepened their knowledge on the Holocaust from a human view-point, so that they were able to understand the mental processes that the Jews experienced as expressed by the interviewees:

"It is very important to learn about the dilemmas because as a society it was difficult to accept the Holocaust survivors in Israel and learning about the moral dilemmas really helped us to understand what happened there and why people acted as they did. This aspect is very important because it is the history of our people, of all of us" (Boaz).

"The Holocaust is a very important part of our past and it is impor-tant to learn about it and not to forget it or to ignore it and simply to go on. It is important to know why people did things, what motivated them, what their considerations were and how they decided what to do"(Miriam).

"It is important to learn from the past for the future and to under-stand how to behave otherwise, both from the behavior of the Jews and

the behavior of the Nazis. It is important to learn about this in order to understand better what our people and my own family experienced. In this way, it is possible to understand their inner experiences" (Pazit).

The second contribution was the beginning of the development of universal moral thinking as expressed by the interviewees:

"In some way it is clear that such situations or similar will reflect upon people in future life, perhaps in a smaller and weaker manner, but they will arrive. If we learn about those dilemmas, we will perhaps not repeat the mistakes of the past" (Dina).

"Dealing with morality could improve my behavior in the future in similar situations. As a result of and thanks to the learning process that I have experienced this year it is a lot clearer and meaningful to me; it influences you to take things in proportion, to understand that things in our lives are actually quite small in comparison to the things as happened in the Holocaust. The research led me to really think and think in a different way. It encouraged me to deliberate more and develop my own moral attitudes" (Elad).

The third contribution was the understanding of the connection between moral behavior in extreme situations and moral behavior in daily life as expressed by the interviewees:

"I think that the Holocaust was an exceptional event that forced people to face situations that they would never otherwise have encountered ... when you think of their moral dilemmas it can teach you about human nature and what you would do when you are in a situation where you have to save yourself or die" (Aia).

"We must gain something from learning about the Holocaust... We must not dismiss it as just another chapter in history. It is important to learn about and draw conclusions from the dilemmas, both those of the Jews and those of the Nazis because they are expressed even in daily matters" (Asaf).

"Learning about the moral dilemmas can help to construct a morality that will prevent such deterioration at least among some of the society. If we deal with the dilemmas of the Holocaust without linking it to present-day reality or to future eventualities there will be no association made between these things. There should be a frame-

work that will tie things together and this should be done by learning about the dilemmas" (Rachel).

"These are large dilemmas but they can also be small and yet they are the same dilemmas in substance. For example if on a class trip we should share food or not with someone who did not bring a sandwich, or joining or not joining a social boycott of someone ... in the Holocaust situations there were people who knew how to make the right decisions in those situations and there were those who did not. It also teaches us a lot about us as individuals. When you mark the solutions for these dilemmas on the questionnaire it teaches you about yourself, what type of human being you are" (Sara).

The fourth contribution was the deepening of self-understanding and self-awareness in relation to moral issues as expressed by the interviewees:

"Learning about the moral dilemmas helps us to understand things relating to morality and may help me in my moral decisions in the future; When you think about the Holocaust usually you think about the incinerators, the 'ghetto', the hunger and so on... you do not think about the person himself, and what he experienced, what the people faced and what they had to decide each day. When you encounter that, you begin to understand the mental difficulty that you might have with yourself if you ever need to cope with these kinds of situations" (Yonat).

"The research made me think how I would act and how others would act in situations like those ... Those things really shocked me and it was difficult for me to cope with them, now it is easier for me than on the first occasion ... the research was very direct ...I really tried to enter into it and to imagine it, to imagine myself and my friends in those situations; It is something that built us as a people and dealing with it is part of our heritage as the Jewish people" (Ronen).

"The entire Holocaust deals with moral dilemmas.... If we do not learn about these dilemmas we will not understand the Holocaust well. This learning could also influence moral decisions that I have to make in the future in society and in my family" (Lily).

. . .

The fifth contribution was the strengthening of Holocaust memory by learning about the moral dilemmas as expressed by the interviewees:

"I am afraid that with time the Holocaust will not be part of our awareness any more that it will be forgotten. It is very important that it should not happen! The superficial way that Holocaust is being taught now may cause a boredom and a lack of interest among young students like ourselves; I think that dealing with and learning about the moral dilemmas will make things more interesting and alive for young students and actually for everyone; in this way, it will contribute to the memory of the Holocaust" (Noa).

It can be concluded that the interviewees strongly valued learning about the moral dilemmas of the Holocaust from five different perspectives. Their estimation related both to their enrichment of knowledge about human and historical aspects of the Holocaust and also to the linkage that they identified between this knowledge and their moral behavior in their present and future life. Another most important contribution is that the students were able to better understand why it is important to remember the Holocaust.

3.5.2 Discussion

The results revealed that the interviewees demonstrated a high level of intellectual and emotional interest in the Holocaust together with a strong desire to talk with survivors in their families about their Holocaust experiences. There was also a mutual difficulty of survivors and their grandchildren to do so. These results correlate strongly with those of Litvak-Hirsch and Brown (2008), Fuchs (2009) and Efrat and Baban (2016b), who all found that there is a strong inter-generational transmission of trauma and memory in Israeli society, with a significant influence on each succeeding generation in a variety of areas and levels. This emotional and intellectual involvement is well represented in the research population since most of the participants in the research, and indeed most of the interviewees were relatives of Holocaust victims or survivors.

The participants' sometimes almost intuitive search for information and desire to understand is emotionally restrained by the mutual difficulty that survivors and their descendants seem to have to touch upon

the sensitive issue of the Holocaust. The personal-family connection
was most significant for the interviewees and created a very influential
emotional-intellectual need to engage with the issue of the Holocaust.
From an inter-generational perspective, the third generation finds it
more difficult to talk about the Holocaust with surviving grandparents
than with their parents, who are the second generation after the Holocaust. Interestingly, as demonstrated by interviewees who did not have
such a personal connection to the Holocaust, the significant emotional-
intellectual interest in the Holocaust is not limited to those who have
relatives who underwent the Holocaust; rather there appears to be a
comprehensive social-national psychological need which is probably
shared by all Israelis and Jews.

The results reveal that family support, school tradition, peer pressure, recognition of the historical-national importance of the journey,
intellectual curiosity but also a personal need constituted the participants' main reasons to go on the journey to Poland. The reasons noted
for deciding not to go on the journey included a lack of family support
due to educational considerations, considerations regarding the participants' age and financial difficulty. Most of these results are quite
similar to those discovered by former investigators (Shalem, 2008;
Rama, 2011; Bondi, 2014; Starkman & Dattel, 2016). However, while
most of the reasons given in favor and against joining the journey can
be classified as "educational", "social", "cultural" or "environmental",
the personal need is different and the most interesting one. The interviewees who talked about this feeling explained that it is related to a
moral attitude which is expressed in the feeling that they need to do
something about the Holocaust. This, together with a feeling of moral
obligation, proved to be a strong emotional motivation stimulus that
affected the decision to go on the journey.

The results reveal a combination of varied and sometimes opposite
cognitive and emotional experiences. The cognitive experiences
included mixed reactions that on the whole described significant
learning processes, increasing knowledge, but also included some
reports of non-significant learning. This picture resembles the findings
reported by Feldman (2001); Romi and Lev (2003); Romi and Lev

(2007) and Cohen (2010). However, the clear reports of what was perceived as non-significant learning during the journey to Poland, which was revealed in this research are a new finding and deserve more investigation.

The present results are also in line with findings of previous research that experiences from the journey to Poland reinforced various emotional reactions towards the Holocaust, such as identifying with the victims and feeling a greater affinity to Jewish heritage (Mimouni-Bloch, Rostami & Bloch, 2012). Other researchers have emphasized different emotional reactions of Jewish-Israeli youth who participate in the journey to Poland. Among them there were positive reactions towards Holocaust victims (Mimouni-Bloch, Rostami & Bloch, 2012) but negative feelings towards Poles and Arabs (Davidovich & Hazan, 2011; Kimchi, 2011). However, the present study revealed other previously unmentioned emotional reactions: a feeling of pleasure regarding the social experience of the journey and a deep feeling of disappointment due to the "not appropriate" emotional reactions to the sights in Poland. Both experiences engendered guilt fillings among the participants, but this was especially so with the lack of "appropriate" response. We can assume that other participants in previous research did not mention these kinds of feelings because probably they considered them as "inappropriate feelings"; while in the present research, on the other hand, participants probably felt that they were encouraged to express their true emotions openly. The feeling of pleasure due to the social experiences in the journey is quite natural and understood. However, returning home with feelings of guilt and disappointment regarding the emotional reactions to the sites in Poland is rather bothering. It seems that certain kinds of messages and expectations could cause unnecessary and unjustified guilt feelings.

As mentioned before the experience of coping with Holocaust moral dilemmas through learning was a new experience for the participants in the research. The reason is that this issue is not included in Holocaust learning programs. It was therefore important and relevant to study its results and to draw conclusions.

Our interviewees found connections between Holocaust moral

dilemmas and morality in general. This finding is supported by the finding of Mimouni-Bloch, Rostami and Bloch (2012) that students who participated in Holocaust experiential learning had an evident sense of increased identification with the victims and also with general liberal values.

'The creation of moral attitudes through learning seems to have occurred because participants in the program were able to develop a deeper understanding of human feelings and the complexity of the interaction between emotions and moral decisions. This result correlates with the conclusions of recent studies supporting the natural assumption that when an individual is exposed to the experience of harming other people, it triggers strong emotional reactions, expressed at the cognitive and emotional levels which will influence his/her moral judgment and potentially his/her actions (Cushman, Young, & Hauser, 2006; Greene et al., 2007).

Learning about Holocaust moral dilemmas was a new experience for the participants due to the lack of general knowledge and specific exposure to Holocaust moral dilemmas in school. Thus, the exposure to moral dilemmas stemmed mainly from the students' participation in the research. It is again noted that Holocaust moral dilemmas are not an integral part of the Holocaust studies curricula in Israel (In the paths of memory, (Ministry of Education, 2015a).

3.5.3 Conclusions

The first conclusion that we present is that all the characteristics of personal connections to the Holocaust which have been described are expression of the authentic psychological need to get to know and to understand the Holocaust. Dealing with Holocaust proved to be an inter-generational need that can help collectively recovering the process from the trauma.

The second conclusion is with regard to the ongoing debate on the journey to Poland. We conclude that early expectations "to feel bad" among the students before the journey led to strong feeling of disappointment because in reality their real emotions did not comply with these expectations. This might be prevented by a beater understanding of the multi-faceted nature of psychological reactions to this kind of journey.

The third conclusion is that learning about specific and realistic human experiences such as are depicted in the moral dilemmas of the Holocaust, help participants to develop a wider moral perspective and understanding of human behavior. It encouraged the development of universal moral thinking and deepening self-understanding and awareness of moral issues. That will potentially have an effect on their moral judgment and actions in the present as well in the future.

The fourth conclusion is that not only the participant's knowledge but also their emotional involvement with regard to the issue of Holocaust was strengthened by their exposure to Holocaust moral dilemmas. Therefore "Holocaust moral dilemmas" is an important subject that should be included in future Holocaust Learning Program curricula.

CHAPTER 4- GENERAL DISCUSSION AND CONCLUSIONS

This chapter presents further discussion and conclusions from the research relating to the studied issues of Holocaust moral dilemmas, the Holocaust Learning Program and lessons learned from these studies. It presents the contributions and the limitations of the research and indicates possible new directions for further investigation. The chapter concludes by presenting possible future directions of Holocaust learning.

4.1. Overview of our main results and conclusions

For the Jews who lost 6,000,000 of their people during World War II (1939-1945) the Holocaust is a terrible tragedy and national trauma that has produced very strong influences and implications even today. The Jewish Holocaust has also become the subject of a very wide field of knowledge and has been studied from many perspectives over many years and in many countries, especially in the USA, Israel and Germany (Browning, 2004; Farabstein, 2002; Goldhagen, 1998; Zimerman, 2013). Main Jewish attention concerning the Holocaust has usually focused on the narrative of the mass murder of Jews and the question: how could it happen? Ethical issues and dilemmas involved in the Jews' behavior mainly during but also after the Holocaust were barely discussed and investigated. This is not surprising because dealing with this most difficult issue entails picking at a very deep and still open wound (Weinrab, 1984, Blady Szwaiger, 2000).

This research was an innovative effort to investigate some of the moral dilemmas faced by the Jews during and after the Holocaust, from the viewpoint of Israeli high-school students participating in the Holocaust Learning Program. This chapter discusses the main results and conclusions of the five research studies.

Study 1 investigated the initial moral attitudes of the participants towards dilemmas of the Holocaust and post-Holocaust eras. Holocaust era dilemmas occurred in "high-conflict" threatening situations with a clear and concrete risk to life. These dilemmas are also defined as "harm to save" (H2S) moral dilemmas in which a person must decide whether to kill another person in order to save himself or others (Koenigs et al., 2007). The results from study 1 suggest that, in general, when participants deliberated between supporting deontological versus survival moral solutions of Holocaust era dilemmas they were usually uncertain how to decide. The main conclusion is that at that point of time when the Holocaust Learning Program had just started, it was actually very difficult for the participants to move from their conventional deontological moral conception and to adapt to the survival moral attitude which was needed for the Jews to survive the Holocaust. Post-Holocaust moral dilemmas relate to the Jewish struggle to cope with the continuous memory, consequences and the effects of the Holocaust in following peace time. The results from study 1 suggest that in general, when participants deliberated between supporting the "acceptance" or the "judgmental" moral attitude towards Jewish resistance to the Nazis, they usually adopted the "acceptance" moral attitude but with much difficulty. **The main conclusion** is that at that point of time when Holocaust learning program had just started, the participants usually tended to agree more with the more accepted attitude in the Israeli discourse today concerning Jewish resistance to the Nazis – it should not be judged retrospectively. It means that when coping with the most disturbing question for the Jews: ***"why did we not strongly resist the Nazis",*** participants tended to take the stand that it is not morally justified to accuse the Jews who suffered the Holocaust as having been "weak" or as the famous expression describes them: "they went like lambs to slaughter".

Study 2 aimed to look for a possible evolution and changes in the initial moral attitudes of the participants through the three different research stages parallel to their studies in the Holocaust Learning Program. In general, the results indicate that the evolution of Holocaust-era moral attitudes through learning represents an increase in the participants' agreement with the survival moral solutions and at the same time, a decrease in their agreement with deontological moral solutions. The final result was that they gave more support to the survival moral solutions at the end of learning process.

These results lead to two main conclusions: 1. Learning process was the main cause for this evolution and it means that enhancement and deepening of knowledge together with emotional adjustment and understanding of the unique reality of the Holocaust appears to lead to this change. 2. It seems that both emotionally and cognitively, it was easier for the participants to decrease their agreement with deontological moral solutions than to increase their agreement with survival moral solutions. With regard to post-Holocaust moral dilemmas, the results revealed an increase in the participants' agreement with the 'acceptance moral solution' concerning Jewish resistance to the Nazis. **The main conclusion** here is the same as for Holocaust era dilemmas - a combination of emotional and cognitive processes through the learning period had led the participants to greater understanding and acceptance of the way that Jews resisted Nazis during the Holocaust.

The main research aim of **Study 3,** which was conducted at the end of the Holocaust Learning Program, was to identify the perceived moral lessons that emerged from learning about the Holocaust and the moral dilemmas that the Jews faced. The results reveal that the overall extent of participants' agreement with the 'humanist-liberal moral lessons' was much higher than with the' national-utilitarian lessons'. **This leads to the conclusion** that learning about Holocaust moral dilemmas helped the participants to adapt 'humanist-liberal lessons' concerning the Holocaust. However, the results also reveal significant differences between boys and girls in relation to the extent of agreement with 'nationalist-utilitarian lessons', such that boys expressed a significantly higher extent of agreement than the girls with these lessons. **It is concluded** that this particular result can be explained mostly by psychological gender differences.

The main research aim of **Study 4,** which was also conducted at the end of the Holocaust Learning Program, was to examine whether participants' moral attitudes are associated with perceived moral lessons derived from the learning process. The results revealed that a significant linear connection (correlation) was found between the attitudes of the participants towards both Holocaust and post-Holocaust dilemmas and the different lessons they perceived to learn from Holocaust Learning Program and learning of Holocaust moral dilemmas. In relation to Holocaust era dilemmas we found that agreement with the survival moral solutions led to agreement with 'humanist-liberal moral lessons'. **The main conclusion** is that exposure to Holocaust moral dilemmas reinforced moral thinking and understanding of human difficulties and needs. In relation to Post-Holocaust era moral dilemmas we found that insofar as the moral attitude is more critical, then the lessons learned will be more radical and at the same time, when the moral attitude is more compassionate then the lessons learned will be less radical. Following those results, **we concluded** that learning about Holocaust moral dilemmas increases students' support of universal lessons such as the duty to help the weak. This insight reinforces the approach that universal humanistic lessons can be learned from the Holocaust.

Study 5 was based on individual in-depth interviews conducted at the end of the learning process. Its main aim was to understand the meanings constructed through the participants' narratives regarding their different personal experiences of Holocaust Learning Program. The main results indicate that interviewees felt that their learning of Holocaust moral dilemmas had deepened their knowledge on the Holocaust mainly from a humanist viewpoint. As a result, they were able to better understand the mental processes that the Jews experienced during the Holocaust. **The conclusion** is that the participants' cognitive and especially emotional involvement with the issue of the Holocaust was strengthened by their exposure to Holocaust moral dilemmas. This leads to the understanding that "Holocaust moral dilemmas" is an important subject that should be included in new future Holocaust Learning Program curricula. Another most important result was the contribution of Holocaust moral dilemmas learning to the development of participants' independent humanistic universal moral thinking. **The conclusion** is that learning about specific and realistic human experiences, such as are depicted in Holocaust moral dilemmas, helped students to develop a wider moral perspective and understanding of human behavior. It also encouraged the development of their universal moral thinking and deepened their self-understanding and awareness. This process will potentially have a beneficial effect on their moral judgment and actions in the present and even more important- in the future as adults.

4.1 Contributions of the present thesis

The following paragraphs summarize and review the main theoretical, methodological and empirical contributions of the present thesis to the extant corpus of knowledge in the relevant fields.

- In the literature review new innovating step of clarifying the domain of Jewish moral dilemmas during and after the Jewish Holocaust was presented. The concept "Survival Morality" was used here for the first time as an original concept to describe a most important element of Jewish moral behaviour during the Holocaust. Furthermore, we clarified some of the important processes which explain both the moral behaviour of the Jews in the Holocaust and the development of the Jewish-Israeli national recovery process after the Holocaust **(Chapter 1).**
- For the first time in the field of research on Holocaust moral dilemmas, complex statistical procedures, which included an exploratory research design combined with longitudinal

research procedures and specific research tools, were used
to fulfil the research aims. In addition, a new research tool
for investigated Holocaust Moral Attitudes was used.
(Chapter 2).

- This study was the first to investigate moral attitudes
  towards Jewish Holocaust moral dilemmas among Jewish-
  Israeli high school students. Therefore, for the first time, we
  have initial results regarding this most important but not yet
  investigated topic. We revealed the participants' strong
  deliberation between supporting the deontological versus
  the survival moral solutions, at the initial stage at the
  beginning of the Holocaust Learning Program *(Study 1)*.

- This study was the first to investigate the existing Holocaust
  Learning Programs in Israel as a factor forming moral
  attitudes among Jewish-Israeli high school students towards
  Jewish moral dilemmas during Holocaust and post-Holocaust
  eras. The three measurements during the learning process
  enabled us to examine the evolution of the participants'
  attitudes over time. The final results regarding the impact of
  Holocaust Learning Program on the creation and development
  of the participants' moral attitudes constitute a new and
  important contribution to knowledge. We now know that this
  learning process caused more support for the survival moral
  attitude towards Holocaust moral dilemmas at the end of the
  learning process. At the same time, there was also an increase
  in participants' support for the 'acceptance moral solution'
  concerning Jewish resistance to the Nazis. A new contribution
  to the field of moral research is the conclusion that it is easier
  to reduce support for deontological solutions than to increase
  support for survival moral solutions *(Study 2)*.

- Moral lessons perceived by the participants as stemming
  from learning about the Holocaust were identified and
  discussed for the first time. Our results demonstrated that
  the Holocaust Learning Program and especially learning

about Holocaust moral dilemmas strengthened the adoption of 'humanist-liberal' moral lessons learned by the participants *(study 3)*.

- New investigating of associations between moral attitudes and moral lessons stemming from Holocaust learning allowed us to find, for the first time, significant correlations between these two dimensions. This finding provides the foundation for the determination that there is a linear connection between moral attitudes and moral lessons in regard to Holocaust moral dilemmas *(Study 4)*.

- The results from the interviews show that learning about Holocaust moral dilemmas can contribute to the participants' understanding of the feelings, thoughts and actions of the Jews in the most terrible situations of the Holocaust. These results also taught us that learning about Jewish Holocaust moral dilemmas can contribute to the participants' understanding of their own moral behavior. In addition, participants reported that as a result of their learning they improved their moral judgment in present situations. Now they think more about how they would potentially act in the same situations as those of the Jews during the Holocaust and even more important - how they can act in future similar situations, in which they will be either on the weak or the strong side. This may be considered as education's most important contribution to high school students – learning how to think more and deliberate more before taking action and obeying orders *(Study 5)*.

4.3 Research limits

This was an exploratory research which, as far as we could ascertain, was the first study on the subject of Jewish Holocaust moral dilemmas. Therefore there were no other results from similar research studies that we could compare with our results. This limitation could be overcome by future research.

4.4 Future directions of investigation

The research reported here increased our knowledge regarding the moral attitudes of Jewish-Israeli youth towards Jewish moral dilemmas during and after the Holocaust. This is new knowledge gained from this innovative research. It is suggested that future studies should continue to investigate this subject in different ways. Several directions for such projects can be suggested:

1. Repeat this research with Jewish high school students outside Israel to look for possible similarities or differences.
2. Repeat this research but add more dilemmas. This will produce more data, results and conclusions.
3. Additionally, it could be very interesting and useful to perform similar research among German youth concerning German moral dilemmas during the Nazi era and the way that Germany is coping with the consequences of the Holocaust. It would be very interesting to compare the German research results with the results of the Jewish and Israeli research and then to compare and integrate all findings. This research could be informing another step towards normalization of relations between Jews and Germans and emphasizing the importance of universal morality.
4. Given the fact that the subject of moral dilemmas is not part of both formal and experiential Holocaust learning programs in Israeli schools today, the exposure of the participants to this subject stemmed from three sources: their former personal knowledge, the Holocaust Learning Program and their participation in the research itself. We suggest that if the subject of moral dilemmas were to be taught thoroughly as part of Holocaust learning programs, it

would be interesting and worthwhile to repeat this research
with other students who learn about the moral dilemmas as
an integral part of their Holocaust studies.

4.5 Future directions of Holocaust learning

4.5.1 "Holocaust Three-dimensional learning program"

Theoretical background:

In Chapter 1 we discussed the intense debate that continues to be
waged concerning new directions for the learning of the Holocaust
(Cohen, 2010) and especially with regard to the necessity and effectiveness of the journeys to Holocaust sites in Poland (Bondi, 2014).
The present Holocaust Learning Program – the compulsory learning
program for the matriculation exams and students voluntary participation in the journey to Poland provide partial answers to fundamental
questions and especially to the question that seem to bother Jews above
all – ***"why did we not strongly resist the Nazis"*** (In the paths of
memory, Ministry of Education, 2015a; Ministry of Education, General
Manager's Directive, 2014; Soen & Davidovich, 2011; Romi & Lev,
2007; Rama, 2011; Rama, 2011; Bondi, 2014). This reality encouraged
us to suggest the following learning program.

The program rational:

Based on the results and conclusions of this research we propose an
educational initiative, a new Holocaust learning program named
"Holocaust Three-Dimensional Learning Program". This program is
based on the conception that we should learn about the Holocaust not
only from the Jewish particular perspective but also from a more
universal perspective. The program can also possibly be used in other
places in the world to cope with the educational challenges involved in
coping with catastrophic national events. Future use of the program
should also need to be investigated and evaluated through academic
research.

The program's educational goals:

1. To enable students to acquire comprehensive knowledge about
the Jewish Holocaust and similar genocides. 2. To teach students to ask

moral questions and to cast doubt on what appears to be certain 3. To develop the student's independent and critical moral thinking. 4. To encourage students to adopt humanistic, democratic values, draw informed conclusions and derive varied lessons out of their own independent thinking.

The program's foundations:

The program has four main foundations: A. Combine different learning methods. B. Use of survivor's narratives. C. Making comparisons. B. Deducing different lessons. We shall now discuss these four foundations.

A. Combine different learning methods:

Our results (Study 5) revealed that learning about horrific phenomena necessitates a certain kind of emotional distancing because otherwise learners might be flooded emotionally and this would disrupt learning. On the other hand, in order to really grasp and understand this highly complex issue of the Holocaust and particularly the Holocaust moral dilemmas, an emotional connection to the situations described is also needed. These elements can be achieved by combining different learning methods - 'formal class learning' with ' experiential learning' in the field. A good combination between the journeys to Poland being the experiential learning together with formal class learning is performed today.

B. Use of survivor's narratives: When we look at the way that the Holocaust has been taught over the years in Israel, we can observe two main learning disciplines involved – the first deals with the main historical events and facts, we shall call it "the frame story". The second deals with the 'narrative story' which concentrates on the survivors' personal narratives, we shall call this "the inner story" (Shapira, 1997, Soen & Davidovich, 2011, Efrat and Baban, 2016b). Based on our results (Study 5), we concluded that the 'inner story' could be best learned through exposure to the Holocaust moral dilemmas. The dilemmas clarify and illustrate what really happened, making the experiences more concrete – something that the students can really understand emotionally and with which they can empathize.

C. Deducing different lessons:

The Jewish people perceive the Holocaust as an additional event along the sequence of continuous attempts by different empires, peoples and dictators to harm and destroy the Jewish people and in the present time - the State of Israel. It is easy to understand how this perception of reality leads to the deduction of lessons such as: "we must be strong in order to survive" or "a strong Israel will prevent the next Holocaust", which are widely accepted in Israel (Machman, 1996b). These are "national-utilitarian" lessons or, in another definition –"Jewish-particular" lessons, which indicate that the Jewish people need an independent state with a strong army to protect itself from another Holocaust. Another kind of lessons that can also be derived from Holocaust learning are the "Humanist-liberal" lessons which indicate that when we the Jewish people are strong they must preserve morality, and not harm, but instead protect those who are weak (Baron, 1994). The results of this research (Studies 3+4) indicate that learning about Holocaust moral dilemmas helped participants to develop not only moral thinking and attitudes but also different moral lessons, so that they expressed more support for the "Humanist-liberal" lessons after their learning. As a result, we believe that the adoption of Humanist-liberal moral lessons and their implementation in different policies can provide a psychological-educational barrier against the rise of negative ideologies of nationalism, militarism and racism.

D. Making comparisons:

Our results (Studies 1+2) indicated that many of the participants agreed that in order to understand, draw conclusions and learn lessons about Holocaust, it is better to compare it to similar phenomenon (other genocides). The way to implement this insight is when learning about Holocaust, to open up discussion, enhancing awareness of the different lessons and using comparison to distinguish them one from the other. This could be done by using the "Holocaust Three-Dimensional Learning Program," which includes the consideration of historical, phenomenological and psychological components.

Figure 4.1 provides a visual description of the four above-mentioned foundations of this program:

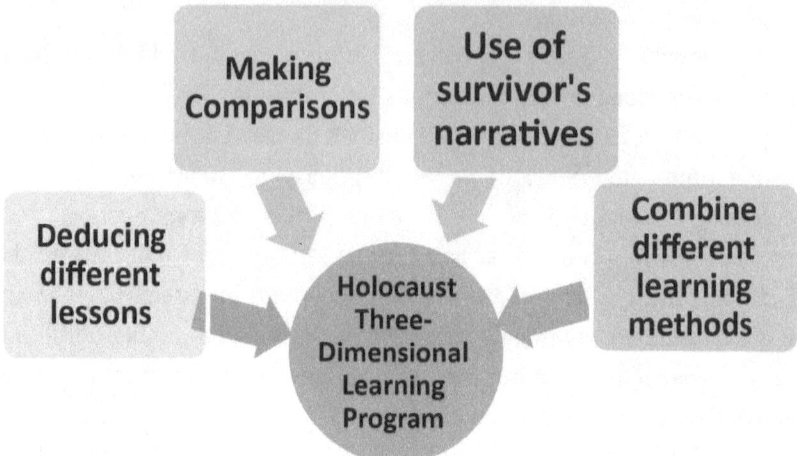

Figure 4.1 –"Holocaust Three-Dimensional Learning Program" foundations

The structure of the "Holocaust Three-Dimensional Learning Program":

"The program would include the following three parts which are defined as "dimensions":

*The first dimension is the **"Chronological Dimension"** –* <u>Focusing on the historical timeline</u> of the Holocaust. This is a historical-chronological perspective; meaning that there is an attempt to go back and learn about the Holocaust from a longer time perspective which would include:

1. The roots of anti-Semitism, its development and implications in Europe during 19th and early 20th century (1800-1914).
2. World War I and its outcomes for Germany (1914-1923).
3. The rise of the Nazis to power in Germany, Nazi ideology and its implementation on the Jews in Germany (1923-1939).
4. World War II and its connection to the Holocaust (1939-1945).
5. Main events of the Holocaust throughout Europe and in North Africa (1939-1945).
6. Israel-Germany relations after the Holocaust (1945-2015).
7. The trials of Nazi war criminals in Germany and German understanding of the Holocaust (1949-2015).
8. The ways in which Israeli society has coped with the Holocaust and its implications (1940-2016).

*The second dimension is the **"Phenomenological Dimension"** –* Focusing on genocide: This is a phenomenological expansion of Holocaust learning comparing the Holocaust to similar events in modern history. Other similar phenomena which should be included in this learning are:

- The Armenian Genocide in Turkey (1914-1923)
- The Genocide of the Romani people in Europe (1941-1945)
- The Tutsi Genocide in Ruanda-Africa (1994)

The learning program should also consider the acts of mass murders by certain governments against their own citizens. Examples are the "Great Hunger" in Soviet Ukraine (1932-1933), the "Euthanasia" program in Nazi Germany (1939-1941) and the Cambodian Genocide (1975-1979).

*The third dimension is the **"Psychological Dimension"**,* Focusing on Moral Dilemmas. Here we go deeply into complex psychological processes to produce a sharper and more focused perception of Holocaust events. This should be accomplished by learning about moral dilemmas faced not only by the Jews but also by other people and nations during World War II. This will include the Allies who fought against Nazi Germany governments and military command, the Nazi regime, the armed Nazi forces, German civilian population and non-Jewish population in the territories conquered by Nazi Germany at that time. The big advantage of learning about moral dilemmas is that this learning necessitates the use of a combination of emotional and analytical thinking. On the one hand, the moral dilemmas expose the learners to the most painful weakness of the human soul, while on the other hand, they must make an analytical cognitive evaluation and balanced judgment in order to form their own moral attitudes.

Figure 4.2 below summarizes the three dimensions:

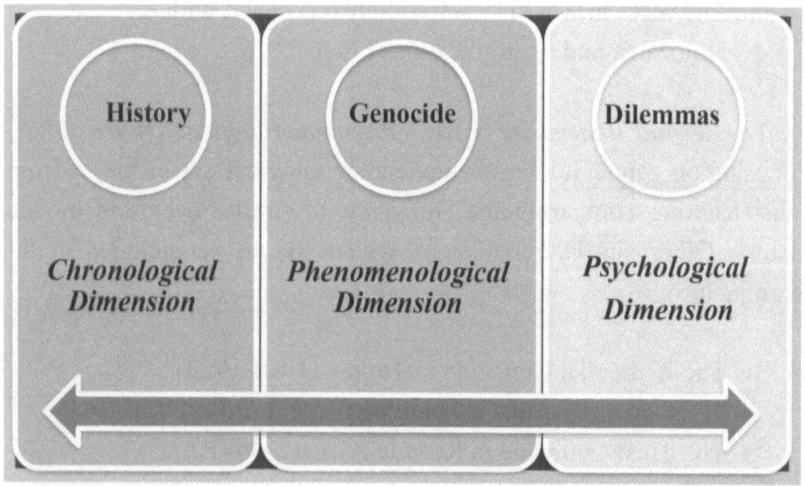

Figure 4.2 - "Holocaust Three-Dimensional Learning Program" structure

Practical implication of the program:
Our results (Study 5) indicate that participants needed much time to adjust themselves to deal with Holocaust learning and especially Holocaust moral dilemmas. We concluded that this is because Holocaust is

such a complicated issue to learn both cognitively and emotionally which needs time and sufficient maturity. Therefore, the duration of such a program should be two full academic years in Grades 11 and 12 when the students are socially, cognitively and psychologically mature enough. The extent of teaching hours should be 2-4 hours per week with an intensive one-day workshop, once a month. This program should include class learning along with experiential outdoor learning such as a journey to Holocaust sites in Poland or an alternative journey discussed below. Students' requirements for matriculation should include formal knowledge exams, personal research work on a selected topic and active participation in class debates and workshops. The teachers in the program should be the school's history teachers and homeroom teachers, who should undergo special academic training.

4.5.2 An optional alternative for the "Journey to Poland"

In Chapter 1 we noted the fact that not all high school students in Israel participate in the journey to Poland for many reasons - financial, educational, lack of motivation and others (Rama, 2011). In addition, our results (Study 5) demonstrated that some of the students came back from the journey with feelings of disappointment regarding their emotional reaction to the sites in Poland. As an option to solve these problems we suggest that Holocaust experiential learning does not necessitate the journey to Poland. This could be achieved in a journey in Israel using the many Holocaust learning centers which are spread over the country.

The journey to Holocaust memorial sites in Poland can be replaced by ***"The Journey to Holocaust memory in Israel"***. We suggest that this journey should take place towards the end of school studies in Grade 12 as the peak of two full academic years of Holocaust learning, when high school students' maturity is at its highest. This kind of journey would not focus solely on the Holocaust. It would also include the story of the Jewish rehabilitation from the Holocaust and the ways in which Israeli society and Holocaust survivors cope with its memory and recover from the trauma. In this way, the story will be told until its end. Of course, this journey can become part of the "Three -Dimensional Holocaust Learning Program". To conclude this part we emphasize the serious interest, importance and significance involved by going in person to see with one's own eyes the extermination sites in Poland, where the horrors happened. In our opinion, this is really a unique, irreplaceable experience, an experience that can benefit every Jew. However, in order to learn and understand the Holocaust, it is not necessary to take this journey at school. It can be done later in life as a mature and independent decision after more life experience.

Summary In the preface to this thesis Professor Gideon Greif (p-9) wrote:

"There is educational value in discussing questions of human behavioral practices in extreme situations, in order to examine ourselves, to think about these situations close-up, to try to reconstruct a particular historical reality and perhaps to come closer to the victims and to identify with them". Our results indicated that participants did expand their knowledge and understanding of Holocaust particular reality by learning about Jewish moral dilemmas. They also reinforced their emotional bond to Holocaust memory and felt closer to its victims. Furthermore, they declared that they felt more aware of moral considerations and behavior. No doubt, there will always be a gap between moral attitudes and moral behavior, especially in extreme situations and conditions. Nevertheless, based on our results and conclusions, we can assume that learning of moral issues and educational "practice" in solving moral dilemmas may increase the probability that later in real life, former students will make better moral decisions. This may improve their moral thinking and enhance interpersonal behavior in everyday life. In a wider perspective, it may even contribute to more humane and reasonable political behavior which might prevent future man-made catastrophes for humanity.

REFERENCES

Abrahamov, Binyamin (2006). *Studies in Arabic and Islamic culture II.* Israel: Bar-Ilan University Press. [Hebrew]

Aharonson, M. (1999). *Memory as history and history as memory,* Israel: Ramat Gan Museum.

Aleman A., & Swart M (2008) Sex differences in neural activation to facial expressions denoting contempt and disgust. *PLoS One 3*(1), e3622.

Alicke, M. D. (2000). Culpable control and the psychology of blame. *Psychological Bulletin, 126,* 556–574.

Amnesty International (2015). *Who remembers the Armenian genocide today?* Library of education for human rights. Amnesty International. Retrieved from: http://amnesty.org.il/CategoryID=396&ArticleID=1197&dbsAuthToken.

American Psychiatric Association (APA) (2014). *Diagnostic and Statistical Manual of Mental Disorders* –DSM-5, Retrieved from: http://www.dsm5.org/Pages/Default.aspx

Andresen, L., Boud, D., & Cohen, R. (2000). Experience-based learning. *Understanding adult education and training, 2,* 225-239.

Aquino, K., & Reed, A. (2002). The self-importance of moral identity. *Journal of Personality and Social Psychology, 83*(6), 1423-1440.

Baltman, Daniel (Ed.) (2002). *Selection of underground newspapers 1940-1943.* Jerusalem: Yad VaShem.

Bar, M. (1978). *The Auschwitz scroll.* Israel: Sifriat Hapoalim. [Hebrew]

Barley, Michael (2007). *The third Reich, a new history.* Trans. Edit Zartal. Tel Aviv: Zemora-Bitan and Yavne Publishers

Bar Natan, R. (2004). *A background document regarding youth delegations to Poland, submitted to the Knesset's Education and Culture Committee.* Retrieved from: http–www.knesset.gov.il-mmm-data

Barnea, Arieh (2014). Why remember? *Mizkar, Journal for Holocaust Matters, Uprising, Memory and Memorial. January, 42,* 27. Petach Tikva, Publication of the Center for Holocaust Survivor Organizations in Israel. [Hebrew]

Bar-On, Dan (1994). *From fear to hope.* Israel: The Ghetto Fighters House and the Kibbutz Hameuhad. [Hebrew]

Bar-Zohar, M. (1991). *On the day of vengeance, the case of Jewish vengeance against the Nazis.* Israel: Teper-Magal Publications. [Hebrew]

Bauer, Yehuda (1982). *The Holocaust – Historical aspects.* Tel Aviv: Shocken Publishers. [Hebrew]

Bauer, Y. (1983). *Reactions during the Holocaust – Attempts to stand up, resist, rescue. theoretical aspects of the study of genocide.* Tel Aviv: Ministry of Defense Publications. [Hebrew]

Beauchamp, Tom L (1991), *Philosophical ethics: An introduction to moral philosophy.* 2nd ed. New York: McGraw Hill.

Ben-Orveh, Y. (1983). *The War of Independence (1947-1949).* Israel: Keter Publications. [Hebrew]

Berger, Israel (2012). *Effects of the heritage expedition to Poland on pupils at the Ort Bialik Educational Campus.* Ph.D. Thesis, Babes Bolyai University, Cluj Napoka, Faculty of Sociology.

Bitts, D. (2004). *Youth delegations to Poland: Trends and directions.* Retrieved from: www.gordon.ac.il/mahad/abroad/poland_journey.htm

Bjorklund, F., Haidt, J., & Murphy, S. (2000). Moral dumbfounding: When intuition finds no reason. *Lund Psychological Reports, 2,* 1-23.

Blady Szwaiger, Adina (2000). *I remember nothing more. Memories of a Jewish doctor in the Warsaw ghetto hospital.* Trans from Polish Avraham Sarid. (Testimony, Pamphlet 3, pp. 17-22). Tel Aviv: Yad Vashem Publications, [Hebrew]

Blair, R. J. R. (1995). A cognitive developmental approach to morality: investigating the psychopath. *Cognition, 57,* 1-29.

Bondi, R. (2014). In the name of the future. *Mizkar, Journal for Holocaust Matters, Uprising, Memory and Memorial. January, 42,* 28. Petach Tikva, Publication of the Center for Holocaust Survivor Organizations in Israel. [Hebrew]

Bogner, N. (2000). *Thanks to the grace of strangers. Rescue of Jews by borrowed identities in Poland.* Jerusalem: Yad Vashem Publications. [Hebrew]

Bowker, J. W. (2002). *The Cambridge illustrated history of religions.* New York City: Cambridge University Press. ISBN 0-521-81037-X. OCLC 47297614

Brand, Yoel & Brand, Hanzi (1960). *The devil and the soul.* Tel Aviv: Ledori Publishers. [Hebrew]

Braun, Virginia, & Clarke, Victoria (2006). Using thematic analysis in psychology. *Qualitative Research in Psychology, 3,* 77-101. Retrieved from: www.QualResearchPsych.com

Bredeson, Dean (2011). *Utilitarianism vs. dentological ethics .Applied business ethics: A skills-based approach.* Cengage Learning. ISBN 978-0-538-45398-1.

Brody, L. R., & Hall, J. A. (2000). Gender, emotion, and expression. In M. Lewis & J. M. Haviland-Jones (Eds.), *Handbook of emotions: Part IV: Social/personality issues.* 2nd ed., (pp. 325– 414). New York: Guilford Press.

Browning, R., Christopher (1992). *Ordinary men: Reserve police battalion 101 and the final solution in Poland.* New York: Harper Collins.

Browning, R, Christopher (2004). *The origins of the final solution: The evolution of Nazi Jewish policy, September 1939-March 1942, with contributions by Jurgen Matthaus.* Lincoln: University of Nebraska Press; Jerusalem: Yad Vashem, Jerusalem.

Bruns, R. A. (1986). *Introduction to a more perfect union: The creation of the United States Constitution.* Washington, DC: Published for the National Archives and Records Administration by the National Archives Trust Fund Board, 1986.

Bullis, C., & Horn, C. (1995). Get a little closer: Further examination of nonverbal comforting strategies. *Communication Reports, 8,* 10-17.

Carmi, I. (1961). In the path of the warriors. *Maarachot,* Jerusalem: Ministry of Defense Publishers. [Hebrew]

Christensen, J. F., & Gomila, A. (2012). Moral dilemmas in cognitive neuroscience of moral decision-making: A principled review. *Neuroscience and Biobehavioral 1348 Reviews, 36*(4), 1249–1264. Doi: 10.1016/ j.neubiorev.2012.02.008

Christensen, J. F., Flexas, A., Calabrese, M., Gut, N.K., & Gomila, A. (2014) Moral judgment reloaded: A moral dilemma validation study. *Front. Psychol. 5,* 607. doi:10.3389/fpsyg.2014.00607

Ciaramelli, E., Muccioli, M., Ladavas, E., & di Pellegrino, G. (2007). Selective deficit in personal moral judgment following damage to ventromedial prefrontal cortex. *Social Cognitive Affective Neuroscience, 2,* 84-92.

Cohen, H. (2010). *Teaching the Holocaust in state schools in Israel. Educational research 2007-2009.* Jerusalem: Bar Ilan University, School of Education. [Hebrew]

Cohen, M. (2004). *The reflection of the Holocaust in the curriculum. A comparative analysis of curricula in literature and history for 7ᵗʰ – 12ᵗʰ grades in secular and religious education.* M.A. thesis. Bar Ilan University. [Hebrew]

Conway, P., & Gawronski, B. (2013). Deontological and utilitarian inclinations in moral decision-making: A process dissociation approach. *Journal of Personality and Social Psychology, 104,* 216-235.

Creswell, J. W., & Plano Clark, V. L. (2011). *Designing and conducting mixed-methods research.* Thousand Oaks, CA: Sage Publications, Inc.

Christensen, J. F., Flexas, A., Calabrese, M., Gut, N.K. & Gomila, A. (2014) Moral judgment reloaded: A moral dilemma validation study. *Frontiers in Psychology 5,* 607. doi:10.3389/fpsyg.2014.00607

Cross, S. E., & Madson, L. (1997). Models of the self: Self-construals and gender. *Psychological Bulletin, 122,* 5-37.

Cushman, F. (2008). Crime and punishment: Distinguishing the roles of causal and intentional analyses in moral judgment. *Cognition, 108,* 353–380.

Cushman, F., & Greene, J. D. (2010). Our multi-system moral psychology: Towards a consensus view. In J. Doris, G. Harman, S. Nichols, J. Prinz, W. Sinnott-Armstrong & S. Stich (Eds.), *The Oxford handbook of moral psychology.* Oxford University Press.

Cushman, F., & Greene, J. D. (2012). Finding faults: How moral dilemmas illuminate cognitive structure. *Social Neuroscience, 7,* 269–279. Doi:10.1080/17470 19.2011.614000.

Cushman, F., Young, L., & Hauser, M. (2006). The role of conscious reasoning and intuition in moral judgment: Testing three principles of harm. *Psychological Science, 17,* 1082–1089. doi:10.1111/j.1467- 9280.2006.01834.x

Czerniakow, Adam (1968). *Warsaw ghetto diary, 6.9.1939-23.7.1942.* Jerusalem: Yad Vashem. [Hebrew]

Damasio, A. (1994). *Descartes' error.* Boston, MA: Norton.

Davidovich, N., Amir, D. & Heskel, A. (2011). Witnesses in uniform. In: N. Davidovich, D. Soen & A. Heskel (Eds.) *Memory of the Holocaust – Issue and challenges* Jerusalem: Ariel. [Hebrew]

Davidovich, N. & Hazan, Y. (2011). Youth journeys to Poland: For and against. In N. Davidovich, D. Soen & A. Heskel (Eds.) *Memory of the Holocaust – Issue and challenges.* Jerusalem: Ariel. [Hebrew]

Davidovich, N., Soen, D. & Haber, L. (2014). The memory begins within us. *Mizkar, Journal for Holocaust Matters, Uprising, Memory and Memorial. January, 41,* 17-18. Petach Tikva, Publication of the Center for Holocaust Survivor Organizations in Israel. [Hebrew]

De Souza Lauretto, M., Nakano, F., De Bragança Pereira, C. A., & Stern, J. M. (2012), Intentional sampling by goal optimization with decoupling by stochastic perturbation. *AIP Conference Proceedings, 1490*, 189-201.

Dushenik, L., & Sabar Ben-Yehoshua, N. (2002). Ethics of qualitative research. In N. Sabar Ben-Yehoshua (Ed.), *Traditions and genres in qualitative research. ,* (pp. 334-368). Or Yehuda: Dvir. [Hebrew]

Efrat, Shay & Baban, Adriana. (2015). The Little Smuggler, Psychological-moral aspects of Jewish parents` dilemmas and decisions in the Warsaw ghetto during World War II: Coping with their children's food smuggling, Edited by: Chis, Vasile, Albulescu, Ion & Bocos, Musata.In *Proceedings of the International Conference on Education Reflection and Development*, Babes-Bolyai University Cluj-Napoca, Romania, Department of Educational Sciences, Doctoral School, "Education, Reflection, Development", 2nd edition 2015, (pp 473-482). ISSN 2457-4643.

Efrat, Shay & Baban, Adriana. (2016a). Holocaust moral attitudes among Israeli high school students, In Kathelin A Moore, Petra Buchwald, Fadia Nasser-Abu Alhija, Moshe Israelashvili, (Eds), *Stress and Anxiety, Strategies, Opportunities and Adaptation* (pp93-100). Berlin: Logos, Verlag. ISBN 978-3-8325-4288-7.

Efrat, Shay & Baban, Adriana. (2016b). I Should Have Felt Bad: Emotional Experiences of Israeli Youth from the Journey to Jewish Holocaust Memorial Sites in Poland. Edited by: Chis, Vasile & Albulescu, Ion. *The European Proceedings of Social & Behavioural Sciences EpSBS* (pp-588-595). Volume XVIII, 22 December 2016, The European Proceedings of Social & Behavioural Sciences EpSBS, e-ISSN: 2357-1330, ©2016 Published by the Future Academy, ERD 2016 - Education, Reflection, Development, Fourth

Edition, Dates: 08 - 09 July 2016, Babes-Bolyai University Cluj-Napoca – Romania.

Eisenberg, N., & Lennon, R. (1983). Sex differences in empathy and related capacities. *Psychological Bulletin, 94*, 100–131.

Elliott, G.R., & Feldman, S.S. (1990). Capturing the adolescent experience. In: S.S. Feldman & G.R. Elliott, (Eds.) Adolescents. *Sociology of Education, 58,* 154-165.

Erikson, E.H. (1968). *Identity: Youth and crisis,* New York: Norton.

Erikson, E. H. (1987), *Youth identity and crisis*. Tel Aviv: Sifriat Poalim. [Hebrew]

Evers-Emden, B. (2000). *Shattered life: Conversations with Jewish parents from Holland, who gave their children to strangers during the Holocaust period*. Tel Aviv :Tachnusder Ltd. [Hebrew]

Farabstein, Esther (2002). *Hidden in thunder. Philosophy and leadership in the days of the Holocaust*. Jerusalem: Rav Kook Institute. [Hebrew]

Farber, K. (2007*). Ulkaniki, Radin, Vilna: From the diary of a son. The torah in the Holocaust and before*. Publication of the author's children. [Hebrew]

Feldman, J. (2001). *In the footsteps of holocaust survivors and Israelis: Youth delegations to Poland and national identity*. M.A thesis, Beersheba University.

Feldman, L.G. (1984). *The special relationship between West Germany and Israel*. Boston: Allen & Unwin, Presidential Library & Museum.

Fink, L.D. (2010). *What is significant learning?* University of Oklahoma Significant Learning Website, Program for Instructional Innovation at the University of Oklahoma. Retrieved from: www. Ou. Edu/pii/significant/WHAT% 20IS. Pdf, 3.

Fischer, A. H., & Manstead, A. S. R. (2000). The relation between gender and emotion in different cultures. In A. H. Fischer (Ed.), *Gender and emotion: Social psychological perspectives* (pp. 71–96). Cambridge, UK: Cambridge University Press.

Fisherman S., & Kaniel, S. (2004). Changes in adolescents' self-identity following the visits to Poland. *Dapim, 37*, 182-202. [Hebrew]

Foot, P. (1967). The problem of abortion and the doctrine of double effect. *Oxford Review, 5*, 5–15.

Frankl, Viktor (1981). *Man's search for meaning: Introduction to Logotherapy*. Tel Aviv: Dvir Publications. [Hebrew]

Freiberg, Dov (1988). *To survive Sobibor*, Jerusalem & New York: Green Publishing House, Gefen.

Friedland, Shaul (1997). *Nazi Germany and the Jews: The years of persecution, 1933-1939.* Tel Aviv: Sifriat Ofakim and Am Oved Publishers. [Hebrew]

Friesdorf, Rebecca , Gawronski, Bertram, &; Conway, Paul (2014) Gender differences in responses to moral dilemmas: A process dissociation analysis, *Personality and Social Psychology Bulletin, 41*(5), 696-713.

Frister, Roman (1993). *Self-portrait with a scar.* Tel Aviv: Dvir Publications. [Hebrew]

Fuchs, Nicole (2009). Your history is part of me: American Jews second and third generation Holocaust survivors and the trans-generational transmission of memory, trauma and history. *Anthology of the Heritage of the Holocaust and Anti-Semitism 4*(87), December, 9-39. Publication of Moreshet, Mordechai Anilevich House of Testimony, the Stefan Roth Institute for the Study of Anti-Semitism and Racism, University of Tel Aviv. [Hebrew]

Fumagalli, M., Ferrucci, R., Mameli, F., Marceglia, S., Mrakic-Sposta, S., Zago, S., Lucchiari, C., Consonni, D., Nordio, F., Pravettoni, G., Cappa, S. & Priori, A. (2010). Gender-related differences in moral judgments. *Cognitive Processing, 11*, 219-226.

Gampel Yolanda, 2005. *My parents live through me. Children of the war.* Jerusalem: Keter Books Ltd. [Hebrew]

Ganor, L. (2006). *IDF and the Holocaust – The Education Unit's consideration of the design of memory of the Holocaust among soldiers 1987-2004.* Doctoral thesis, the School of History, Bar Ilan University, Israel. [Hebrew]

Gay, John (2002), Concerning the fundamental principle of virtue or morality. In J. B. Schneewind, *Moral philosophy from Montaigne to Kant.* Cambridge University Press. ISBN 978-0521003049.

Gelber, Yoav (2004). *Resurrection and Nakhba: Israel, Palestinians and Arab states, 1948.* Israel: Kinneret Publishers. [Hebrew]

Gibton, D. (2002). Field grounded theory: Meaning of the data analysis process and construction of theory in qualitative research. In N. Sabar Ben-Yehoshua, ed. *Traditions and genres in qualitative research. ,* (pp. 195-227). Or Yehuda: Dvir. [Hebrew]

Gillath Omri, McCall, Cade, Shaver Phillip & Blascovich Jim

(2008), What can virtual reality teach us about prosocial tendencies in real and virtual environments? Retrieved from: http://dx.doi.org/10. 1080/15213260801906489,

Goldhagen, Daniel, Jonah (1998). *Hangmen by choice, serving Hitler, ordinary Germans and the Holocaust.* Israel: Yediot Ahronot and Sifrei Hemed. [Hebrew]

Goren, Y. (1997). *War of independence.* Tel Aviv: Ilan Publishers. [Hebrew]

Gottwein, D. (1998). *Privatization of the Holocaust: Politics, memory and historiography.* Pages for the research of the Holocaust. Collection 15. Israel: Institute for the Research of the Holocaust Period, University of Haifa and Ghetto Fighters House Publications. [Hebrew]

Graham, J., Iyer, R., Nosek A. B., Haidt, J., Koleva S., & Ditto H. P. (2011), Mapping the moral domain, *Journal of Personality and Social Psychology, American Psychological Association 101*(2), 366–385, 0022-3514/11/$12.00 DOI: 10.1037/a0021847

Greene, J. C. (2007a). *Mixed methods in social inquiry* (Vol. 9). New Jersey, US: Jossey-Bass, Wiley.

Greene, J. D. (2007b). Why are VMPFC patients more utilitarian? A dual-process theory of moral judgment explains. *Trends in Cognitive Sciences, 11*, 322-323.

Greene, J. D. (2008). The secret joke of Kant's soul. In W. Sinnott-Armstrong (Ed.), *Moral psychology 3*, 35–80). Cambridge, MA: MIT Press.

Greene, J. D. (2011). Emotion and morality: A tasting menu. *Emotion Review, 3*(3), 1–3. doi:10.1177/ 1754073911409629

Greene, J. D., & Haidt, J. (2002). How (and where) does moral judgment work? *Trends in Cognitive Science, 6*, 517-523.

Greene, D. J., Morelli, A. S., Lowenberg, K., Nystrom, E. L., & Cohen, D..J. (2007), Cognitive load selectively interferes with utilitarian moral judgment, *Cognition 107* (2008) 1144–1154, doi:10.1016/j.cognition.2007.11.004

Greene, J. D., Nystrom, L. E., Engell, A. D., Darley, J. M., & Cohen, J. D. (2004). The neural bases of cognitive conflict and control in moral judgment. *Neuron, 44,* 389–400. doi:10.1016/j.neuron.2004.09.027

Greene, J. D., Sommerville, R. B., Nystrom, L. E., Darley, J. M., & Cohen, J. D. (2001). An fMRI investigation of emotional engagement in moral judgment. *Science, 293,* 2105–2108. doi:10.1126/science.1062872

Greenspan, Y. (2012). *Hinduism: A short introduction.* Tel Aviv: University of Tel Aviv. . [Hebrew]

Greif, G. (1998). Daily life of Auschwitz prisoners. *In Memoriam, 28.* Jerusalem: Yad Vashem Publications. Central School for Holocaust Studies. [Hebrew]

Greif, Gideon (1999). *We wept without tears . . . Testimonies of the Jewish Sonderkommando from Auschwitz.* Jerusalem: Yad Vashem. [Hebrew]

Greif, Gideon, Weitz, Yechiam, & Machman, Dan (1983). *In the days of the holocaust.* Units 1-2. Jerusalem: Open University. [Hebrew]

Gross, J. J., & John, O. P. (1998). Mapping the domain of expressivity: Multimethod evidence for a hierarchical model. *Journal of Personality and Social Psychology, 74,* 170-191.

Guglielmo, S., & Malle, F. Bertram (2010) Enough skill to kill: Intentionality judgments and the moral valence of action, *Cognition Journal, 117,* 139-150. Brown University, United States, doi:10.1016/j.cognition.2010.08.002

Guglielmo, S., Monroe, A. E., & Malle, B. F. (2009). At the heart of morality lies folk psychology. *Inquiry, 52,* 449–466.

Gunnar, Heinsohn (2000). What makes the holocaust a uniquely unique genocide? *Journal of Genocide Research,* 2(3), 411–430.

Gurani, Y. (2015) *From Auschwitz to Jerusalem.* Tel Aviv: Am Oved in collaboration with the Ben-Gurion Heritage Center.

Gutman, I. (1979a). *Image of Jewish leadership in countries under Nazi control, 1933-1945.* Jerusalem: Yad Vashem Publications. [Hebrew]

Gutman, I. (1979b). *Totalitarianism and Holocaust.* Jerusalem: Zalman Shazar Centre Publications. [Hebrew]

Gutman, I. (1983). *The Holocaust and its meaning*. Jerusalem: Zalman Shazar Centre Publications. [Hebrew]

Gutman, I. (Ed.) (1990a). Kastner, Roj'ie (Rudolf) Israel (1906-1957). In *Encyclopedia of the Holocaust* (Vol. A: A-B) Jerusalem: Yad Vashem – Authority for the Memory of the Holocaust and Heroism and Sifriat Hapoalim. [Hebrew]

Gutman, I. (Ed.) (1990b). *Encyclopedia of the Holocaust*. Yad Vashem and Hakibbutz Haartzi Publications. (In Hebrew).

Guterman, B., Yablonka, H., & Shalev, A. (Eds.) (2008). *We are here – Holocaust survivors in the State of Israel*. Jerusalem: Yad Vashem Publications. [Hebrew]

Hadawi, Sami (1970) *Village statistics 1945, Classification of land and area ownership in Palestine*. Beirut: Palestine Liberation Organization Research Center.

Haidt, J. (2001). The emotional dog and its rational tail: A social intuitionist approach to moral judgment. *Psychological Review, 108*, 814-834.

Haidt, J. (2007). The new synthesis in moral psychology. *Science, 316*, 998–1002. doi:10.1126/science.1137651

Haidt, J., & Joseph, C. (2007). The moral mind: How 5 sets of innate intuitions guide the development of many culture-specific virtues, and perhaps even modules. *The Innate Mind, 3*, 367–391. New York, NY: Oxford University Press.

Hall, J. A., & Schmid Mast, M. (2008). Are women always more interpersonally sensitive than men? Impact of goals and content domain. *Personality and Social Psychology Bulletin, 34*, 144-155.

Hamilton, V. L. (1978). Who is responsible? Towards a social psychology of responsibility attribution. *Social Psychology, 41*, 316–328.

Harter, S. (1990). Self and identity development, In S. Feldman and G. Elliott (Eds.), *At the threshold: The developing adolescent* (pp. 352-387). Cambridge, MA: Harvard University Press.

Hatis-Rolf, S. (1998). The Kastner affair. In *Political Lexicon of the State of Israel*. Jerusalem: Keter and Jerusalem Publication House. [Hebrew]

Hauser, M. D. (2006). *Moral minds: How nature designed a universal sense of right and wrong*. New York: Harper Collins.

Hauser, M., Cushman, F., Young, L., Jin, R. K.-X., & Mikhail, J. (2007). A dissociation between moral judgments and justifications. *Mind & Language, 22*(1), 1–21. doi:10.1111/j.1468-0017.2006.00297.x

Hausner, Gideon (1988). *The Holocaust as reflected in the law*. Tel Aviv: Am Oved. [Hebrew]

Heberer, Patricia (2011). *Children during the Holocaust*. Holocaust Memorial Museum's Center, , Maryland: Altamira Press.

Heider, F. (1958). *The psychology of interpersonal relations*. New York: Wiley.

Heilbruner, Oded & Zimeman, Moshe (Eds.) (1995). *Chapters from Adolph Hitler's "My struggle/Mein Kampf"*. trans. Dan Yaron. Tel Aviv: Akademon Publishers. [Hebrew]

Heskel, A. (2012). *The prison guard from block 11*. Tel Aviv: D.O.L. Ltd. Publishers. [Hebrew]

Heskel, A. (2015). How is the collective memory of the Warsaw Ghetto Uprising shaped? *Mizkar, Journal for Holocaust Matters, Uprising, Memory and Memorial. January, 44*, 21-26. Petach Tikva, Publication of the Center for Holocaust Survivor Organizations in Israel. [Hebrew]

Holevski, S. (2001). *Rebellion and partisan fighters*. Jerusalem-Tel Aviv: Yad Vashem – Authority for the Memory of the Holocaust and Heroism and Mordechai Anilevitch Testimony House [Hebrew]

Ilem, Yigal (1990) *Those who obey orders: Identity card*. Israel: Keter Publishers. [Hebrew]

Jaffee, S., & Hyde, J. S. (2000). Gender differences in moral orientation: A meta-analysis. *Psychological Bulletin, 126*, 703.

Kamm, F. M. (1996), *Morality, mortality: Vol. II: Rights, duties, and status*. New York: Oxford University Press.

Kaplan, Haim (1961). *A tale of agony: Warsaw ghetto diary*. Tel Aviv: Am Oved. [Hebrew]

Kassan, L., & Kromer-Nevo, M., (Eds.) (2010). *Data analysis in qualitative research.* Beer Sheva: Ben Gurion University in the Negev. [Hebrew]

Katz, Y. (2009). *At the expense of the victims.* Jerusalem: Ministry of Defense Publishers. [Hebrew]

Katz, Y., Ben Ami, M. & Ilan, H. (2005). *Award of the Vilna ghetto committee in the Holocaust: The Jewish cultural life according to diaries and memories.* Jerusalem: Ministry of Defense Publishers. [Hebrew]

Keren, N. (1985). *The influence of public opinion shapers on the one hand and Holocaust research on the other hand on the development of educational discussion and curricula pertaining to teaching the Holocaust in high schools and informal education between 1948 – 1981.* Ph.D. Thesis. Hebrew University, Jerusalem. [Hebrew]

Keren, N. (1987). *The subject of the Holocaust in Israeli society and in the education system 1948-1981.* Israel: Moreshet Publications. [Hebrew]

Keren, N. (1998). Preserving memory in oblivion: The struggle for Holocaust studies in Israel. In *Times*, 64, 56-64. A quarterly publication of History, Columbia University Press, Center for Educational Technology.

Kermish, Yosef (Ed.) (1966). *The Warsaw ghetto uprising in the enemy's eyes. The reports of General Jurgen Stroop.* Jerusalem: Yad Vashem. [Hebrew]

Kermish, Y. (Ed.) (1989). *Jewish underground journalism in Warsaw.* Vol. 4: November 1941-February 1942. Jerusalem: Yad Vashem. [Hebrew]

Kidder, L. (2003). *How good people make tough choices. Resolving the dilemmas of ethical living.* Revised Ed: New York: Harper Collins. ISBN 0-688-17590-2

Kimchi, S. (2011). Journey to Poland strengthens Israeli and Jewish identity and extremism toward the Arab minority. In Ben-Artzi (Ed.), *Line education – the information data base. 547.* Retrieved from: http://portal.macam.ac.il/ArticlePage.aspx?id=3818

Kischke, M. (2013) *The second generation, things I did not tell to my father*. Tel Aviv: Hargol Publishers and Modan Publishers. [Hebrew]

Klausner, I. (1975). *The history of Zionism*. Tel Aviv: The Zalman Shazar Centre for Israeli History. [Hebrew]

Knobe, J. (2003a). Intentional action and side effects in ordinary language. *Analysis, 63,* 190–193.

Knobe, J. (2003b). Intentional action in folk psychology: An experimental investigation. *Philosophical Psychology, 16,* 309–324.

Knott, K. (2008). *Hindouisme*. Trans. Roni Parchuk. Israel: Mishkal Publishers and Sifrei Tamar. [Hebrew]

Kochavi, Arieh, I. (2006). *The path to the Nuremburg trials – Consolidation of punitive policies towards war criminals*. Jerusalem: Yad Vashem Publications. [Hebrew]

Koenigs, M., Young, L., Adolphs, R., Tranel, D., Cushman, F., Hauser, M., & Damasio, A. (2007). Damage to the prefrontal cortex increases utilitarian moral judgments. *Nature, 446,* 908–911. Doi: 10.10 38/nature05631

Kohlberg, L. (1969). Stage and sequence: The cognitive-developmental approach to socialization. In D. A. Goslin (Ed.), *Handbook of socialization theory and research* (pp. 151-235). New York: Academic Press.

Kohlberg, L. (1973). The claim to moral adequacy of a highest stage of moral judgment. *Journal of Philosophy 70*(18), 630–646.

Kolb, D. A. (1984). *Experiential learning: Experience as the source of learning and development*. New Jersey: Prentice-Hall.

Kolett, A. (2014). Teaching the Holocaust – what next? *Mizkar, Journal for Holocaust Matters, Uprising, Memory and Memorial. January, 42,* 16. Petach Tikva, Publication of the Center for Holocaust Survivor Organizations in Israel. [Hebrew]

Konforti, Yitzhak (2006). *Past times: Zionist historiographies and the shaping of national memory*. Jerusalem: Ben-Zvi Memorial Publications. [Hebrew]

Kovner, A. (1981*). On a narrow bridge*. Israel: Hakibbutz Haartzi. [Hebrew]

Kovner, A. (2002*). Letter to the partisan guards*. Tel Aviv: Moreshet. [Hebrew]

Laor, D. (2009). *The struggle for remembrance –Essays on literature, society and culture* . Tel Aviv: Ofakim Books, Am Oved Publishers. [Hebrew]

Larue, G. A. (1991). Ancient ethics. In P. Singer (Ed.), *A companion to ethics.* (pp. 29–40). Malden, MA: Blackwell.

Leibovitch, I. & Lavie, T. (1997). *What is above and what is beneath.* Israel: Sifriat Maariv. [Hebrew]

Lev, M. (2007). Teenagers travel into memory. In M. Shmida & S. Romi (Eds.), *Education in formal reality changes* (pp. 219-239). Jerusalem: Magnes Press – Hebrew University.

Lev, M., Shadmi, H., & Ben-Ezra, J. (2006). *A journey of a man following people*. Israel: Ministry of Education, Psychological-Counseling Services in cooperation with the Director of Social Education. (In Hebrew).

Levi, Primo (2011). *If this is a man?* Tel Aviv: Am Oved and Sifriat Afeqim. [Hebrew]

Levine, Itamar (2002). *Signs of fire, testimony from the holocaust period in religious literature.* Tel Aviv: Yedioth Aharonoth Publications. [Hebrew]

Levine, Itamar (Ed.) (2005). *Lexicon of the Holocaust.* Tel Aviv: Yediot Ahronot Publishers with Hemed Books. [Hebrew]

Levine, Itamar (2015). *Kapo in Allenby, bringing Jews to trial in Israel accused of assisting the Nazis.* Jerusalem: Yad Yitzhak ben Zvi – Anilevitch House of Testimony, Givat Haviva. [Hebrew]

Levine, S. (1979). *Morality and the shaping of moral character.* Tel Aviv: Otsar Hamoreh. [Hebrew]

Levracht, H. (1973). *Reparations from Democratic Germany.* Israel: Shonot Publishers. [Hebrew]

Lindenstrauss, M . (2012). *The State Comptroller's Report for 2011.* The State of Israel.

Litvak-Hirsch, T. & Braun, D. (2008). Three generations of mothers after the Holocaust: Trans-generational transmission from a grandmother Holocaust survivor to her daughter and granddaughter. In R. Fisher (Ed.) *In the spaces of memory, creativity of the second and third generations of Holocaust survivors*. Israel: Ghetto Fighters House, Laor Publishers and Keter Publishers. [Hebrew]

Lomski-Feder, E. (1997). Stories of former soldiers: The interaction between personal memory and social memory of war. In *Theory and criticism. Jerusalem* (pp. 59 – 79). Jerusalem: Van Leer Institute and Hakibbutz Hameuchad Publications, 11. [Hebrew]

Lorach, N. (1976). *The historiography of the War of Independence*. Tel Aviv: Cathedra for the History of the Land of Israel and its Settlement. [Hebrew]

Lubotkin, Zvia (1979). *In the days of annihilation and rebellion*. Tel Aviv: Ghetto Fighters House Publication. [Hebrew]

Lurie, Shani (2015). *For the memory, 2,* Jerusalem: Yad Vashem Publications. [Hebrew] Retrieved from: www.yadvashem.org/yv/he/education/units/for.../magazine10_educ.pdf

Machman, D. (1996a). The Arabs and the Holocaust according to Azmi Bashara: indeed a political bond. Israel: *Zmanim – A Quarterly on History*. [Hebrew]

Machman, D. (1996b). *The Holocaust in Jewish history, awareness and interpretation*. Tel Aviv: Moreshet Publications. [Hebrew]

Machman, D. (1998*). The Holocaust and its research – Conceptualization, terminology and fundamental issues*. Tel Aviv: The Mordechai Anilevitch House of Testimony. [Hebrew]

Malle, B. F., Moses, L. J., & Baldwin, D. A. (2001). Intentions and intentionality: Foundations of social cognition. Cambridge, MA: MIT Press.

Maltz, Judy (2016), Why Israelis are refusing to send their kids on school trips to Auschwitz? *Haaretz Newspaper*, May 5th, 2016. Retrieved from http://www.haaretz.com/israel-news/.premium-1.717866,

Mason, J. (1996). *Qualitative researching*. London: Sage Publications.

Mayseless, O., & Solomon, G. (2005). *Characteristics of Israeli youth – Contradictory and complementary poles, self-confidence and sense of pressure, proximity and friction, and conformity – compliance.* Tel-Aviv: Tel-Aviv University, Israel.

Mazower, Mark (2015). *Hitler`s empire. How the Nazis ruled Europe.* Israel: Modan Publishers [Hebrew]

Mendez, M. F., Anderson, E., & Shapira, J. S. (2005). An investigation of moral judgment in front temporal dementia. *Cognitive and behavioral neurology, 18*(4), 193-197.

Meyer, N. D., & Tormala, Z. L. (2010). "Think" versus "feel" framing effects in persuasion. *Personality and Social Psychology Bulletin, 36,* 443-454.

Mimouni-Bloch A., Rostami S., & Bloch Y. (2012). *Can Holocaust memorial journeys cause PTSD?* Paper presented to the Sackler Faculty of Medicine, Tel-Aviv: Tel-Aviv University, Israel.

Ministry of Education (2014) *General Manager`s Directive.* Etz Madorim Programs. 9.10 Holocaust studies. Set regulations 9/4(a) 3-10 "Memory for Me" Multi-age education program. Retrieved from: http://cms.education.gov.il/EducationCMS/Applications/Mankal [Hebrew]

Ministry of Education (2015a). *In the paths of memory. Education program on the subject of the Holocaust: nursery, elementary, junior high and high school.* Retrieved from: http://cms.education.gov.il/educationCMS/units/moe/shoa/hpnew.htm [Hebrew]

Ministry of Education (2015b). *New study program on the Holocaust from 2014-2015.* Retrieved from: http://cms.education.gov.il/EducationCMS/Units/ /History

Ministry of Education (2015c). *Journeys to Poland.* Jerusalem: Ministry of Education, Social and Youth Department. [Hebrew] Retrieved from: http://cms.education.gov.il/EducationCms/Units/Noar/ MinhelethPolin/ChomreiHadracha/MipinkasiShelmadrich.htm

Moll, J., & de Oliveira-Souza, R. (2007). Moral judgments, emotions and the utilitarian brain. *Trends in Cognitive Sciences, 11,* 319–321. doi:10.1016/j.tics.2007.06.001

Moore, A. B., Clark, B. A., & Kane, M. J. (2008). Individual differences in working memory capacity, executive control, and moral judgment. *Psychological Science, 19,* 549–557.

Moras, D. (1972). *And the world remained silent while six million were slaughtered.* Kibbutz Lohamei Haghettaot: The Yitzhak Katznelson Ghetto Fighters' House. [Hebrew]

Morgan, D. L. (1988). *Focus groups as qualitative research.* Beverley Hills: Sage Publications.

Nachmias, H. (1998). *Research methods in the social sciences.* Tel Aviv: Am Oved. {Hebrew]

Nasmith, S. (1983*).* *The battle of the ghetto.* Kibbutz Lohamei Haghettaot: The Yitzhak Katznelson Ghetto Fighters' House. [Hebrew]

Neistatt, Meir (1944). Story of a 13 year old youth. In *Holocaust and rebellion*, 1953. Jerusalem: Ministry of Education.

Neuberger, B. (1994*). Genocide Ruanda 1994 – Genocide in the land of a thousand hills.* Tel Aviv: The Open University. [Hebrew]

Neuman, M. (2010). Mental influence of the Holocaust. In A. Elitsur, S. Tiano, H. Munitz, H. & M. Neuman (2010). *Selected chapters in psychiatry.* 5th ed. Tel Viv: University of Tel Aviv with Papyrus Publishers. [Hebrew]

Nimsovitch, Y. (1968*). Thanks to them – Figures from the notebook.* Jerusalem: The Ministry of Defence. [Hebrew]

Ofer, D. (2007*).* The remnants of the diaspora in Israeli histography. In *Studies on the establishment of Israel, A collection of Zionist, the Yishuv and State of Israel problems, 17,*465-511. [Hebrew]

Ohtsubo, Y. (2007). Perceived intentionality intensifies blameworthiness of negative behaviors: Blame–praise asymmetry in intensification effect. *Japanese Psychological Research, 49,* 100–110.

Orbach, A. (2010). *Survivors.* Jerusalem: Yad Yitzhak Ben-Zvi. [Hebrew]

Oron, Y. (1995a). *The banality of indifference.* Tel Aviv: Dvir Publishers. [Hebrew]

Oron, Y. (1995b). *The internationality of apathy – consideration of the Yishuv and the Zionist Movement to the Armenian genocide.* Tel Aviv: The Kibbutz Seminar College. [Hebrew]

Oron, Y. (2003). *From a viewpoint of pain – Issues in the teaching of the Holocaust and genocide.* Tel Aviv: The Open University. [Hebrew]

Oron, Y. (2005). *Denial – Israel and the Armenian genocide*. Kfar Saba: Maba Publishers. [Hebrew]

Oron, Y. (2006). *Genocide – Thoughts on the unimaginable, theoretical aspects of the study of genocide*. Tel Aviv: The Open University. [Hebrew]

Piaget, J. (1965/1932). *The moral judgment of the child*. New York: Free Press.

Piaget, J. (1972). Intellectual evolution from adolescence to adulthood. *Human Development, 15*, 1-12. New York.

Piaget, J., & Inhelder , B. (1973). *Memory and intelligence*. New York: Basic Books.

Pizarro, D. (2000). Nothing more than feelings? The role of emotions in moral judgment. *Journal for the Theory of Social Behavior, 30*, 355–375. doi:10.1111/1468-5914.00135

Pizarro, D. A., Uhlmann, E., & Bloom, P. (2003). Causal deviance and the attribution of moral responsibility. *Journal of Experimental Social Psychology, 39*(653-660).

Radlich, E. (1983*). Living as if.* Tel Aviv: Kibbutz Lohamei Haghettaot and Hadekel Publications. [Hebrew]

Ring, I. (1999). *Morality for what*? Israel: Sifriat Hapoalim and HaKibbutz Hameuhad, Hashomer Hatzair. [Hebrew]

Rama – State Authority for Measurement and Assessment in Education (2011). *Assessment of youth journeys to Poland in 2009: Cognitive, moral, and emotional influences*. Retrieved from: http://rama.education.gov.il

Rest, J. (1983). Morality. In P.H. Mussen (Ed.), *Handbook of child psychology* (Vol 3, 4th ed.). New York: Wiley.

Romi , S., & Lev, M. (2003). *Adolescents' feelings and attitudes to the Holocaust: Changes following the journey to Poland*. Israel: Bar Ilan University. [Hebrew]

Romi, S. & Lev, M (2007) Experiential learning of history through youth journeys to Poland: Israeli Jewish youth and the Holocaust. *Research in Education*, 78, 88-102.

Sabar Ben-Yehoshua, N. (2002). Ethnography in education. In N.

Sabar Ben-Yehoshua, eds. *Traditions and genres in qualitative research.* (pp. 101-139). Or Yehuda: Dvir, 101-139. [Hebrew]

Sagi, N. (1986). *German reparations: A history of the negotiations.* Trans. D. Alon, Jerusalem: MPG Books, London.

Schatzker, C. (1973). *Didactical issues in Holocaust teaching.* Israel: Masua Publishing, Tel Yitzhak. [Hebrew].

Schatzker, C. (1980). The teaching of the Holocaust: Dilemmas and considerations. *The Annals of the American Academy of Political and Social Science, 450* (1), July, 218-226.

Schatzker, C. (1998). Teaching the Holocaust – A sequence of dilemmas. In Y. Rapel (Ed.), *Memory and awareness of the Holocaust in Israel.* Israel: Masoa Publishing.

Schatzker, C. (1999). Holocaust teaching: Contemporary issues. In E. Etkes & R. Feldhay (Eds.), *Education and history: Political and cultural contexts* (pp. 447-455). Jerusalem: The Zalman Shazar Center for Jewish History.

Schweder, D., & Haidt, J. (1993). The future of moral psychology: truth, intuition, and the pluralist way. *Psychological Science, 4,* 360-365.

Segev, T. (1991*). The seventh million.* Jerusalem: Keter. [Hebrew]

Shalem, M. (2008). Defending the trips to Poland. In *The Echo of Education* (pp. 84-87). Tel Aviv: Hed Hahinuch.

Shapira, A. (1997). *The Holocaust: Private memory and public memory. New Jews, old Jews.* Tel Aviv: Ofakim Library, Am Oved Publishers. [Hebrew]

Shapira, Anita (2009). *Historiography of Zionism and the Land of Israel.* Jerusalem: The Israeli Historical Society and the Shazar Centre. [Hebrew]

Shasha, Shaul (2012), *Mizkar, memorandum, Publication on the Holocaust, Jewish people, anti-Semitism and democracy,* July 2012 , 34, 7. Abstract of the medical committee reports, Published by the Center of Organizations of Holocaust Survivors in Israel.

Shaver, K. G. (1985). *The attribution of blame: Causality, responsibility, and blameworthiness.* New York: Springer.

Shields, Patricia. M., & Rangarajan, Nandhini (2013). A play book for research methods, integrating conceptual frameworks and project management. United States of America, Stillwater OK: New Forums Press Inc..

Shkedi, A. (2003). *Words that attempt to touch, Qualitative research - Theory and*

implementation. Tel Aviv: Ramot. [Hebrew]

Snarey, John, Kohlberg, Lawrence, & Noam, Gil (1983). Ego development in perspective: Structural stage, functional phase, and cultural age-period models. *Developmental Review, 3*(3), 303-338, doi:10.1016/0273-2297(83)90018-7, ELSEVIR

Snyder, Timothy (2012). *Europe between Hitler and Stalin*. Keter Publishers. Jerusalem. [Hebrew]

Soen, D., & Davidovich, N. (2011). *Teens Travel to Poland: Pros and cons, in memory of the Holocaust – Issues and challenges*. Israel: Ariel University Center of Samaria.

Solomon, Zahava (2012), *Mizkar, memorandum, Publication on the Holocaust, Jewish people, anti-Semitism and democracy, July 2012 , 34*, 6 , Abstract of the medical committee reports. Published by the Center of Organizations of Holocaust Survivors in Israel.

Sorensen, R.A., 1988. *Blind spots*. Oxford University Press, Oxford.

Sroufe, A., Coope, R., & DeHart, G. (1998). *Child development, its nature and course*. Tel Aviv: The Open University. [Hebrew]

Starcke, K., Ludwig, A. C., & Brand, M. (2012). Anticipatory stress interferes with utilitarian moral judgment. *Judgment and Decision Making, 7*(1), 61–68.

Starkman, Rotem, & Dattel, Lior (2016). What really happens on Israeli students' holocaust trips to Poland? http://www.haaretz.com/israel-news/.premium-1.718360

Steev, I. (2002). *Jewish demography of our times: Zionism and the establishment of the state*. Tel Aviv: Jewish Agency. [Hebrew]

Stebbins, Robert. A (2001), Exploratory research in the social sciences. *Qualitative Research Methods, 48,* Thousand Oaks, London, New Delhi: Sage Publications, International Educational and Professional Publisher.

Styron, T. (Ed.) (1979). *Sophie's choice*. Random House, New York.

Szekely, D. R., & Miu, C, A., (2014). *A cognitive neuroscience laboratory*, Romania: Department of Psychology, Babeş- Bolyai University, Cluj-Napoca.

Tal, Y. (2006). *Buddhism: A short introduction*. Israel: Mapa Publications and University of Tel Aviv. . [Hebrew]

Tal, Z. (2000). *Footsteps of a man – Jewish resistance during the Holocaust period*. Teacher's Guidebook. Kibbutz Lohamei Haghettaot: Ghetto Fighters' House Publications. [Hebrew]

Talmi, D., & Frith, C. (2007). Neurobiology: Feeling right about doing right. *Nature, 446,* 865–866. doi:10.1038/446865a

Tassy, S., Oullier, O., Duclos, Y., Coulon, O., Mancini, J., Deruelle, C., & Wicker, B. (2012). Disrupting the right prefrontal cortex alters moral judgment. *Social Cognitive and Affective Neuroscience, 7,* 282–288. doi:10.1093/scan/nsr008

Tassy, S., Oullier, O., Mancini, J., & Wicker, B. (2013). Discrepancies between judgment and choice of action in moral dilemmas. *Frontiers in Psychology, 4,* 250. doi:10.3389/fpsyg.2013.00250

Turiel, E. (1983). *The development of social knowledge: Morality and convention. Cambridge: Cambridge University Press.*

Valdesolo, P., & DeSteno, D. (2006). Manipulations of emotional context shape moral judgment. *Psychological Science, 17*(6), 476-47.

Waller, Bruce N. (2005). *Consider ethics: Theory, readings, and contemporary issues*. New York: Pearson Longman.

Weiner, B. (1995). *Judgments of responsibility: A foundation for a theory of social conduct*. New York: Guilford.

Weinfeld, M. (2001). *The ten commandments and recitation of the "Hear O Israel" prayer: Evolution of declarations of faith*. Israel: HaKibbutz Hameuhad. [Hebrew]

Weinrab, A. (1984). *Three days we walked*. Tel Aviv: Ghetto Fighters House and Kibbutz Hameuhad. [Hebrew]

Weiss, Shalom (2013). *The character of humanity, three generations try to understand*. Haifa: Pardess Publishers. [Hebrew]

Weissmandel, M. D. (1960). *From the depths*. 3rd ed. Jerusalem: The Author's Sons.

Weitz, Y. (1995). *The man who was murdered twice – The life, trial and death of Dr. Israel Kastner*, Tel Aviv: Dvir Publishers. [Hebrew]

Weitz, Y. (1997). *From vision to revision*. Tel Aviv: Zalman Shazar Centre for Israel History. [Hebrew]

Weitz, Yehiam (2005). Moshe Sharett and the reparations agreement with Germany, 1949-1952. *Cathedra 115*, 2005, Israel: Yad Yitzhak Ben Zvi. [Hebrew]

Weitzberg, B. (1996). *From the gallows to Shaar Hagai: Chapters in the diary, memories and records from the days of the Holocaust and afterwards till the establishment of the State of Israel.* Israel: Carmel Publishers. [Hebrew]

Wheatley, T., & Haidt, J. (2005). Hypnotic disgust makes moral judgments more severe. *Psychological Science, 16*(10), 780-784.

Wiesenthal, S. (2012). *The murderers among us*. Tel Aviv: Levine-Epstein. Publishers. [Hebrew]

Worgen, Y. (Ed.) (2008). *Youth Delegations to Poland*. A document submitted to the Knesset Education Committee. The Knesset Research and Information Center.

Yablonka, H. (1996). *The Law to bring Justice against the Nazis and their Collaborators: Another aspect of the Israeli question, the survivors and the Holocaust.* Jerusalem: Cathedra Publishers. [Hebrew]

Yablonka, H. (2000). *State of Israel v. Adolf Eichman.* Jerusalem: Yediot Ahronoth [Hebrew]

Yablonka, H. (2008), Warriors discourse. In R. Fisher (Ed.) (2008). *In the spaces of memory, creativity of the second and third generations of Holocaust survivors.* Israel: Ghetto Fighters House, Laor Publishers and Keter Publishers

Yerushalmi, E. (1995). *Journal: Diary from a Lithuanian ghetto.* Jerusalem: Yad Vashem Publishers. [Hebrew]

Youssef, F. F., Dookeeram, K., Basdeo, V., Francis, E., Doman, M., Mamed, D., & Legall, G. (2012). Stress alters personal moral decision making. *Psychoneuroendocrinology, 37*, 491–498. Doi: 10.1016/j. psyneuen.2011.07.017

Zimerman, Moshe (2013). *Germans against Germans. The fate of the Jews 1938- 1945*. Jerusalem: Am Oved Publishers. The Hebrew University in Jerusalem. The R. Kavner Center. [Hebrew]

Zuckerman, Yitzhak (2009). *Those seven years*. Tel Aviv: Hakibbutz Hameuhad. [Hebrew]

APPENDICES

Appendix 1: Moral Attitudes Questionnaire

Dear participant

The questionnaire presents several moral dilemmas that faced Jews during and after the Holocaust.

You are requested to choose and mark your personal attitude concerning the suggested solutions for each dilemma on the options scale (1-5) where 1 = strongly disagree, 5= strongly agree. You can alternatively mark the response "I have no opinion" or write a solution of your own. It is very important that you won't skip any of the dilemmas.

In this questionnaire there are no grades for your responses and there is no correct or incorrect response; each solution that you choose and write is respected and legitimate exactly like any other solution.

You should know that these are dilemmas and solutions, which actually occurred in reality.

In order to comply with ethical requirements, please sign the consent form attached to the questionnaire before beginning to respond to it.

Thank you for your cooperation!

Best wishes Shay Efrat, the Researcher

Questionnaire investigating moral attitudes towards the Holocaust (No`)

Date of questionnaire completion _________________

A. Personal details

1	Date of birth	
2	Sex	M / F
3	Religion	1. Secular Jewish, 2.Traditional Jewish, 3.Religios Jewish, 4.Other:_____________
4	Place of residence	
5	School	
6	Class	
7	4 last numbers of mobile phone number	
8.	Do you have or did you have family members who were Holocaust survivors or victims?	Yes / no

Part I – Moral dilemmas and Jews coping strategies during the Holocaust

Instructions: The dilemmas presented here are dilemmas that faced Jews during the Holocaust. Try as far as possible, despite the difficulty, to imagine yourself in place of Jews during the Holocaust and to think as if you were them.

1. **The Judenratt Dilemma**: The head of the Judenratt – the Jewish leader in the ghetto, did all he could to save as many Jews as possible. In order to do this he was forced to perform acts of cooperation with the Germans, for example, by transmitting lists of Jews who lived in the ghetto, who were designated for transportation to the death camps. The head of the Judenratt hoped each time that these would be the last Jews who would be transferred…

The dilemma is whether I, as the head of the Judenratt should prepare and transmit the demanded lists to the Germans or not?

Solution A: I will transmit the lists because in this way I will perhaps save the rest of the Jews or at least postpone their death.

Strongly disagree	Disagree	Uncertain	Agree	Strongly agree		I have no opinion
1	2	3	4	5		[ ]

Solution B: I will not transmit the list, although I know that the Germans will probably kill me for that.

Strongly disagree	Disagree	Uncertain	Agree	Strongly agree		I have no opinion
1	2	3	4	5		[ ]

Solution C: Another solution of your own

___

2. **The Sonderkommando Dilemma**: The "Sonderkommando" were Jewish prisoners who were forced by the Germans to perform different jobs for them in the operation of the incinerators at Auschwitz-Birkenau death camp, such as: helping the Jews to undress before entering the gas chambers, evacuating the bodies from the gas chambers after death, extracting teeth of those murdered, burning the bodies in the incinerators and grinding the Leftovers bones of the dead.

The dilemma is: Should I agree to serve in the Sonderkommando or refuse, knowing that refuse will probably cause immediately execution?

Solution A: I will refuse to work and take the risk that I will be immediately executed.

Strongly disagree	Disagree	Uncertain	Agree	Strongly agree		I have no opinion
1	2	3	4	5		[ ]

Solution B: I agree to work because I have no option and thus, perhaps I may be saved.

Strongly disagree	Disagree	Uncertain	Agree	Strongly agree		I have no opinion
1	2	3	4	5		[ ]

Solution C: Another solution of your own

____

3. The dilemma of the hat: In concentration and death camps the Germans would punish any "crime" with death, such as standing without a hat at the formation.

The dilemma is: My hat was stolen. Should I steal another prisoner's hat or not? If I steal it, he will die and if I don't steal it, I will die.

Solution A: I won't steal the hat of another Jew because that would be immoral and would lead to his/her death.

Strongly disagree	Disagree	Uncertain	Agree	Strongly agree		I have no opinion
1	2	3	4	5		[ ]

Solution B: I will steal it in order to survive.

Strongly disagree	Disagree	Uncertain	Agree	Strongly agree		I have no opinion
1	2	3	4	5		[ ]

Solution C: Another solution of your own

____

4. The Crying Baby Dilemma: In cases of real unambiguous risk of death faced by a group of Jews, who were in hiding and faced discovery by the Germans, there were parents who killed their babies or infants because they cried and it was impossible to calm them. The parents did this in order to save the other people hiding with them from death.

   The dilemma is: whether I should kill my child in order to save the other people or not?

Solution A: I shall kill my child because the lives of the majority are more important than the life of a single person.

Strongly disagree	Disagree	Uncertain	Agree	Strongly agree		I have no opinion
1	2	3	4	5		[ ]

Solution B: I will not kill my child because I cannot / unwilling to do this, even if we all die.

Strongly disagree	Disagree	Uncertain	Agree	Strongly agree		I have no opinion
1	2	3	4	5		[ ]

Solution C: Another solution of your own

5. The Little Smuggler Dilemma: The Jews in the ghettos suffered from the Germans' deliberately starvation and were dying from hunger. In these dire straits there were parents who allowed their children (who usually volunteered to do this), to smuggle in food from the "Aryan" area to the family imprisoned in the ghetto, although the smuggling children were mostly killed instantly if caught. Only children who were physically small and nimble enough could climb under the fence or through the narrow gaps in the wall and escape from the ghetto in order to bring food. Thus, the use of the children was essential because adults could not do this.

The dilemma is: Should I permit my child to go out of the ghetto for smuggling food or not?

Solution A: I permit that my child should go because there is no alternative, if he doesn't bring food, we will die anyway, all of us, from starvation.

Strongly disagree	Disagree	Uncertain	Agree	Strongly agree		I have no opinion
1	2	3	4	5		[ ]

Solution B: I will not permit my child to go so that his life will not be endangered.

Strongly disagree	Disagree	Uncertain	Agree	Strongly agree		I have no opinion
1	2	3	4	5		[ ]

Solution C: Another solution of your own

____

6. The Rebellion Dilemma: In the ghettoes there were Jews (relatively few for the size of the imprisoned population), who rebelled against the Germans with weapons in organized groups and sometimes in personal initiatives. These Jews did not ask and also did not receive any authorization from the other Jews in the ghetto for their armed rebellion, although their actions endangered the lives of all the Jews because it was clear that the Germans would take a collective revenge.

The dilemma is: should I join the armed rebels and fight the Germans without the permission of the other Jews?

Solution A: I will not join them because it is not right to fight with arms against the Germans without the consent of the other Jews in the ghetto and risk their life.

Strongly disagree	Disagree	Uncertain	Agree	Strongly agree		I have no opinion
1	2	3	4	5		[ ]

Solution B: I will join them because in any case, the Germans will murder us all and it is important to rebel.

Strongly disagree	Disagree	Uncertain	Agree	Strongly agree		I have no opinion
1	2	3	4	5		[ ]

Solution C: Another solution of your own

7. Giving away Children Dilemma. During the Holocaust there were Jewish parents, who gave their young children to Christian religious institutions or to private individuals (non-Jews) under payment or not, so that they would raise the children and thus perhaps save their lives.

The dilemma is: Should I give up my child and transfer the responsibility for his/her fate to a stranger with no guaranty to his destiny?

Solution A: I am entitled to give him/her up to non-Jews because this is the only way that I can perhaps save his/her life.

Strongly disagree	Disagree	Uncertain	Agree	Strongly agree		I have no opinion
1	2	3	4	5		[ ]

Solution B: I must not give up my child to non-Jews because it's impossible to know what they will do with him/her.

Strongly disagree	Disagree	Uncertain	Agree	Strongly agree		I have no opinion
1	2	3	4	5		[ ]

Solution C: Another solution of your own

Part II – Jews' Moral dilemmas after the Holocaust

Instructions: The following are dilemmas that Jews have coped with and cope with today in periods after the Holocaust. Please try to define your attitudes towards the different solutions offered for the following dilemmas from a present-day viewpoint.

1. "They went like lambs to Slaughter" dilemma: The phrase "went like sheep to slaughter" is often heard and interpreted as an accusation relating to the passive behavior of the Jewish masses who were murdered in the Holocaust. This definition was strongly accepted in Israel, especially until the trial of Eichman (1961) and is still heard today.

The dilemma is: Is it morally right or wrong to accuse those murdered of going "like sheep to slaughter"?

Solution A: It is right because it is correct that they acted in this way and we should tell the truth.

Strongly disagree	Disagree	Uncertain	Agree	Strongly agree		I have no opinion
1	2	3	4	5		[ ]

Solution B: It is wrong because they did not all go "like sheep to slaughter".

Strongly disagree	Disagree	Uncertain	Agree	Strongly agree		I have no opinion
1	2	3	4	5		[ ]

Solution C: Another solution of your own

2. The Kapo Dilemma: Following the end of the Second World War and the Holocaust, Jewish survivors who served as Kapo (work managers) or in similar jobs in the concentration and death camps were brought to trial in Israel and accused by Holocaust survivor witnesses of physical and mental abuse of Jewish prisoners in the camps.

The dilemma is: Is it right or wrong to judge Holocaust survivors who acted in the most extreme conditions of the concentration and death camps?

Solution A: It is wrong to judge them because they have suffered enough as it is and the Germans are the ones who cause and were responsible for everything.

Strongly disagree	Disagree	Uncertain	Agree	Strongly agree		I have no opinion
1	2	3	4	5		[ ]

Solution B: It`s right to judge them because if they are guilty, they should pay for their acts.

Strongly disagree	Disagree	Uncertain	Agree	Strongly agree		I have no opinion
1	2	3	4	5		[ ]

Solution C: Another solution of your own

3. The Revengers Dilemma: In the first years after the Holocaust there were Holocaust survivors who performed individual or organized acts of revenge and killed Germans who were suspected of murdering against Jews during the Holocaust. These actions were not preceded by any investigation or legal and official trial.

The dilemma is: Is it permissible to kill Germans suspected of murdering Jews in the Holocaust without any investigation or legal and official trial?

Solution A: It is permissible because they are loathsome murderers and revenge should be carried out against them, as our duty to those who were murdered.

Strongly disagree	Disagree	Uncertain	Agree	Strongly agree		I have no opinion
1	2	3	4	5		[ ]

Solution B: This is forbidden because it is against the law and there may be mistakes in identification and killing of innocent people.

Strongly disagree	Disagree	Uncertain	Agree	Strongly agree		I have no opinion
1	2	3	4	5		[ ]

Solution C: Another solution of your own

4. The Kastner Dilemma: Dr. Israel Kastner, one of the Jewish leaders in Hungary during the Holocaust, had personal contact with some of the senior Nazi officers in Hungary. He bribed them and gave them recommendation letters so that they would agree to save some of the Jews of Hungary. By doing that he was actually able to save the lives of at least 1,500 Jews. In 1954, he was brought to trial in Israel and accused of collaboration with the Germans. During the trial, the judge Benjamin Halevi described Kastner as one who had "sold his soul to the devil" because of the bribery and the recommendation letters.

The dilemma is: It is morally possible to define him in this way?

Solution A: It is forbidden to do this because he only did that to save Jews.

Strongly disagree	Disagree	Uncertain	Agree	Strongly agree		I have no opinion
1	2	3	4	5		[ ]

Solution B: It is permissible because it is a matter of personal perception and it is possible to express any opinion.

Strongly disagree	Disagree	Uncertain	Agree	Strongly agree		I have no opinion
1	2	3	4	5		[ ]

Solution C: Another solution of your own

5. The Reparations Dilemma: After the Holocaust the Germans paid financial reparations to the State of Israel (that was very impoverished at that time), and also paid personal reparations to individual Holocaust survivors. The reparations were for the German Nazi crimes against Jews during the Holocaust. In Israel, there were people who claimed that it was morally forbidden to take money from the Germans and strongly opposed this, claiming that, in fact, this expressed forgiving and forgetting the Holocaust and that it is impossible to ever pardon the Germans.

The dilemma is: should the reparations be accepted or rejected?

Solution A: The reparations should be accepted because at least there will be some compensation for the terrible crimes that the Nazis carried out against the Jews. It does not mean that we have forgiven them.

Strongly disagree	Disagree	Uncertain	Agree	Strongly agree		I have no opinion
1	2	3	4	5		[ ]

Solution B: It is forbidden to accept the reparations because this expresses forgiveness for the Germans.

Strongly disagree	Disagree	Uncertain	Agree	Strongly agree		I have no opinion
1	2	3	4	5		[ ]

Solution C: Another solution of your own

6. The Resistance Dilemma: In the literature and discourse on the Holocaust there is a dispute concerning the issue of what it is more important to highlight: the "active" resistance against the Nazis, meaning the rebellion and armed uprisings or the "passive" resistance that included escape, hiding, forced labor for the Germans, bribery, etc. It is a historical fact that most of the Holocaust survivors survived due to "passive" resistance.

The dilemma is: should active or passive resistance be highlighted?

Solution A: Most of the Jewish survivors were saved due to passive resistance and so this should be highlighted.

Strongly disagree	Disagree	Uncertain	Agree	Strongly agree		I have no opinion
1	2	3	4	5		[ ]

Solution B: Active armed resistance is more important since we want to educate the younger generation to values of armed resistance and battle against those who want to exterminate us and so we need to highlight this.

Strongly disagree	Disagree	Uncertain	Agree	Strongly agree		I have no opinion
1	2	3	4	5		[ ]

Solution C: Another solution of your own

7. The Holocaust Comparison Dilemma: Historians debate whether to view the Jewish Holocaust as a one-time unique event such as cannot be compared to any other event in history or whether it is part of a series of similar historical events such as the Armenian`s genocide by the Turkish.

The dilemma is: can the Holocaust be compared to other events in history?

Solution A: the Holocaust is genocide and can be compared to other similar events in history.

Strongly disagree	Disagree	Uncertain	Agree	Strongly agree		I have no opinion
1	2	3	4	5		[ ]

Solution B: The Holocaust is so unique in its scope and strength and the extent of horrors that it is incorrect to compare it to anything else.

Strongly disagree	Disagree	Uncertain	Agree	Strongly agree		I have no opinion
1	2	3	4	5		[ ]

Solution C: Another solution of your own

____

Appendix 2: Perceived influences and lessons learned questionnaire

Part 1 – Perceived influences on the moral attitudes

Below is a list of possible perceived influences that may have affected your moral attitudes towards Jews' moral dilemmas during and after the Holocaust. Please mark the extent of influence of each factor on a scale of possibilities from 1-5 where 1 = it did not influence me at all, 5 = had a very strong influence.

Perceived influences	No influence 1	Little influence 2	Medium influence 3	Strong influence 4	Very strong influence 5	Not relevant
Knowledge and experiences that I experienced before Grade 11&12						
Holocaust studies for matriculation						
The trip to Poland including preparation						
My family						
My friends						
Participating in this research						

Another possible influence:

____

Part 2 – Perceived moral lessons from Holocaust learning

Below is a list of possible perceived moral lessons that you may have gained from your Holocaust learning. Please mark the extent of your agreement with each lesson on a scale of possibilities from 1-5, where 1 = totally disagree and 5 = strongly agree

Perceived lessons	Totally disagree 1	Do not agree 2	Slightly agree 3	Agree 4	Strongly agree 5
Since we have been harmed, we have the right to harm others					
If we do not act morally, we may end up being like the Nazis					
Moral dilemmas are irrelevant in times of war					
Since we are strong, we must not harm the weak					
It's important to learn about Holocaust moral dilemmas					

Another lesson

____

Appendix 3: Interview Guidelines

1. Do you have a personal connection to the Holocaust?

2. Please explain this connection (if you do have one).

3. Did you participate in the journey to Poland?

4. Please explain your decision about the journey.

5. How was the trip for you?

6. Were there certain meaningful experiences that you wish to share? What were they?

7. Please tell me about the moral meanings that you found in your Holocaust learning.

8. What do you think about your learning on the Holocaust moral dilemmas?

9. Please tell me about your experiences and insights from coping with Holocaust moral dilemmas through learning.

Appendix 4: Interviewees' main characteristics

N	Interviewee name (fictive)	Gender	Relative of Holocaust survivors	Participated in the journey to Poland
1	Yonat	Female	Yes	Yes
2	Pazit	Female	Yes	Yes
3	Noa	Female	Yes	Yes
4	Lily	Female	No	Yes
5	Rachel	Female	Yes	Yes
6	Miriam	Female	No	Yes
7	Sara	Female	Yes	No
8	Aia	Female	No	Yes
9	Dina	Female	Yes	No
10	Boaz	Male	No	Yes
11	Elad	Male	Yes	No
12	Asaf	Male	Yes	No
13	Ronen	Male	No	Yes

Appendix 5: Student Consent form for participation in the research

Date: ____________________________

Dear Participant.

Please fill in your name and sign the following consent form:

I know that I am to participate in a research conducted by Shay Efrat on the subject of moral attitudes towards the Holocaust that is being carried out solely for research, learning and educational purposes, and that my name will be kept anonymous and my privacy will be maintained by the researcher and my details will not be published in any form. I hereby declare that I agree to participate in the research without any coercion being enforced on me and out of my own free choice, consent and will.

Name: ____________________________

Signature: __________________________

Appendix 6: Parents' consent form for the participation of child in the research

10.11.2014

Request to obtain permission from parents of Grade 11 to allow their children to participate in a research study on Holocaust studies

Dear parents of Grade 11 students

My name is Shay Efrat. I am a member of Kibbutz Shamir, a teacher and educational counselor by profession. At present, I am also studying for a doctorate in the Psychology Department of Cluj University, Romania. The subject of my doctoral research is the development and shaping of moral attitudes of Israeli students during Holocaust studies in school and during the preparation for and the actual journey to Poland. The research hypothesis is that moral attitudes towards the Holocaust develop, alter and are shaped during this learning process in Grades 11 and 12.

The purpose of the research is therefore to identify and characterize these moral attitudes, the way in which they develop and the factors that influence these processes. The participants in the research will be students in Grade 11 in the academic year 2015 from "Hill and Valley "school, "Jordan Springs School" and Hulla Valley" school. Participation in the research is a right and not an obligation and depends on the consent of both the student and their parents. The research tools are attitudes questionnaires, individual interviews and documentary analysis. The questionnaires are anonymous. Students who agree to participate in interviews or to share personal documents such as letters or diaries will provide strong assistance to the research and in each case the identity of the writer will remain confidential and will only be known to the researcher, who will not use students' names and they will not appear in any place in writing. The research structure is longitudinal meaning that the questionnaires and interviews will be conducted at three different points in time: approximately at the beginning of the student's studies in December 2014, after returning from Poland – September/October, 2015 and towards the end of their school studies – February/March 2016.

I would be grateful if you would confirm the participation of your son/daughter in this research on the attached consent form and return it to the school. I will be glad to answer any questions and to explain everything in greater detail.

Thank you for your cooperation

Shay Efrat – Telephone 050-5914899

____

I/ We (first name and surname)

____

Consent to the participation of our son/daughter

____

in the research study conducted by Shay Efrat on Holocaust studies in Israel that is being performed solely for scientific purposes.

Mother's signature _________________

Father's signature _________________